Frontier
FLIES

Ken Morrish Photo

TROY BACHMANN

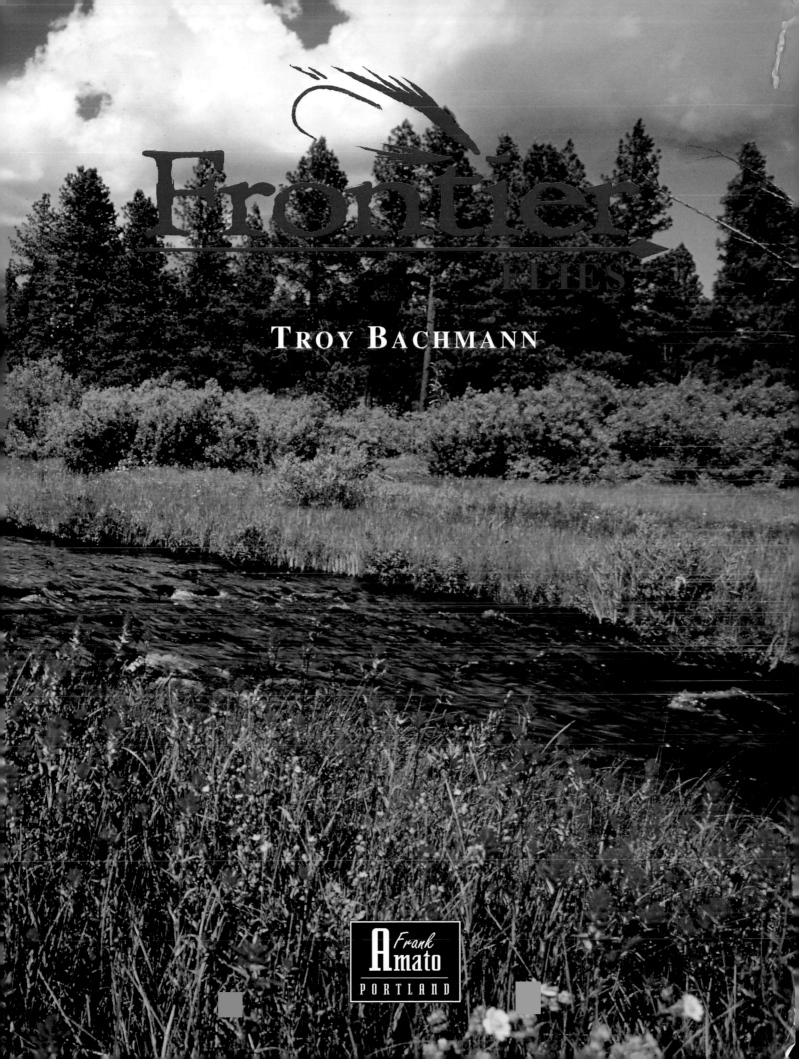

Frontier
FLIES

TROY BACHMANN

Frank Amato PORTLAND

ACKNOWLEDGMENTS

I would like to specially thank those who were involved in making this book. Frank, Nick and Tony Amato for sharing the vision and appreciation of our quality and unique fly patterns. Without their sense of adventure, this book would never have come about.

The guest writers: Their stories and knowledge add dimension and enthusiasm to our wonderful sport.

The Fly Fishing Shop in Welches, Oregon, with which I have had the pleasure of growing up. Without their dedication and artistic approach to the sport both in teaching fly tying and fishing, I may not been involved with this remarkable industry. Their high standards, sometimes unbearable, allowed me to persevere without compromise.

To my parents Mark Bachmann and Patty Barnes, who shared their passion of this wondrous sport, which gave birth to my own.

To those special friends who have always given a helping hand when it was needed, always with positive and creative support Cathy Byers, Dick Crossley, Kevin Jurgens, Janelle McFarland and family, Brad Shiley, Brian Silvey, Mark Stensland, Bob Sterne.

Photography: Kevin Jurgens, Kenny Morrish, and Brian O'Keefe who capture the colorful playing field of this sport so we can all rejoice and reflect in our most precious memories. Jim Schollmeyer: who captures such detail on film, subjects which the majority of us often overlook.

To those dealers who had the courage to do business with a start-up company. They understand that quality, innovation, and service is valuable and they are dedicated to providing the very best to their customers. A list of our dealers is provided in Appendix A, our products are available through them.

To the fly fishermen, especially those who give and work to preserve, protect, and restore native biodiversity of fish habitat.

To Mexico, the wonderful and colorful culture of the people. A very special thanks to Efrain Del Toro Garcia, G.M. of Mexican operations, his dedication to this dream has been unmatched with perseverance and honesty. A true friend and partner. Thanks also to his family who have always had support and belief.

Author with an Alaskan rainbow.

A special thanks to Tom Robinson and crew at Rainbow King Lodge in Iliamna, Alaska. When the lodge was built in 1973, the rainbow trout fisheries were at risk due to mismanagement and overfishing by the public. Rainbow King Lodge leased the land from the Alaska Peninsula Corporation and imposed healthy regulations to preserve the wildlife and fisheries. Through proper stream stewardship the population and size of rainbow trout has increased to enviable proportions. A fishing trip at Rainbow King Lodge is one no one should miss.

Published in 1998 by:
Frank Amato Publications, Inc.
PO Box 82112 • Portland, Oregon 97282 • (503) 653-8108

Softbound ISBN: 1-57188-129-8 Softbound UPC: 0-66066-00328-7 • Spiral Hardbound ISBN: 1-57188-130-1 Spiral Hardbound UPC: 0-66066-00329-4

Photography:
Jim Schollmeyer: cover, pages 6-11, fly plates
Ken Morrish: frontispiece, title page

Book Design: Tony Amato
Printed in Hong Kong, China

3 5 7 9 10 8 6 4 2

CONTENTS

FOREWORD

By the summer of 1984, when I was in my mid-thirties, I was ready to leave the Bay Area of California. Since childhood it has been clear mountain streams and rivers with spotted trout that this soul has been drawn to. I had been fly fishing since the age of fourteen but infrequently and without fishing buddies or teachers. A move to the Pacific Northwest made sense and would be good for me on a number of levels, one of which would be to live where there were lots of fish close to home and a large community of fly fishers to meet and learn from.

I arrived in Portland and got settled by early October. Within a week, I found my way out of town and explored up Highway 26 towards Mount Hood. Past the town of Sandy, the road climbs into the fir and cedar I remembered from a family vacation in 1963 and follows the Sandy River which is in a deep canyon and can't be seen. Seventeen miles on, the road crosses the major tributary to the Sandy, the Salmon River, and within a few miles passes through a cluster of five little villages consisting of vacation cabins, a resort, permanent homes of the locals, and a few stores providing basic services. These villages lie in a valley at the foot of the mountain where five major freestone streams that head from different glaciers, snow fields or alpine wetland meadows converge to form the main stem of the Sandy River. The upper Sandy, the Zig Zag, Camp Creek, Still Creek, and the lower Salmon flow on all sides of the villages. Other lesser tributaries—too numerous to name—flow from all the valley boundary slopes to join their part of the Sandy system.

The Sandy thus drains the entire west and south flanks of Mount Hood and its adjacent watersheds, forming an ancient navigable river that carries nutrient-rich glacial till some fifty miles in a northwest trend to its confluence with the Columbia

River at a point many miles below Bonneville Dam where the Columbia is still tidal. The Sandy is therefore connected directly to the sea and suffers no restriction to the migration of anadromous fish.

While fish stocks are not nearly what they were decades ago, the Sandy system still spawns and rears spring, fall and unique winter Chinook, coho salmon, spring, summer, fall and winter steelhead, resident rainbow trout, and resident coastal cutthroat trout. Many of these fish are of hatchery origin, but many are wild. Some of these stocks spawn in the lower river, but most either reside or migrate to the upper reaches into the valley of the five villages.

As I drove through the villages, a painted wooden sign with a large image of a steelhead fly caught my eye. The little store was a run-down, shingled cabin that shared a muddy parking lot with a shabby-looking tavern next door. Although I felt like a greenhorn who knew a lot less about fly fishing than these Northwest boys, I had to stop and check out the little shop. About all I expected to find was an older guy or two tying local patterns for sale. What I discovered instead was a high-tech fly fishing specialty shop in its third year of business that was founded and staffed by professional white-water trout and steelhead guides. I had landed at The Fly Fishing Shop in Welches. I introduced myself to the dark-haired man across the counter, admitted my California origins, and announced that I wanted to learn and get into the sport in a serious way. Mark Bachmann shook my hand and made me feel welcomed in his store.

Mark explained that the store only stocked the brands of new graphite rods, reels, fly lines, waders, boots, and other equipment that stood up to the field-testing that he and his partners put them through while guiding year-round. If an item had a great image from its advertising but didn't prove

itself in the field, they didn't stock it. The hallmark of the shop was "quality."

This philosophy extended to the fly selection just as rigorously. I had been in a number of shops around the West over the years and had picked over lots of flies in lots of fly bins. Something was different about this shop's fly selection. As I looked closer I could see that some of the shop's patterns were of the commercially tied type and quality I was used to, had seen in other shops, and accepted as good product. Some bins, however, held flies that were tied with a perfection that stood out. These flies had exact, correct proportion and a consistency of color, material handling, amount of dressing, and overall finish that made them stand out. The flies were also distinguished by their uniformity. The flies were so like each other in their bin that they were interchangeable, and one did not have to pick through six to find two really good ones—they were all alike and crafted as if by the hand of a jeweler. With that observation I left the shop and headed down the mountain for another week of work. But I had made the connection I needed to make; I had found a home base for my sport, and people who would become teachers and new friends.

The next weekend I was back in the shop to see Mark, ask more questions, and buy a new three-weight trout rod. As I entered, I noticed two teenage boys sitting at the yellow round table in the corner. They both were wearing headphones connected to their tape cassette players, were bobbing their heads at different tempos in time with different rock songs, and were each tying flies at ninety miles an hour. One kid was right-handed and the other left. Each had fur, feather, and ribbing materials laid out in super neat, organized stacks on their respective convenient sides out of each other's way. Most significantly, each had a hatch of two

or three dozen finished flies piled up on the far side of his respective vise. One was tying a large steelhead pattern and the other was knocking out a production run of a dry-fly trout pattern. I bought my new rod and was in a hurry to go fishing over near Bend, but before I left Mark introduced me to the two kids. The lefty tying the steelhead flies was Brian Silvey whose recent steelhead pattern innovations appear in the following pages. The other young man was Mark's son Troy, who would grow and develop his skilled knowledge of fly tying to now author this book.

A few weeks later, in early November, I hired Mark as a guide to take me steelhead fishing on the rivers near the shop. Mark selected the Salmon River as the place to try because its water level was perfect that day and it held lots of summer steelhead. I landed my first steelhead on a fly on that trip with Mark. The following weekend Mark was booked but suggested I hire Troy who he said could do just as good a job.

Getting to know Troy that day, I found I was in the company of a teenager who not only had been fishing these waters intensively for eight years but who had an aptitude for all aspects of fly fishing. Here was that happy case where a person's natural gifts coincide with the location and family activity into which he is born. Troy was already a gifted fly angler and a student of all aspects of the sport who was born into a family and place where he had full access to everything he needed to excel. By age eighteen, Troy was the president of his high school steelhead club and had spent thousands of hours under all conditions and all times of year exploring the local rivers with a fly rod. Like any child who is passionate about a hobby or strong interest, Troy learned his fishing by the personal experience of inventive trial and error. He studied aquatic bugs and all other kinds of things that live under rocks in a river and began accumulating observations that would

later be expressed in a prolific talent for developing hundreds of innovative new fly patterns. Not knowing what was considered possible or impossible, traditional knowledge or unheard of, he tried and experimented with whatever came to mind.

Without knowing it, Troy broke the rules of convention and took steelhead with all kinds of methods not yet written about or popularized. At a time when most anglers considered fly fishing as the least likely way to catch steelhead, Troy took many summer fish on a size 12 Wulff pattern which he skated on hackle points on glassy runs, and with size twelve trout fly caddis pupae emergers which he dead-drifted subsurface on a floating line into deep pools against steep lava walls. Troy once spotted a twelve-pound summer steelhead rising in a pool and took it on a size 14 Blue-wing Olive Parachute on six-pound 3X tippet.

By the time I met him, Troy knew every rock and pool, riffle and run in his home valley that he could get to on his bike or, later, his first car. He had landed well over two hundred steelhead with all kinds of large and small wet and dry flies in all kinds of holding water and knew the nature of the fish superbly well. Few people could spot steelhead under white-water bubbles or through choppy surfaces in a flowing river like Troy, or could select the right fly and make the right presentation for each situation. I saw that Troy approached steelhead fishing in his cascading home waters the way a pro golfer assesses each hole of a championship golf course picking the best club and approach to suit whatever conditions prevail at the time. I had never met anyone who was so creative and freestyle in his approach to trout and steelhead fishing.

On the day Troy was guiding me, he took me to a pool that required a long hike through the woods. Upstream, a long stretch of pocket water and riffles settled against a bedrock wall at the top of the pool. The current was forced to torque bottom to top in a way that it cut a deep slot and dropped the gravel it excavated to the near side, forming a long bar with a drop-off shoulder. Troy looked the pool over in ways I had yet to learn and made decisions about where I should start, what fly to use, and what presentation to make. My second steelhead, a fifteen-pound summer buck, followed my sunken fly as it swept up the shoulder of the bar on my third cast and took it with an explosive turn that sent water flying.

The fish was hooked and racing downstream and out of the pool before I could react. Troy immediately commanded me to keep the rod high and barked that I had to follow the fish or be spooled. He surprised me with his drill sergeant-like authority, and I saw that there was deep experience behind his instructions to his much-older client. In a riffle, one hundred yards downstream, the fish tried to stay in the heavy current around the outside of a large boulder. Troy warned me to turn him to the inside or say good-bye. I turned the fish at the boulder and we landed him in a shallow back channel. (I still have the picture.) I appreciated Troy as an exceptional young man that day and from then on took an interest in his growing up.

The months that followed brought more fishing trips with both Mark and Troy, and the early days of a lasting friendship with the whole family. I discovered that both Mark and Troy were talented artists who drew and painted in watercolors and oils. Becoming a regular around the shop on weekends, I began to see the nature of the business and its routine. The largest retail department was the sale of flies, which had to be restocked as they sold out. Mark had managed the hunting and fishing departments of a large sports center down in Portland and knew the business. To make his own shop work,

he had trained Troy, Brian Silvey, and two other teenage boys to tie most of the hundred or so trout and steelhead patterns the store carried.

It was Mark's artistic eye for color and form and his own observations of insect life, that was behind the quality of those perfect flies and design of the unique patterns I had noticed my first time in the store. Troy and the other boys were earning money as tiers for the shop. Troy's specialty was production of the trout dry flies. Mark would give him a pattern and Troy had to tie whatever number of dozen were needed. Troy was paid by the dozen, but only for each dozen that passed Mark's merciless inspection. In the early years as Troy was getting started (three years before I came on the scene), Mark would often only accept half the flies his son or the other tiers produced. The rejects had to be cut down with a blade to salvage the hook and be redone. There were glum faces of disappointment on every occasion that flies were rejected, but the boys responded to the challenge and focused their young minds on how to improve, and how to beat the old man.

By the time I came along in the late fall of 1984, Troy and the others could knock out ten dozen perfect flies in a full work day. Troy was producing a total of a thousand dozen small trout flies of varied patterns a year to earn his school and car money. While it was Mark's instruction that taught Troy and specified the details of the patterns to be tied, it was Troy's extraordinary hand-eye coordination, his own artistic sense and his own observations of naturals on the river, that produced the jeweler's flies that drew customers from all over the region to the shop.

As the years went by, Troy was exposed to the styles and techniques of other master fly tiers who put on clinics at the shop, so that his own trademark style developed from many teachers and examples. A summer guiding for a prominent lodge in Alaska taught him to know that regional fishery and the fly patterns that could be used there.

Troy also put himself through college producing flies for the family shop. He has personally tied well over twenty-thousand dozen flies, mostly for trout and steelhead. In time, with increasing maturity and mastery, Troy rose to putting on clinics of his own and began teaching the craft to others. In the last five years, Troy has distinguished himself as a leading innovator and designer of new patterns that are expanding the sport.

When Troy started his wholesale production business, Frontier Fly Company, he faced established competition. Because of the good reputation he earned in the industry, he was able to make a success where many others have failed. He could do so because he offers over four-hundred unique pattern variations that he has developed so that retail shops can offer new and effective patterns to their customers.

This book about the flies of the Frontier Fly Company has lots of great information about new flies, how they can be tied, and how to fish them. For me, however, having seen Troy develop and having underestimated him a number of times, this book is also a public testament to the coming of age of a brilliant artist and innovator. Troy Bachmann is the most creative person I know. He will keep studying, keep exploring the sport he loves, and keep thinking up new things that can be done with fly-tying materials to craft new imitations that fool fish. While this book is Troy's achievement, he wrote it for you. If you get ideas of your own from this book, spend pleasant hours at a vise tying his patterns, or find these patterns in a fly shop and catch fish with them, Troy will be pleased. He wishes you the best of luck.

Jim Barlow
Welches, Oregon
December 12, 1997

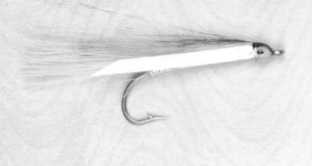

INTRODUCTION

Over the years I have met a lot of men and women who love to fly fish. We have shared a lot of conversation about the sport, and I have learned that we do not all come to the river for the same reasons, the same outlook, or the same philosophical approach. We do not all enjoy the same type of fly fishing, some just fish trout, others fish trout and steelhead, and some rogue purists just fish steelhead. Quite a few fishermen concern themselves with bass and lily pads. Still others are lured by flats and blue water where two-hundred-pound fish will take a fly, and rinsing the salt from their reels each night is merely the end of an exhilarating day.

A friend once summed up his view of the sport in one sentence: "fly fishing is the pursuit of personal excellence." Anglers must be knowledgeable about fish behavior and feeding habits. This is the basis of what fly to select and how to present it. There is a lot of study involved. This is why fly fishing is a sport that continually offers new challenges. It is a contest of wits between fisher, surroundings, circumstances, and fish. The fisher needs to gather as much information and develop as many skills as possible in order to be successful. Still, no one can completely master the sport. There is always something more to learn about this complex pastime, and a greater challenge to pursue.

We choose to fish the way we do because it supplies us with stimulation, grounding, or relaxation. Personal preferences have such a great influence, we must conclude that fly fishing is a very subjective sport. And yet after fly rods and fly lines, there is one common denominator—fly fishing boils down to a selection of flies. The flies in your box had better be the right patterns for the time and place, and they had better be well made.

We spend countless hours researching and developing imitation fish food, so we can intelligently fool our quarry. Fishing methods, techniques and equipment only accommodate the food we present—the food is the key to success.

For those of us involved in the production of this book, fly fishing is more than a sport, it is our livelihood. We are professionals who have the opportunity to spend a great deal of time on the water during all of the seasons. Our observations and field experience lead to the creative process of designing new fly patterns that are innovative advances from the classical patterns of yesterday.

This book is a window into the complexities of the many species and forms of natural fish foods that the hundreds of patterns in the pages and plates that follow attempt to imitate. The design and layout should help readers build a more complete approach in their quest to take fish. Each section is designed with the experienced fly fisher in mind. My goal is not only to help the novice fly fisher in advancing their fly tying techniques and patterns base, but to build on the understanding of entomology and its importance to the sport.

The fly fisher with fishing skills (casting, wading, knots, etc.) and fishing knowledge (reading water, spotting fish, general insects, etc.) is a two-dimensional fisher. The study of insects and fish behavior brings in a third dimension. Fly tying allows the fly fisher to explore this dimension intimately, thus becoming more adept at catching fish. Use this book as a guide to acquire the third dimension.

The "Mayflies" dry section (page 13) is presented in a unique reference method using the scientific classification of family names in alphabetical order. Each family name is accompanied with the common name. We use scientific classification names to provide clarity should one need to pursue more information through scientific publications. Each species is then dissected into life cycle stages, excluding nymphs, so that the fly tier can further understand and develop his knowledge from the bench to the water.

Included in "Dry Flies for Trout" are patterns other than mayflies. These are mainly attractor patterns not represented in the mayfly class, and are considered universal for taking cutthroat, brown, and rainbow trout.

"Caddis flies for Trout" is laid out in similar format, with the addition of the first life cycle stage. The life cycle layout follows the insect through its developmental metamorphosis: larva, pupa, emerger, and adult. The fly fisher should also understand that this is the way the insect moves through the water column. Fish key on certain insects and their life cycle stages, and the fisher should understand at what stage the fish are feeding to catch them.

The "Stonefly Dries for Trout" section represents the most commonly found species throughout the world. We have developed new and proven hi-tech patterns that more closely imitate the real insect. Fishing dry stoneflies is fascinating, but can be very technical. How high or low the pattern sits on the water surface can make a tremendous difference. Since stonefly hatches can be diversified, a variety of patterns is recommended.

Fishing often overlooked terrestrial insects can prove very productive. Many times their hatches are immense and of a long duration, supplying a great amount of fish food. During hot summer months, both lakes and rivers experience terrestrial hatches, and the species generally overlap. Our fly selection is limited to the most popular patterns.

The "Nymphs and Wet Flies for Trout" section represents an assortment of flies generally found on the bottom of the water column, or in the insect's first life cycle stage. The range of diversity, and overlapping of application for each fly in this section, limits the ability to organize, so they are presented in alphabetical order. The scientific classification can be used to obtain additional information from other publications regarding the appropriate fly for a specific need.

Some believe that steelhead fly fishing is the ultimate fresh water challenge. Whether you are using a standard single-handed rod or a Spey rod, ample skills are needed to perform this formidable task. Steelhead, although usually located in moderate conditions, are temperamental creatures and few in number, making their pursuit daunting to the most courageous fly fisher.

The "Steelhead and Salmon Flies" section is also presented in alphabetical order. There are many theories as to why steelhead come to the fly, none of which have been scientifically proven. The most popular theories suggest aggressive instinct, habitual feeding behavior, or the triggering of search images of saltwater organisms.

Within this section, some patterns do not mimic food, but rather, the unfolding of trial and error by dedicated steelheaders. Other patterns imitate the size, color and movements of the marine creatures that sustained steelhead while they grazed at sea.

Steelhead fly fishers examine their flies as works of art that possess vitality. A steelhead fly must have a soul born of form, function, and fine craftsmanship, which breathes confidence to the angler. It has to provide the kind of confidence that breeds the discipline to make that dozen more casts at the end of a tough day. Most steelheaders tie their own flies because production flies lack these qualities.

The steelhead flies in this book weren't included because of a tier's fantasy or that they were just pretty to look at, but because they are proven high-percentage scorers.

Saltwater fly fishing is the new frontier in our sport. Fly fishers are seeking the new challenges found on the flats, lagoons, rivers, reefs, and in the blue water. The diversity of saltwater fly fishing surpasses that of freshwater fly fishing due to the large number of fish species and the available fishing areas. The "Saltwater Flies" section was compiled by professional saltwater anglers who have put as much study into their passion as their freshwater counterparts.

Where specific histories and attitudes have largely influenced the evolution of freshwater trout, steelhead, and salmon tying techniques and materials, the majority of saltwater fly tying history has yet to be written. It is new and fascinating, and it is easy to become captivated by the unique openness of the fly tying techniques and applications. Saltwater tiers approach it with vigor and an "anything goes" attitude.

The birth of innovative saltwater fly fishing techniques and fly patterns occurs daily. The unparalleled variety of ocean organisms has stimulated the unconventional development of this new fishing frontier. However, there has already been a great deal of study and development in patterns and fishing techniques to date, and the demands of saltwater are no less critical than that of fresh water perhaps even more so.

The fly fisher looking to develop a three-dimensional approach to the sport will greatly benefit from the addition of fly tying. Those fishers and tiers looking to keeping up with current innovations will find new and exciting patterns to apply from this book. It is our goal to push the envelope on quality and innovation using the latest scientific research both in insect understanding and the development of new materials.

Troy Bachmann
Welches, Oregon
January 1998

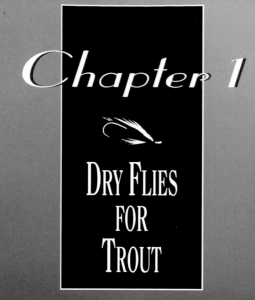

Chapter 1

Dry Flies for Trout

MAYFLIES

Rick Hafele

The world of the trout is largely an unknown world. After 30 years of fishing in streams, snorkeling in streams, and studying streams and the creatures that live in them, I find that most answers still remain a mystery. First, it is terribly difficult for our species to enter the world of the trout. Covered in neoprene and breathing through a snorkel, we can enter a cold, mountain trout stream for short periods of time. While there, we might be able to see this world as a trout does. Shimmering shafts of light dizzily dancing on bottom rocks and roots. Waves and currents pushing us left or right and up and down. But try as we might, we are not fish. We don't spend the night hidden in a tangle of roots, or mate in fast cold water, or spend the winter under a layer of ice, and we don't hunt the river for tiny morsels of food. We are simply visitors from another world hoping to satisfy our curiosity and appreciation for things beautiful and wild.

Trout are more restricted. They can't visit our world as we can theirs, but they can see into it. It's a good thing too, or dry-fly fishing wouldn't exist! The nature of light, however, adds a twist to the view a trout gets. Due to refraction, the bending of light rays as they pass from air into water, trout see out of the water's surface through a small circular window that increases in diameter as they sink deeper into their watery world. As they rise towards the surface, the window shrinks in diameter. It is through this window that we try to pass our dry flies with the hope that a trout is looking up. Fly fishers pass many types of flies through the trout's window. I would be willing to bet though, that through the history of fly fishing the most common type of dry fly ever passed through the window of the trout is the mayfly.

Mayflies are as closely linked to the history of fly fishing as a fly is to your tippet. Light Cahill, Quill Gordon, March Brown, Blue-Winged Olive, are names every fly fisher knows as well as his or her own. My own fascination with fly fishing took hold when I witnessed a huge mayfly hatch from a small farm pond in Illinois.

Why have mayflies been such a central part of fly fishing? I believe the first reason is that they present an ideal creature of nature to imitate with a fly. Nymphs mostly hide in the bottom rocks and debris while young. Once mature and ready to transform into the winged stage, they leave the safety of the stream or lake bottom and swim rather helplessly to the water's surface where gradually the winged "dun" stage escapes the hard exoskeleton of the nymph, and then rides buoyantly on the surface before taking flight. Mayfly duns float with wings upright and tails tilted up, and are thus obvious to both fish and fisherman.

Second, mayflies are abundant and diverse, found only in clean cold waters, the same type of waters that best satisfies the needs of trout. Thus, where the best hatches of mayflies occur, the best numbers of trout likewise occur. Finally, duns not eaten by fish or birds fly off the water and remain hidden for one or two days in the safety of shoreline trees and shrubs. There they transform into their final but brief form, the "spinner." Spinners have only one thing in mind—sex! And they must be quick about it for they live as little as an hour, two days at the most. After mating in swarms over the water, the females drop to the water's surface to lay eggs, offering themselves one more time to fish looking out their window to the world above.

Because mayfly duns and spinners offer an ideal food for trout, they offer an ideal insect to imitate with dry flies. The fly tier must then ask, "What characteristics of the dun or spinner are most important to imitate with a fly?" Trout after all are wild creatures fighting for survival, and are often difficult to fool. It has long been known that trout see color, and fly tiers spend hours working on just the right mix of colors for their flies. But is color the most important key to a successful fly? The shape of mayfly duns and spinners is distinct from other common dry flies like caddisfly or stonefly adults. But is shape the most important factor for our flies? The rich diversity of mayfly species in any single stream also means they occur in a rich variety of sizes. Some are small enough to test the eyesight of a teenager, while others are almost too big to fit in a trout's mouth. But how important is size when selecting your fly pattern? There are other subtle aspects of a fly. How does it float on the surface, low with the body touching the water, or high supported only by its legs and tails? What are the proportion of wings, legs, body and tails? Proper answers to these questions result in successful fly patterns.

In my opinion size and shape are the most critical aspects of a successful dry fly, or any fly pattern. Trout, over and over again, respond critically to size. If trout are selecting a natural, 4 millimeters long and your fly pattern is 6 mm long, be ready for disappointment. Likewise, if the natural's wings stand straight up, a fly pattern with wings flat along the body will be shunned by trout even when size and color exactly match the natural. How the fly floats is also very important, for this leaves a significant impression on the water's surface (the trout's window). Large flies float with more of their body on the surface, and fly patterns should match this character. Color, though important, falls at the bottom of my list. This is largely due to the fact that naturals of the same species vary in color. Just as people have different hair color and skin tones, so too insects of the same species vary slightly in body or wing color. As a result, the color of your fly cannot match the color of all the insects emerging. I try to use a fly that approximates the dominant color of the natural, and then don't worry about color further.

How exact of an imitation is exact enough? This depends on a great many variables. Clarity of water, type of water (flat or riffle?), time of day, type of weather, size of hatch (heavier hatches generally result in more selective feeding), fishing pressure (more anglers mean more selective trout), and species of fish (brown trout don't have a reputation as selective feeders for nothing) can all affect how trout respond to a particular fly pattern. As I said at the beginning, the world of the trout is largely unknown. Because of these unknowns, fly fishing is filled with mysteries and challenges, and the need for a variety of fly patterns. I don't believe this will ever change. And I thank God for that!

Baetis CDC Loop Wing Emerger

Color: Gray/olive
Hook: Daiichi 1150
Thread: Olive
  Flymaster
Tail: Blue dun hackle
  fibers
Body: Dun-dyed
  goose biot quill
Rib: Lime green
  Krystal Flash
Thorax: Olive Super
  Fine Dubbing
Shellback: White CDC

Note: The wing is tied in at the thorax, pushed back and tied in at the eye to create a bubble. Excess CDC is tied back for legs and floatation.

Baetis Emerger CDC, Egger's

Color: Gray
Hook: Daiichi 1180
Thread: Gray Flymaster
Tail: Dun Microfibetts,
  two split
Body: Gray Super Fine
  Dubbing
Rib: Green Krystal
  Flash
Thorax: Gray Super
  Fine Dubbing

Wing: Dun-dyed CDC/pearl Krystal Flash/gray closed-cell float foam
Note: Can imitate an emerger or a dun trapped in the surface film. The CDC helps with floatation, but mainly imitates unfolding wings trapped in the surface film. The float foam ensures the fly's ability to stay afloat after several fish takes.

Baetis Floating Emerger

Color: Slate green
Hook: Daiichi 1180
Thread: Olive
  Flymaster
Tail: Blue dun hackle
  fibers
Body: Slate green
  Super Fine Dubbing
Legs: Dun Microfibetts,
  two split
Wing: Gray synthetic
  dubbing ball

Note: Creating the dubbing ball for the wing is somewhat difficult. Take proper portion of gray dubbing, dub onto thread, hold thread vertically above and slide dubbing down thread. It should bunch up inside your finger on top of the body. Secure and shape with a few turns of thread. Cover thread with more olive dubbing and tie in legs at eye of hook.

Baetis Sparkle Dun

Color: Green
Hook: Daiichi 1180
Thread: Olive
  Flymaster
Tail: Dark olive
  Antron yarn
Body: Slate green
  Super Fine Dubbing
Wing: Natural deer
  hair
Note: It is important to
create a slim elegant body in order to imitate a mayfly properly.

Baetis Sparkle Dun

Color: Slate gray
Hook: Daiichi 1180
Thread: Gray
  Flymaster
Tail: Dark olive
  Antron yarn
Body: Slate gray Super
  Fine Dubbing
Wing: Natural deer
  hair

Baetis Cripple, Quill Body

Color: Dun/slate green
Hook: Daiichi 1180
Thread: Gray
  Flymaster
Tail: Gray Antron yarn
Body: Medium-dun
  goose biot quill
Rib: Copper fine wire
Collar Hackle: Blue
  dun dry-fly hackle
Thorax: Green pearl
  Flashabou/slate green Super Fine Dubbing
Wing: Natural deer hair

Note: Cripples imitate the adult as it is emerging from the nymphal shuck. This is often the most vulnerable stage of the life cycle. The green Flashabou represents the air pocket used by the nymph to reach the water's surface.

Twilight Baetis Cripple

Color: Dun/orange
Hook: Daiichi 1100
Thread: Gray Flymaster
Tail: Blue dun hackle
  fibers/light gray
  Antron yarn
Body: Slate gray Super
  Fine Dubbing
Rib: Copper fine wire
Collar Hackle: Blue
  dun dry-fly hackle
Thorax: Dun synthetic dubbing

Wings: 1st: Natural deer hair. 2nd: Orange highly visible Antron yarn
Note: Use only one or two turns of hackle, this is only to imitate legs and stabilize the fly; we don't want the fly floating too high. The orange Antron is added to improve visibility in low-light conditions.

Twilight Baetis Extended Body Compara-dun

Color: Slate green
Hook: Daiichi 1100
Thread: Olive Flymaster
Tail: Gray Microfibetts
Body: Monofilament
  and Microfibetts for
  base of extended body.
  Olive Super Fine
  Dubbing overwrap.
Wing: Gray-dyed
  natural deer
  hair/chartreuse highly visible Antron yarn

Note: The extended body can be difficult to master. The use of an extended body tool is a must. Create a loop with 3-pound monofilament. Tie a loop in at the bend of the hook and attach to extended body tool. Tie in four Microfibetts of the length needed. Wrap thread up and down Monofilament and Microfibetts to create extended body. Next tie in the deer hair wing and add the Antron. Before applying dubbing for the body, make sure under body of thread is completely smooth.

Baetis CDC Dun

Color: Slate green
Hook: Daiichi 1180
Thread: Olive
  Flymaster
Tail: Dun Microfibetts,
  four split
Body: Slate green
  Super Fine Dubbing
Wings: 1st: Blue dun-
  dyed CDC. 2nd:
  White CDC 3rd:
  Pearl Flashabou

Note: This is a silhouette-based pattern. The white CDC and flash helps the fisherman locate the fly.

Baetis Traditional Dun

Color: Blue dun
Hook: Daiichi 1180
Thread: Gray
  Flymaster
Tail: Blue dun hackle
  fibers
Body: Slate gray Super
  Fine Dubbing
Collar Hackle: Blue
  dun dry-fly hackle
Wing: Blue dun hen
  neck hackle tips

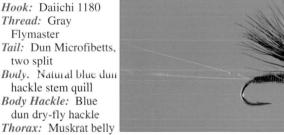

Note: The body hackle needs to be compact for highest floating function.

Baetis, Hair Wing Dun

Color: Blue dun
Hook: Daiichi 1180
Thread: Gray
  Flymaster
Tail: Dun Microfibetts,
  two split
Body: Natural blue dun
  hackle stem quill
Body Hackle: Blue
  dun dry-fly hackle
Thorax: Muskrat belly
  dubbing
Wings: 1st: Dun-dyed deer hair. 2nd: White highly visible Antron
  yarn

Note: Use only three turns of body hackle. Cut V-shape out of bottom so fly lies flat on water.

Baetis Thorax

Color: Olive
Hook: Daiichi 1180
Thread: Olive
  Flymaster
Tail: Blue dun hackle
  fibers split with a
  figure-eight of thread
Body: Olive Super
  Fine Dubbing
Body Hackle: Blue
  dun dry-fly hackle

Wings: Valley quail body plumes paired, cupped together, and tied
  upright
Note: The body hackle is not intended to be dense. It is tied in separated wraps; just enough to keep it afloat and imitate legs. If you cut a V-shaped wedge out of the bottom of the hackle, it will help the fly float upright. Not considered a high-floating dry-fly, but a flush floater.

Twilight Baetis Hairwing Dun

Color: Blue
  dun/orange
Hook: Daiichi 1100
Thread: Gray
  Flymaster
Tail: Dun Microfibetts,
  two split
Body: Natural blue dun
  hackle stem quill
Body Hackle: Blue
  dun dry-fly hackle
Thorax: Muskrat belly dubbing

Wings: 1st: Dun-dyed deer hair. 2nd: Orange highly visible Antron
  yarn
Note: The silhouette of this pattern is excellent for fooling fish, but if you have poor eyesight, it is hard for you to see. The highly visible Antron will allow you to watch the fly adrift, down to size #22 and in low-light conditions.

Twilight Baetis Parachute

Color: Green/
  chartreuse
Hook: Daiichi 1100
Thread: Olive
  Flymaster
Tail: Blue dun hackle
  fibers
Body: Olive Super
  Fine Dubbing
Body Hackle: Blue
  dun dry-fly hackle

Wings: Chartreuse highly visible Antron yarn
Note: The Antron yarn is looped with a bodkin. Don't make the loop post too high; just enough for you to see it but concealed from the fish.

Twilight Baetis Parachute

Color: Slate gray/pink
Hook: Daiichi 1100
Thread: Gray
  Flymaster
Tail: Blue dun hackle
  fibers
Body: Slate gray Super
  Fine Dubbing
Body Hackle: Blue
  dun dry-fly hackle
Wings: Fluorescent
  pink highly visible Antron yarn.

Baetis CDC Angel Wing Spinner

Color: Slate gray
Hook: Daiichi 1180
Thread: Gray
  Flymaster
Tail: Blue dun hackle
  fibers
Body: Slate gray Super
  Fine Dubbing
Wings: 1st: Blue dun-
  dyed CDC. 2nd:
  White Antron yarn.
  3rd: Silver pearl Sparkle Flash

Baetis CDC Angel Wing Spinner

Color: Slate green
Hook: Daiichi 1180
Thread: Olive Flymaster
Tail: Blue dun hackle fibers
Body: Slate gray Super Fine Dubbing
Wings: 1st: Blue dun-dyed CDC. 2nd: White Antron yarn. 3rd: Silver pearl Sparkle Flash

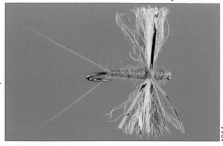

Baetis Spinner, Polywing

Color: Dun
Hook: Daiichi 1180
Thread: Gray Flymaster
Tag: Gray Super Fine Dubbing
Tail: Dun Microfibetts, two split with a figure-eight of thread
Body: Dun-dyed turkey biot quill
Rib: Same as thread
Thorax: Gray Super Fine Dubbing
Wing: White poly yarn
Note: The tail is split with a figure-eight of thread and a dubbing ball. Poly wings are used to imitate the translucent wing of a spent spinner while adding floatation to the fly.

CALLIBAETIS

Callibaetis Loop Wing Emerger

Color: Gray
Hook: Daiichi 1180
Thread: Gray Flymaster
Tail: Blue dun hackle fibers
Body: Gray Super Fine Dubbing
Rib: Lime green Krystal Flash
Collar Hackle: Grizzly dry-fly hackle
Thorax: Gray Super Fine Dubbing
Wing: White poly yarn
Note: This fly style is designed to sit suspended in the surface film with the tail and body submerged while the wing and thorax are above and visible to the angler. The loopwing pattern is perfect for imitating the mayfly emerging from the nymph's shuck.

Callibaetis Sparkle Dun

Color: Gray
Hook: Daiichi 1180
Thread: Gray Flymaster
Tail: Dark olive Antron yarn
Body: Gray Antron dubbing
Rib: Silver fine wire
Wing: Natural elk hair
Note: The tail is the

most crucial part of the fly. The colors and proportions are important: it imitates the nymphal shuck. Do not dress the tail or body too heavily. The rib adds segments to the body.

Callibaetis Cripple

Color: Gray
Hook: Daiichi 1180
Thread: Gray Monocord
Tail: Gray marabou
Body: Gray marabou
Rib: Silver fine wire
Body Hackle: Grizzly hackle, two wraps
Thorax: Gray Super Fine Dubbing
Wing: Natural deer hair

Note: Tie in tail and body material as one. To create taper it should be tied in tip first. Do not overdress tail or body, a bad habit of some tiers. The body needs an elegant taper and the barbs of the marabou need to be fluffy and clean to imitate the abdominal gills. It is always best to study the insect in your fishing area to ensure proper imitation.

Adams Traditional

Color: Gray
Hook: Daiichi 1180
Thread: Gray Flymaster
Tail: Mixed brown and grizzly hackle fibers
Body: Gray Super Fine Dubbing
Body Hackle: Brown and grizzly dry-fly hackle
Wing: Grizzly hen neck hackle tips

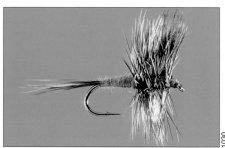

Note: Match the wing tips. Pair together so the cups of the feather tips are on the outside and split with a figure-eight of thread.

Callibaetis CDC Compara-dun

Color: Gray/speckled
Hook: Daiichi 1180
Thread: Gray Flymaster
Tail: Light gray Microfibetts
Body: Gray goose biot quills
Thorax: Gray Super Fine Dubbing
Wing: White or natural CDC/teal flank feather

Note: The wing is tied heavy and vertical and pulled to the sides to give it a Japanese fan look. The teal flank feather is in front to add contrast and proper coloration.

Callibaetis Hairwing Dun

Color: Slate gray
Hook: Daiichi 1180
Thread: Gray Monocord
Tail: Gray Microfibetts
Body: Light-dun goose biot quill
Rib: Gray Monocord thread
Body Hackle: Grizzly dry-fly hackle
Thorax: Muskrat belly dubbing
Wing: Natural deer hair

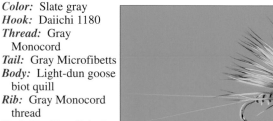

Note: When using goose or turkey quill for the body, it is a good idea to secure it with a rib to decrease the chance of the quill unraveling on sharp little fish teeth.

Callibaetis Thorax

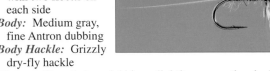

Color: Gray
Hook: Daiichi 1180
Thread: Gray
Flymaster
Tail: Gray
Microfibetts. Split tail
with two fibetts on
each side
Body: Medium gray,
fine Antron dubbing
Body Hackle: Grizzly
dry-fly hackle
Thorax: Gray Antron dubbing, slightly coarser than body
Wing: Gray/tan speckled partridge body plume matched, paired and
tied upright
Note: This is a nice imitation of adult mayflies landing to lay eggs. It
is a flush floater. The type of dubbing used is a matter of preference.
I prefer a coarser synthetic dubbing for larger mayfly imitations
because it adds contrast and floatation.

Speckled Wing Dun, Quill Body

Color: Slate gray
Hook: Daiichi 1180
Thread: Gray
Flymaster
Tail: Grizzly hackle
fibers
Body: Peacock quill,
stripped
Body Hackle: Grizzly
dry-fly hackle
Wing: Wood duck-
dyed mallard flank
Note: An Eastern Catskill tie combination of a high-floating and an
attractor concept.

Parachute Adams

Color: Gray
Hook: Daiichi 1180
Thread: Gray
Flymaster
Tail: Mixed brown and
grizzly hackle fibers
Body Hackle: Brown
and grizzly dry-fly
hackle
Wing: White calf body
hair, calf tail or poly
yarn

Twilight Adams Parachute

Color: Gray/Day-
Glo™
Hook: Daiichi 1100
Thread: Gray
Flymaster
Tail: Mixed brown and
grizzly hackle fibers
Body: Gray Super Fine
Dubbing
Body Hackle: Brown
and grizzly dry-fly
hackle
Wing: Day-Glo™ Krystal Flash
Note: The shimmer of the wing can be seen in the daylight, or you can
charge it with a strobe to glow in the dark for low-light conditions.

Twilight Red Adams Parachute

Color: Gray/flame
pink
Hook: Daiichi 1100
Thread: Gray
Flymaster
Tail: Mixed brown and
grizzly hackle fibers
Body: Gray Super Fine
Dubbing
Body Hackle: Brown
and grizzly dry-fly
hackle
Wing: Pink highly visible Antron yarn
Note: The addition of the Twilight Antron post enables many older
fishermen to track their fly.

Speckled Wing Spinner

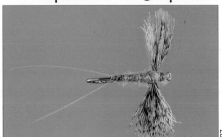

Color: Gray/partridge
Hook: Daiichi 1180
Thread: Gray
Flymaster
Tail: Gray Microfibetts
Body: Gray Super Fine
Dubbing
Wing: White poly
yarn, partridge plume
Note: The partridge
imitates the speckled
wings of the real *Callibaetis* insect.

Twilight Callibaetis Spinner

Color: Slate/Day-
Glo™
Hook: Daiichi 1100
Thread: Gray
Flymaster
Tail: Gray Microfibetts
Body: Gray Super Fine
Dubbing
Wings: 1st: White poly
yarn. 2nd:
Combination of pearl
and Day-Glo™ Krystal Flash
Note: This spinner pattern is much easier to see in all light conditions.

BLUE-WINGED OLIVE

CDC Loop Wing Emerger

Color: Olive
Hook: Daiichi 1510
Thread: Olive
Flymaster
Tail: Natural, blue dun
hackle fiber
Body: BWO Super
Fine Dubbing
Rib: Lime green
Krystal Flash
Body Hackle: Medium
dun CDC
Thorax: BWO Super Fine Dubbing/olive pearl glass bead
Wing: Blue dun-dyed CDC
Note: One of the most effective emerger patterns ever developed.
The curved hook and green pearl rib imitates the adult emerging
from the nymphal shuck, while the trapped air sack that took
the nymph to the surface and the CDC creates the perfect floatation
and color.

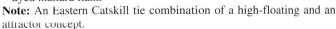

Blue Wing Olive Sparkle Dun

Color: Olive
Hook: Daiichi 1180
Thread: Olive Flymaster
Tail: Dark olive Antron yarn
Body: BWO Super Fine Dubbing
Wing: Natural deer hair

Note: Most anglers prefer vertical Sparkle Dun wings fully fanned out.

Blue Wing Olive Cripple

Color: Olive
Hook: Daiichi 1180
Thread: Olive Flymaster
Tails: 1st: Dark olive Antron yarn. 2nd: Olive marabou tips
Body: Olive marabou
Rib: Copper fine wire
Body Hackle: Olive-dyed grizzly dry-fly hackle
Thorax: Lime green Krystal Flash/olive Super Fine Dubbing
Wing: Dun-dyed deer hair

Note: The lime green Krystal Flash imitates the trapped air in the nymphal shuck as the adult begins to emerge.

Blue Quill Traditional

Color: Blue dun
Hook: Daiichi 1180
Thread: Gray Flymaster
Tail: Blue dun hackle fiber
Body: Peacock quill, stripped
Body Hackle: Blue dun dry-fly hackle
Wing: Mallard duck wing feather

Note: This pattern has been around forever. Tips and techniques that will make tying this pattern easier are: Treat the wing feather with hair spray, and tie in wings as if tying a parachute.

Extended Body Compara-dun

Color: Olive
Hook: Daiichi 1180
Thread: Olive Flymaster
Tail: Dun Microfibetts, four split
Body: Monofilament and Microfibetts for base of extended body. BWO Super Fine Dubbing over wrap
Wing: Dun-dyed deer hair

Note: I prefer to use a traditional dry-fly hook, rather than a curved egg hook. The traditional hook tends to have a higher percentage of hooking success. Often, the curved hook's gap is too narrow in smaller sizes.

Twilight Blue Wing Olive

Color: Olive
Hook: Daiichi 1100
Thread: Olive Flymaster
Tail: Blue dun hackle fibers
Body: BWO Super Fine Dubbing
Body Hackle: Blue dun dry-fly hackle
Wing: Day-Glo™ and pearl Flashabou

Note: This is a traditional high-floating dry-fly pattern that has been modified to be highly visible.

Twilight Extended Body Compara-dun

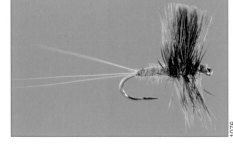

Color: Olive
Hook: Daiichi 1100
Thread: Olive Flymaster
Tail: Blue dun Microfibetts
Body: Monofilament and Microfibetts for base of extended body. BWO Super Fine Dubbing overwrap

Wings: 1st: Dun-dyed deer hair. 2nd: Metallic blue Krystal Flash
Note: The extension of the body is difficult. Use an extended body tool by Griffin Enterprises, and follow their directions.

Blue Wing Olive Thorax

Color: Olive
Hook: Daiichi 1180
Thread: Olive Flymaster
Tail: Gray Microfibetts, four split
Body: BWO Super Fine Dubbing
Body Hackle: Olive-dyed grizzly dry-fly hackle
Thorax: Same as body
Wing: Natural quail plumes, paired, cupped and tied upright
Note: Cut a "V" in the bottom of body hackle to help the fly sit flat on the water's surface.

Blue Wing Olive Parachute

Color: Olive
Hook: Daiichi 1180
Thread: Olive Flymaster
Tail: Blue dun hackle fibers
Body: BWO Super Fine Dubbing
Body Hackle: Blue dun dry-fly hackle
Wing: Gray, silver or white poly yarn

Twilight BWO Parachute

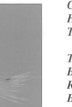

Color: Olive/blue
Hook: Daiichi 1100
Thread: Olive
Flymaster
Tail: Blue dun hackle
fibers
Body: BWO Super
Fine Dubbing
Body Hackle: Blue
dun dry-fly hackle
Wing: Fluorescent blue
highly visible Antron yarn
Note: Since BWOs are predominately early morning and late evening hatches, the highly visible wing gives the angler the great advantage of seeing the fish strike.

BWO Angel Wing Spinner

Color: Olive/Day-
Glo™
Hook: Daiichi 1180
Thread: Olive
Flymaster
Tail: Olive Super Fine
Dubbing
Body: BWO super fine
dubbing
Rib: Light olive #A
rod-wrapping thread
Wings: 1st: Gray poly yarn. 2nd: White Antron yarn
Note: Spinner hatches often happen in blankets, where there are so many spinners on the water that your fly disappears. The highly visible wing (angel wing) helps the angler keep track of his fly.

GREEN DRAKE

Green Drake CDC Loop Wing Emerger

Color: Slate green
Hook: Daiichi 1510
Thread: Olive
Monocord
Tail: Brown and olive
Antron yarn
Body: Dark olive
Super Fine Dubbing
Rib: Metallic green
Krystal Flash
Body Hackle: Natural
blue dun CDC
Thorax: Dark olive Antron dubbing
Wing: Gray poly yarn
Note: This pattern is truly unique. I developed it because there wasn't a successful Green Drake emerger pattern. This pattern is extremely effective because it represents the mayfly's most vulnerable stage when the adult is tied to the shuck in the surface film.

Green Drake Sparkle Dun

Color: Green
Hook: Daiichi 1180
Thread: Green
Monocord
Tail: Dark olive
Antron yarn
Body: Olive Antron
dubbing
Rib: Yellow #A rod-
wrapping thread
Wing: Dun-dyed deer
hair
Note: The color of the wing matches that of the real insect.

Green Drake Cripple

Color: Dark green
Hook: Daiichi 1180
Thread: Green
Monocord
Tail: Olive marabou
Body: Olive marabou
Rib: Copper fine wire
Body Hackle: Olive-
dyed grizzly dry-fly
hackle
Thorax: Olive Antron
dubbing
Wing: Blue dun-dyed deer hair
Note: The tail and the body are the same piece. The rib is reverse-wrapped to prevent unraveling.

Eastern Green Drake

Color: Brown/olive
Hook: Daiichi 1180
Thread: Olive
Flymaster
Tail: Olive-dyed
mallard flank
Body: Mixture of olive
and mahogany
Antron dubbing
Body Hackle: Blue
dun dry-fly hackle
Thorax: Dubbing, same as body
Wing: Valley quail plume
Note: The Eastern Green Drake can be tied in a yellow version also. In many cases Pale Evening Duns will work.

Green Drake Hairwing Dun

Color: Olive/dun
Hook: Daiichi 1180
Thread: Green
Monocord
Tail: Green
Microfibetts, several
split
Body: Olive Antron
dubbing
Rib: Yellow #A, rod-
wrapping thread
Body Hackle: Olive-dyed grizzly dry-fly hackle
Thorax: Olive Antron dubbing
Wings: 1st: Dark blue dun-dyed deer hair. 2nd: White poly yarn
Note: The wing can be tied with or without poly secondary wing, depending on the angler's eyesight.

Midwest Green Drake

Color: Green
Hook: Daiichi 1180
Thread: Green
Monocord
Tail: Moose hair
Body: Green pearl and
dark olive Krystal
Flash twisted around
hook shank
Body Hackle: Blue
dun dry-fly hackle
Wing: Blue dun hen neck hackle tips
Note: The body represents the translucent abdomen of the egg-laying adult.

Green Drake Parachute

Color: Olive
Hook: Daiichi 1180
Thread: Olive Flymaster
Tail: Blue dun hackle fibers
Body: Olive-dyed goose biot quill
Body Hackle: Olive-dyed grizzly dry-fly hackle
Thorax: Olive Antron dubbing
Wing: White poly yarn

Note: Though slightly more difficult to tie, the biot quill adds the look of a segmented body. The poly wing can either be cut or looped over for a cleaner more visible look.

Green Drake Paradrake

Color: Dark olive
Hook: Daiichi 1180
Thread: Olive or brown Flymaster
Tail: Olive-dyed deer hair
Body: Olive-dyed extended deer hair
Rib: Same as thread
Body Hackle: Olive-dyed grizzly dry-fly hackle
Wing: Natural elk hair

Note: The tapering of the body is accomplished by the tension of the thread when ribbed.

Green Drake Angel Wing Spinner

Color: Green
Hook: Daiichi 1180
Thread: Olive Flymaster
Tail: Gray Microfibetts
Body: Olive Super Fine Dubbing
Wings: 1st: White poly yarn. 2nd: Pearl and silver Krystal Flash

Green Drake Spinner

Color: Olive/brown
Hook: Daiichi 1180
Thread: Brown Monocord
Tail: Gray Microfibetts, several split
Body: March brown Antron dubbing
Rib: Yellow #A rod-wrapping thread
Wing: Gray or silver poly yarn

Note: In this last life cycle stage, the adult's body color usually changes. Species in specific regions are different, and the real insect's hatching should be studied for proper imitation.

HENDRICKSON

Hendrickson Dark Sparkle Dun

Color: Light gray
Hook: Daiichi 1180
Thread: Gray Flymaster
Tail: Gray Antron yarn
Body: Gray with a slight pink tint, Antron dubbing
Wing: Natural elk hair

Hendrickson Light Sparkle Dun

Color: Pale pink
Hook: Daiichi 1180
Thread: Cream Flymaster
Tail: Beige Antron yarn
Body: Hendrickson's pink Super Fine Dubbing
Wing: Natural elk hair

Hendrickson Twilight Loop Wing Emerger

Color: Light pink
Hook: Daiichi 1510
Thread: Gray Flymaster
Tail: Blue dun hackle fibers
Body: Hendrickson's pink Super Fine Dubbing
Rib: Lime green Krystal Flash
Body Hackle: Grizzly dry-fly hackle
Thorax: Gray with a slight pink tint, Antron dubbing mixture
Wing: Pink highly visible Antron yarn

Note: Since the style of this pattern is designed to be mostly submerged in the surface film, the wing needs to be made of a highly visible material, and not too tall. The wing helps tremendously in revealing the fly's location when adrift.

Hendrickson Compara-dun

Color: Pale pink
Hook: Daiichi 1180
Thread: Cream Flymaster
Tail: Tan Microfibetts
Body: Hendrickson's pink Super Fine Dubbing
Wing: Natural elk hair

Note: The difference between a Compara-dun and a Sparkle Dun is the tail. Sparkle Duns imitate an emerger. Compara-duns can imitate adults or spinners.

Hendrickson Dark Hairwing Dun

Color: Light gray
Hook: Daiichi 1180
Thread: Gray Flymaster
Tail: Gray Microfibetts, two split
Body: Gray stripped hackle stem
Body Hackle: Grizzly dry-fly hackle
Thorax: Light gray Antron dubbing
Wing: Natural elk hair
Note: Stripped hackle stems make a beautifully slender segmented mayfly body.

Hendrickson Light Hairwing Dun

Color: Beige
Hook: Daiichi 1180
Thread: Beige Flymaster
Tail: Tan Microfibetts
Body: Ginger stripped hackle stem
Body Hackle: Grizzly dry-fly hackle
Thorax: Pink Antron dubbing
Wing: Natural elk hair
Note: Soaking the hackle stem in water prior to use will make it supple and much easier to wrap around the hook shank.

Natural Dark

Color: Gray
Hook: Daiichi 1180
Thread: Gray Flymaster
Tail: Natural blue dun hackle fibers
Body: Light-dun goose biot quill
Body Hackle: Grizzly dry-fly hackle
Thorax: Gray Antron dubbing
Wing: White poly yarn

Natural Light

Color: Pale pink
Hook: Daiichi 1180
Thread: Beige Flymaster
Tail: Ginger hackle fibers
Body: Hendrickson's pink goose biot quill
Body Hackle: Grizzly dry-fly hackle
Thorax: Hendrickson's pink Super Fine Dubbing
Wing: White poly yarn

Twilight Hendrickson Parachute

Color: Pinkish gray
Hook: Daiichi 1100
Thread: Gray Flymaster
Tail: Natural, blue dun hackle fiber
Body: Gray/pink Antron dubbing
Body Hackle: Grizzly dry-fly hackle
Wing: Yellow highly visible Antron yarn

PALE EVENING DUN

PED Sparkle Dun

Color: Pale yellow
Hook: Daiichi 1180
Thread: Pale yellow Flymaster
Tail: Olive Antron yarn
Body: Pale yellow Super Fine Dubbing
Wing: Natural elk hair

PED Compara-dun

Color: Pale yellow
Hook: Daiichi 1180
Thread: Pale yellow Flymaster
Tail: Clear Microfibetts
Body: Pale yellow Super Fine Dubbing
Wing: Natural elk hair

PED Cripple

Color: Tan
Hook: Daiichi 1180
Thread: Tan Flymaster
Tail: Tan Antron yarn
Body: Light tannish yellow Antron dubbing
Body Hackle: Grizzly dry-fly hackle
Thorax: Tan Antron dubbing
Wing: Natural deer hair

Note: Pay close attention to the proportions. The silhouette is the key to a successfully tied cripple.

Compara-dun Sulfur

Color: Bright yellow
Hook: Daiichi 1180
Thread: Yellow Flymaster
Tail: Clear Microfibetts
Body: Fluorescent yellow Super Fine Dubbing
Wing: Natural deer hair

PED Angel Wing Spinner

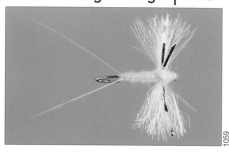

Color: Pale yellow
Hook: Daiichi 1180
Thread: Pale yellow Flymaster
Tail: Clear Microfibetts
Body: Pale yellow Super Fine Dubbing
Wings: 1st: Tan CDC 2nd: White poly yarn. 3rd: Pearl and silver Sparkle Flash

PALE MORNING DUN

PED Cream Puff Parachute

Color: Yellow
Hook: Daiichi 1180
Thread: Pale yellow Flymaster
Tail: Grizzly hackle fibers
Body: Pale yellow Super Fine Dubbing
Body Hackle: Grizzly dry-fly hackle
Wing: White poly yarn
Note: Anglers often prefer to fish parachute-style patterns because of visibility and the addition of the hackles imitating legs.

PMD Emerger

Color: Tan
Hook: Daiichi 1560
Thread: Tan Flymaster
Tail: Natural pheasant tail fibers
Body: Natural-ginger stripped hackle stem
Thorax: Tan opossum dubbing
Wing: White poly yarn
Note: This is a pattern that can be fished wet, well under the surface film, or dressed with floatant to be fished in the surface film. An extremely effective and versatile pattern.

PED Parachute

Color: Pale yellow
Hook: 1180
Thread: Yellow Flymaster
Tail: Natural ginger hackle fibers
Body: Yellow Super Fine Dubbing
Body Hackle: Natural ginger dry-fly hackle
Wing: White calf body hair or poly yarn
Note: This is a traditional color combination used for general applications.

PMD Loop Wing Emerger

Color: Pale green
Hook: Daiichi 1510
Thread: Pale olive Flymaster
Tail: Blue dun hackle fibers
Body: Pale green synthetic dubbing
Rib: Lime green Krystal Flash
Body Hackle: Blue dun dry-fly hackle
Thorax: Pale green Antron dubbing
Wing: White poly yarn, looped
Note: The thorax is of slightly darker and coarser dubbing to imitate the real insect and to add contrast.

Twilight PED Parachute

Color: Yellow/ fluorescent yellow
Hook: Daiichi 1100
Thread: Pale yellow Flymaster
Tail: Grizzly hackle fibers
Body: Pale yellow Super Fine Dubbing
Body Hackle: Grizzly dry-fly hackle
Wing: Fluorescent chartreuse Twinkle

PMD Sparkle Dun

Color: Pale green
Hook: Daiichi 1180
Thread: Olive Flymaster
Tail: Dark olive Antron yarn
Body: Pale green synthetic dubbing
Wing: Natural deer hair

PMD Sparkle Dun

Color: Pale olive
Hook: Daiichi 1180
Thread: Pale olive
Flymaster
Tail: Dark olive
Antron yarn
Body: Pale olive Super
Fine Dubbing
Wing: Natural deer
hair

PMD Sparkle Dun

Color: Pale orange
Hook: Daiichi 1180
Thread: Orange
Flymaster
Tail: Dark olive
Antron yarn
Body: Pale orange
synthetic dubbing
Wing: Natural deer
hair

Twilight Sparkle Dun

Color: Pale olive
Hook: Daiichi 1100
Thread: Pale olive
Flymaster
Tail: Dark olive
Antron yarn
Body: Pale olive Super
Fine Dubbing
Wings: 1st: Natural
deer hair. 2nd:
Fluorescent
chartreuse Antron yarn

Twilight Sparkle Dun

Color: Pale orange
Hook: Daiichi 1100
Thread: Light orange
Flymaster
Tail: Dark olive
Antron yarn
Body: Pale orange
synthetic dubbing
Wings: 1st: Natural
deer hair. 2nd:
Fluorescent orange
Antron yarn

PMD Cripple

Color: Tan
Hook: Daiichi 1180
Thread: Orange
Flymaster
Tail: Tan Antron yarn
Body: Tan-dyed
stripped hackle stem
Body Hackle: Ginger
dry-fly hackle
Thorax: Pale pink
Super Fine Dubbing
Wing: Natural deer hair

Note: Pale morning duns are among the most elegant and slender of the mayfly species. It is critical that the proportions, colors and sizes are exact.

PMD Extended Body Compara-dun

Color: Pale pink
Hook: Daiichi 1180
Thread: Cream
Flymaster
Tail: Clear
Microfibetts, split
Body: Monofilament
and Microfibetts for
base of extended
body. Pale pink Super
Fine Dubbing
overwrap
Wing: Natural elk hair

Note: It is important to create extended bodies that match the size and taper of the insect. It will take practice to perfect tying these bodies.

PMD Extended Body CDC

Color: Yellow
Hook: Daiichi 1510
Thread: Yellow
Flymaster
Tail: Cream large-
cut neck hackle.
Leave split ends
Body: Tail and body
are same piece
Thorax: Yellow
synthetic dubbing

Wing: Yellow CDC/yellow highly visible Antron yarn
Note: There are many things I like about the application of CDC feathers. They are light and lifelike imitating. However, they are fragile and take a high degree of maintenance. Often I will combine CDC with poly or other floating material to expand the variety of fishing applications. For example, this PMD pattern has both CDC and Antron wings. CDC feathers are good for the first fish, but then must be dried out thoroughly before their floating ability is fully restored. This is great if the backeddy only has one fish, but if there are abundant game, the added Antron can be greased and back to fishing immediately.

PMD Hairwing Dun

Color: Pale pink
Hook: Daiichi 1180
Thread: Pale pink
Flymaster
Tail: Clear
Microfibetts, split
Body: Pink-dyed
hackle stem
Body Hackle: Grizzly-
dyed fly hackle
Thorax: Pinkish tan
Antron dubbing
Wing: Natural deer hair

Note: There are many species and color variations of pale morning duns. Often the color that best represents the insect hatching in the particular area you are fishing will be the most effective. Trout are very selective when feeding on small mayflies.

Cream Puff Parachute

Color: Pale orange
Hook: Daiichi 1180
Thread: Orange Flymaster
Tail: Grizzly hackle fibers
Body: Pale orange synthetic dubbing
Body Hackle: Grizzly dry-fly hackle
Wing: White poly yarn

Twilight PMD Parachute

Color: Pale olive
Hook: Daiichi 1100
Thread: Pale olive Flymaster
Tail: Grizzly hackle fiber
Body: Pale olive Super Fine Dubbing
Body Hackle: Grizzly dry-fly hackle
Wing: Fluorescent chartreuse Twinkle

Twilight PMD Parachute

Color: Pale pink
Hook: Daiichi 1100
Thread: Orange Flymaster
Tail: Grizzly hackle fibers
Body: Pale pink Super Fine Dubbing
Body Hackle: Grizzly dry-fly hackle
Wing: Pink highly visible Antron yarn

PMD Poly Spinner

Color: Pinkish orange
Hook: Daiichi 1180
Thread: Orange Flymaster
Tail: Clear Microfibetts, split
Body: Pink/orange Antron Dubbing
Wing: White poly yarn

PMD CDC Spinner

Color: Pale orange
Hook: Daiichi 1180
Thread: Orange Flymaster
Tail: Clear Microfibetts
Body: Pale orange synthetic dubbing
Wing: Tan CDC plumes
Note: Designed for the most selective feeders.

The CDC wings have a captivating appeal of realism that poly does not have, however they lack durability. I have often walked into fishing areas where other fishermen were not catching and been successful with CDC patterns, but they are one-fish flies. A good technique is to have a half-dozen flies and change after each fish. Put the used flies in your hat bill to dry and recycle.

SLATE WING MAHOGANY DUN

Compara-drake Mahogany

Color: Dark brown
Hook: Daiichi 1180
Thread: Dark olive Flymaster
Tail: Brown-dyed deer hair
Body: Brown-dyed deer hair
Rib: Same as thread
Body Hackle: Blue dun dry-fly hackle
Wing: Silver or light-gray poly yarn

Note: Rules to follow for tying Paradrake patterns: Wing height and length of extended body is equal to hook shank. Pinch hair and pull back so that hair is tight and straight. Ribbing is wrapped with medium tension.

Blue Wing Mahogany Dun

Color: Brown/blue
Hook: Daiichi 1180
Thread: Brown Flymaster
Tail: Blue dun hackle fibers
Body: Brown-dyed goose biot quill
Body Hackle: Blue dun dry-fly hackle
Thorax: Brown synthetic dubbing
Wing: Gray poly yarn

Note: Used for imitating smaller sizes. Para-drake patterns are very difficult to tie smaller than #16.

HEXAGENIA

Hexagenia Emerger, Frontier

Color: Yellow/brown
Hook: Daiichi 1270
Thread: Yellow Flymaster
Tail: Brown Antron yarn
Body: Gold Antron dubbing
Rib: Brown, small, round vinyl rib
Body Hackle: Brown Antron yarn as trailing shuck

Legs: Wood duck-dyed mallard flank
Eyes: Black mono eyes, small
Thorax: Same as body
Wing: Four yellow CDC plumes matched, paired and tented back
Note: A fantastic emerger pattern that took years of research. I have most often witnessed this large mayfly preyed upon in the emerger stage.

Brian O'Keefe Photo

Hexagenia Sparkle Dun

Color: Golden
Hook: Daiichi 1180
Thread: Gold Monocord
Tail: Brown Antron yarn
Body: Gold Antron dubbing
Wing: Natural elk hair

Hexagenia Hairwing Dun

Color: Golden
Hook: Daiichi 1180
Thread: Gold Monocord
Tail: Ginger Microfibetts, several split to each side
Body: Gold Antron dubbing
Rib: Copper wire, fine
Body Hackle: Ginger dry-fly hackle
Thorax: Same as body
Wing: 1st: Gold Sparkle Flash. 2nd: Bleached elk hair
Note: Some anglers think the hair wingdun patterns are just like elk hair caddis patterns. This is not true. If you are an experienced tier, it is easy to distinguish the dissimilarities.

Hexagenia Compara-drake

Color: Yellow
Hook: Daiichi 1180
Thread: Tan Monocord
Tail: Gold-dyed deer hair or natural bleached elk rump
Body: Gold-dyed deer hair, extended from eye of hook
Rib: Tan or brown Monocord
Body Hackle: Ginger dry-fly hackle or yellow-dyed grizzly dry-fly hackle
Wing: Bleached elk hair
Note: This is a great pattern if you are fishing large adult Hex's. It is difficult to build a large mayfly pattern, the bigger they become, the harder it is to maintain perfect proportions. *Hexagenia's* vary in color, depending on location. Substitute color of materials as needed.

Hexagenia Parachute

Color: Golden
Hook: Daiichi 1180
Thread: Gold Monocord
Tail: Ginger hackle fibers
Body: Gold synthetic dubbing
Body Hackle: Natural ginger dry-fly hackle
Thorax: Yellow Antron dubbing
Wing: Tan poly yarn
Note: High-tech flies are not always your best choice.

Hexagenia Paradrake

Color: Yellow/brown
Hook: Daiichi 1180
Thread: Brown or yellow Monocord
Body: Wood duck-dyed mallard flank, extended and pulled back, and tied in at half the length of hook shank
Body Hackle: Natural ginger dry-fly hackle
Thorax: Yellow Antron dubbing
Wing: Yellow-dyed mallard flank

Hexagenia Spinner

Color: Yellow
Hook: Daiichi 1180
Thread: Yellow monocord
Tail: Ginger Microfibetts
Body: Tan and yellow braided nylon
Body Hackle: Gold-dyed grizzly saddle hackle
Eyes: Black mono eyes, small
Thorax: Tan synthetic dubbing
Wing: Clear Super Hair and pearl Krystal Flash

MARCH BROWN

March Brown Hairwing Dun

Color: Brown
Hook: Daiichi 1180
Thread: Brown Flymaster
Tail: Dark brown Microfibetts, split
Body: Natural-brown, stripped hackle stem
Body Hackle: Brown dry-fly hackle
Thorax: Brown Antron dubbing
Wings: 1st: Brown-dyed deer hair. 2nd: White poly yarn

March Brown Traditional Dun

Color: Brown
Hook: Daiichi 1180
Thread: Brown Flymaster
Tail: Natural-brown hackle fibers
Body: Brown-dyed goose biot quill
Body Hackle: Brown-dyed dry-fly hackle
Wing: Natural-brown hen hackle tips

Twilight Hairwing Dun

Color: Brown
Hook: Daiichi 1100
Thread: Brown Flymaster
Tail: Dark brown Microfibetts
Body: Brown-dyed stripped hackle stem
Body Hackle: Brown dry-fly hackle
Thorax: Brown Antron dubbing
Wings: 1st: Brown-dyed deer hair. 2nd: Fluorescent red highly visible Antron yarn

Note: This pattern is very effective but nearly impossible to see without the Twilight strip.

March Brown Parachute, Quill Body

Color: Brown
Hook: Daiichi 1180
Thread: Brown Flymaster
Tail: Natural-brown hackle fibers
Body: Brown-dyed goose biot quill
Body Hackle: Brown-dyed dry-fly hackle
Thorax: Brown Antron dubbing
Wing: White poly yarn

Note: The goose biot quill adds slenderness and segments to the body. Tiers tend to tie mayfly patterns too robustly.

Twilight March Brown Parachute

Color: Brown
Hook: Daiichi 1100
Thread: Brown Flymaster
Tail: Natural-brown hackle fibers
Body: Brown synthetic dubbing
Body Hackle: Brown-dyed dry-fly hackle
Wing: Orange highly visible Antron yarn

March Brown Spinner

Color: Gray
Hook: Daiichi 1180
Thread: Gray Flymaster
Tail: Gray Microfibetts
Rib: Gray Monocord thread
Body: Dark gray synthetic dubbing
Thorax: Same as body
Wing: White poly yarn

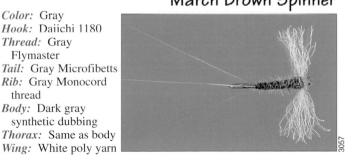

SIPHLONURIDAE

Dark Cahill

Color: Dark brown
Hook: Daiichi 1180
Thread: Brown Flymaster
Tail: Natural-brown hackle fibers
Body: Gray Super Fine Dubbing
Body Hackle: Brown dry-fly hackle
Wing: Wood duck-dyed mallard flank

Note: Wings are tied in a clump with tips toward eye of hook, erected with wraps of thread in front of wing, split in half with a bodkin and tied with several figure-eight wraps.

Light Cahill

Color: Cream
Hook: Daiichi 1180
Thread: Cream Flymaster
Tail: Natural cream hackle fibers
Body: Cream Super Fine Dubbing
Body Hackle: Light ginger dry-fly hackle
Wing: Wood duck-dyed mallard flank

Compara-drake

Color: Brown
Hook: Daiichi 1180
Thread: Dark brown Flymaster
Tail: Brown-dyed extended deer hair
Body: Tail, body and thorax are the same piece
Rib: Dark brown Flymaster thread
Body Hackle: Dark brown-dyed grizzly dry-fly hackle
Wing: Natural deer hair

Note: The trick to tying Compara-drake extended body patterns is spinning the correct amount of deer hair at the eye of the hook. Spin the deer hair so the tips point away from the wing.

Ginger Quill

Color: Tan
Hook: Daiichi 1180
Thread: Beige Flymaster
Tail: Natural ginger hackle fibers
Body: Bleached, stripped peacock quill
Body Hackle: One brown/one ginger dry-fly hackle
Wing: Natural mallard wing feather

Hare's Ear Parachute

Color: Tan
Hook: Daiichi 1180
Thread: Tan Flymaster
Tail: Natural and brown-dyed grizzly hackle fibers, mixed
Body: Natural hare's ear Antron dubbing
Body Hackle: Grizzly dry-fly hackle
Wing: White poly yarn

Spent Spinner, Natural Hare's Ear

Color: Tan
Hook: Daiichi 1180
Thread: Tan Flymaster
Tail: Tan Microfibetts
Body: Natural hare's ear Antron dubbing
Rib: Tan Monocord
Wing: White poly yarn

TRICO

Trico Loop Wing Emerger

Color: Black/white
Hook: Daiichi 1130
Thread: Black Flymaster
Tail: Gray Microfibetts (3), brown Antron yarn, half the length of the Microfibetts
Body: Black Krystal Flash
Body Hackle: Black dry-fly hackle
Thorax: Black Antron dubbing
Wing: White poly yarn

Note: The black Krystal Flash body creates an incredibly realistic fly. The Antron tail imitates the adult's shedding shuck, which makes all the difference when fishing large educated fish.

Gulper Special

Color: Brown
Hook: Daiichi 1180
Thread: Dark brown Flymaster
Tail: Grizzly hackle fibers
Body: Brown Antron dubbing
Body Hackle: Grizzly dry-fly hackle
Wing: White poly yarn

Light Cahill Parachute

Color: Cream
Hook: Daiichi 1180
Thread: Cream Flymaster
Tail: Ginger hackle fibers
Body: Cream Super Fine Dubbing
Body Hackle: Light ginger dry-fly hackle
Wing: White calf hair or poly yarn

Trico High & Dry Dun

Color: Black/Day-Glo™
Hook: Daiichi 1100
Thread: Black 8/0 or 14/0
Tail: Brown Microfibetts
Body: Black goose or turkey biot quill
Body Hackle: Black dry-fly hackle
Wing: Pearl and Day-Glo™ Flashabou looped, one on each side

Note: This is a tight little fly for fishing adults. Tying on a Daiichi 1100, provides the advantage of an oversized eye and a slightly wider gap. I recommend tying any size smaller than a #18 on this hook. Tricos have very clear translucent wings. The pearl and Day-Glo™ Flashabou is the perfect material.

Spent Spinner, Gray Drake

Color: Reddish brown
Hook: Daiichi 1180
Thread: Dark brown Flymaster
Tail: Brown Microfibetts, four split in half
Body: Dark brown synthetic dubbing
Rib: Brown Monocord thread
Wing: White poly yarn

Trico High & Dry Female

Color: Light green/dark brown/Day-Glo™
Hook: Daiichi 1100
Thread: Black 8/0 or 14/0
Tail: Brown Microfibetts
Body: Olive goose or turkey biot quill
Body Hackle: Brown-dyed Coachman dry-fly hackle
Wing: Pearl and Day-Glo™ Krystal Flash looped, one on each side

Note: Male and female Tricociliadae are distinctly different colors. Males are generally all black, while females can vary in shades of tan, brown or green.

Trico Hairwing Dun

Color: Black/silver
Hook: Daiichi 1100
Thread: Black 8/0 or 14/0
Tail: Black Microfibetts
Body: Black stripped hackle stem
Body Hackle: Black dry-fly hackle
Thorax: Black Antron dubbing
Wing: Light gray or silver poly yarn

Note: The difference between using synthetic or Antron dubbing is the effect you are trying to create. In general, I use synthetic dubbing such as Scintilla, Buggy Nymph, Super Fine Dubbing or Fly-Rite, when tying sleek elegant abdomens. Antron-based dubbings are commonly used in mayfly dry thoraxes and nymphs. Antron dubbing traps tiny air bubbles under the thorax and legs, like that of the landing adult mayfly.

Trico Hairwing Dun, Female

Color: Light green/black/silver
Hook: Daiichi 1100
Thread: Black 8/0 or 14/0
Tail: Black Microfibetts
Rib: Lime green Krystal Flash
Body: Green Krystal Flash
Body Hackle: Black dry-fly hackle
Thorax: Black Antron dubbing
Wing: White poly yarn

Note: The Hairwing Dun pattern is one of my all-time favorites. It has all of the imitating qualities of the real insect; split tail, elegant abdomen, slightly larger thorax with legs, a tilted back wing, and it lies flush with the surface of the water.

Trico, Black & White Parachute

Color: Black/white
Hook: Daiichi 1100
Thread: Black 8/0 or 14/0
Tail: Black hackle fibers
Body: Black thread
Body Hackle: Black dry-fly hackle
Wing: White poly yarn

Twilight Trico Parachute

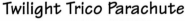

Color: Black/pink
Hook: Daiichi 1100
Thread: Black 8/0 or 14/0
Tail: Black hackle fibers
Body: Black thread
Body Hackle: Black dry-fly hackle
Wing: Pink highly visible Antron yarn

Note: Since the majority of Tricos are under size 18, and hatches are generally large masses, the Twilight wing is a big help in locating your fly. I have witnessed many fishermen thrash their water and put the fish down, because they fish using a general location technique. They cast losing sight of their fly, but knowing its general location. If a fish rises in that location, they strike, and more often than not, come up empty-handed. Twilight flies will provide the means for more precise fishing.

Twilight Trico Parachute, Female

Color: Light olive/black/orange
Hook: Daiichi 1100
Thread: Black 8/0 or 14/0
Tail: Black hackle fibers
Body: Fluorescent green Super Hair
Body Hackle: Black dry-fly hackle
Thorax: Black Antron dubbing
Wing: Orange highly visible Antron yarn

Note: Trico females often have bright green abdomens.

Trico Angel Wing Spinner

Color: Black/Day-Glo™
Hook: Daiichi 1100
Thread: Black 8/0 or 14/0
Tail: Black Microfibetts
Body: Black-dyed hackle stem
Thorax: Black Antron dubbing
Wings: 1st: White poly yarn. 2nd: Silver and pearl Sparkle Flash

Trico Angel Wing Spinner, Female

Color: Light green/black
Hook: Daiichi 1100
Thread: Black 8/0 or 14/0
Tail: Gray Microfibetts
Body: Olive-dyed hackle stem
Thorax: Brown Antron dubbing
Wings: 1st: White poly yarn. 2nd: Silver and pearl Sparkle Flash

Note: Often generic patterns will not fool the fish. An exact imitation is needed to produce takes.

Twilight Trico Parachute Spinner

Color: Dark brown/Day-Glo™
Hook: Daiichi 1100
Thread: Black 8/0 or 14/0
Tail: Gray Microfibetts
Body: Brown synthetic dubbing
Thorax: Same as body
Wings: 1st: White poly yarn. 2nd: Day-Glo™ Flashabou. 3rd: Fluorescent pink Antron yarn

Note: Spinners are often difficult to see in riffles or where the water's surface is not flat. The high visible post sits above the surface like a beacon. The Day-Glo™ wing is not applied to make the fly glow, but to imitate the Tricos translucent, delicate wings.

OTHER DRY FLIES

Adams Trude

Color: Gray/white
Hook: Daiichi 1180
Thread: Gray Flymaster
Tail: Natural golden pheasant crest tippet fibers
Body: Gray Antron dubbing
Collar Hackle: Brown dry-fly hackle
Wing: White calf tail

Beetle Bug Coachman

Color: Red/brown/white
Hook: Daiichi 1180
Thread: Red Flymaster
Tail: Natural elk hair
Body: Red Flymaster
Body Hackle: Brown-dyed Coachman dry-fly hackle
Wing: White calf body hair

Note: A terrific attraction pattern that has a sleeker taper to the body than a Royal Wulff. Wings are tied heavy and forward.

Damsel Dry

Color: Blue
Hook: Daiichi 1510
Thread: Black Flymaster
Tail: Blue and black-dyed braided nylon
Body: Blue Antron dubbing
Eyes: Black plastic mono eyes
Thorax: Same as body
Shellback: White Antron yarn with a black Antron yarn stripe
Wing: Light gray Super Hair
Note: This is the best dry damsel pattern I've seen.

Griffith's Gnat

Color: Peacock
Hook: Daiichi 1180
Thread: Black Flymaster
Body: Peacock herl
Body Hackle: Grizzly dry-fly hackle
Note: Space the hackle out. You are trying to imitate a cluster of midges. You only need enough hackle to make it float. A good Griffith's Gnat is tied hackle forward and with excellent quality peacock.

Hackle Peacock, Brown

Color: Peacock
Hook: Daiichi 1180
Thread: Black Flymaster
Tail: Red strung saddle hackle fibers
Body: Peacock herl
Rib: Silver fine wire
Collar Hackle: Brown, slightly webby saddle hackle

Note: The hackle should be semi-stiff, allowing it to be fished either wet or dry.

Hackle Peacock, Gray

Color: Peacock
Hook: Daiichi 1180
Thread: Black Flymaster
Tail: Red strung saddle hackle fibers
Body: Peacock herl
Rib: Silver fine wire
Collar Hackle: Grizzly, slightly webby saddle hackle

Lime Trude

Color: Lime/white
Hook: Daiichi 1180
Thread: Light olive Flymaster
Tail: Natural golden pheasant crest tippet fibers
Body: Lime Antron dubbing
Collar Hackle: Brown dry-fly hackle
Wing: White calf tail

Mosquito

Color: Black/white
Hook: Daiichi 1180
Thread: Black Flymaster
Tail: Grizzly hackle fibers
Body: Moose mane wrapped around hook shank, tapered
Body Hackle: Grizzly dry-fly hackle
Wing: Grizzly hen neck-hackle tips, paired and matched so cups of feathers point outward
Note: The heavier the collar hackle, the higher the fly will float.

Pink Trude

Color: Pink/white
Hook: Daiichi 1180
Thread: Cream Flymaster
Tail: Natural golden pheasant crest tippet fibers
Body: Pink Antron dubbing
Collar Hackle: Cream dry-fly hackle
Wing: White calf tail
Note: Trudes are very popular cutthroat patterns.

Royal Wulff

Color: Royal
Hook: Daiichi 1180
Thread: Black Flymaster
Tail: Natural elk hair
Body: Peacock herl and red rayon floss
Rib: Silver fine wire
Collar Hackle: Brown-dyed Coachman dry-fly hackle
Wings: White calf tail or white calf body hair

Renegade

Color: Peacock
Hook: Daiichi 1180
Thread: Black Flymaster
Tag: Gold flat #16-#18 Mylar tinsel
Body: Peacock herl
Body Hackle: Brown dry-fly hackle
Collar Hackle: Cream dry-fly hackle

Tarantula, Frontier

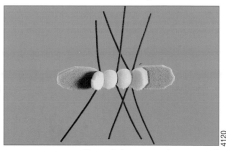

Color: Tan
Hook: Daiichi 1720
Thread: Black flat waxed
Body: Tan/brown/yellow layered closed-cell float foam
Rib: Thread-created segments
Legs: Medium, round rubber legs
Note: A very popular attractor pattern for rainbow, cutthroat, and brown trout. The body is light enough to design and color with Pantone® pens.

Royal Coachman Trude

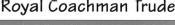

Color: Royal
Hook: Daiichi 1180
Thread: Black Flymaster
Tail: Natural golden pheasant crest tippet fibers
Body: Peacock herl and red rayon floss
Rib: Silver fine wire
Collar Hackle: Brown-dyed Coachman dry-fly hackle
Wing: White calf tail
Note: Caution; materials and proportions determine the difference between a well-tied fly and a poorly tied fly. Compromises on materials only lower quality.

Gray Wulff

Color: Gray
Hook: Daiichi 1180
Thread: Gray Flymaster
Tail: Dark moose body hair
Body: Gray Super Fine Dubbing
Body Hackle: Blue dun dry-fly hackle
Wings: Natural elk hair

Chapter 2

CADDISFLIES FOR TROUT

CADDISFLIES

Troy Bachmann

Darren and I sat in "position" trying to catch our breath. The sun was still high and warm enough to dry out our clothes. We were the first to reach our favorite back-eddy and sat high on the bank to ensure our visibility to other anglers.

We were teenagers, working our summers tying flies and driving shuttle for the local fly shop. We discovered this special spot the previous summer and knew every current, rock, and every fish in the area. This particular back-eddy rivaled any of the other fishing spots on the lower one hundred miles of the Deschutes River.

It was midday as we headed for our favorite spot in search of hungry redband rainbow trout. Since the boats were on the river with their clients and it would be an hour after dusk before they pulled into the boat launch area, we were confined to one side of the river.

At dusk we had our favorite riffle. It tapers off an island about a mile up from our pick-up area. It allowed us good fishing and we were able to see the arriving boats in plenty of time to meet them. The riffle was long, with perfect water depth and bottom structure to house an abundant area of rainbows. It was hot and arid; perfect conditions for caddisfly hatches. Deschutes River is famed for its wildness, steelhead runs, resident hybrid redband rainbow trout, stonefly, caddisfly and mayfly hatches. The caddisfly hatches are enormous and initiate half-witted, out-of-control feeding behavior. Match the hatch and chances are you will have to buy a new cotton mesh for your net.

Darren and I were standing in our island riffle preparing to fish. One boat gently pulled into our riffle and the guide asked if he could fish his single client there. "Of course," we replied. As if we had a choice! We were shuttle drivers at the bottom of the totem pole, and the two-hour trip back was a lot easier if the clients were happy.

We found ourselves standing across from a back-eddy on the other side of the river that we had not noticed before. It was barely visible but our trained ears tuned in to the frantic rising of a large number of fish. We stopped, noticing the working fish simultaneously. They were many, and they were untroubled and feeding as if it was Thanksgiving. We found a high bank where we could study the eddy for the rest of the evening.

The eddy was large and appeared deep, with a high opposing bank and overhanging alders for casting. We discussed the topography and concluded that the reason we had not seen anyone fishing it before was that it was "a bitch of a spot" to get to. The stakes were high; lots of big fish and lots of work. We planned our strategy for the next day, swearing to secrecy.

The next day we were on the river at 4:30 a.m. putting in a group of fishermen. We wasted no time fishing our way to the pick-up area, arriving before noon. We needed to study the back-eddy in full sunlight in order to see the bottom's structure.

The swim was cool and refreshing. We stood with clothes dripping, high on the outcrop, relishing the full view of our newly discovered playground. "Not many fish or much insect activity this time of day," Darren said. There were just a few small fish cruising around about a foot under the surface. We sat and dissected the eddy. It was bigger and deeper than we had thought. Stretching forty yards long and equal in width, the structure was heaven for fish. Seams, upwellings, overhanging trees, tailing riffles, deep water for cover, and plenty of food!

I like to think of every fishing spot as a magic locked box, then I strive to figure out how to unlock its secrets to get to the treasure and reap the wealth. This place was magical. In the middle of this grand eddy was a gravel bar, perfectly designed for the experienced wader. The gravel bar began underneath the overhanging trees and was completely hidden by the greenish water; it extended out to the middle of the eddy ending with a perfect casting platform. The current was swift, turning in such a way that it had built the bar to accommo-

date an angler on each side. I volunteered to go first. It was a little soft in places, but for the most part secure.

We knew that casting on an inactive back-eddy would cause the fish to go deep so we agreed to wait for the fish to start rising before casting. The systematic approach we had learned from the professional guide staff would be our strategy. Casting not to the biggest fish but to the closest fish. They called it "cherry picking." If you cast to a fish that is far away when fish are feeding at your feet, chances are you will catch your selected fish, but you will lose the opportunity of catching the fish close in. They will be spooked and you'll have to move out or cast further for the next one. Select the fish closest to you and work your way out.

Since that first evening of "spectacular" fishing, we have refined our approach and casting techniques. Tonight, as we sit waiting for the eddy to turn on, we reflect on our past fishing experiences. "Wouldn't it be great to be a shuttle driver and fly tier for the rest of your life?" I asked Darren. We both took a deep breath of cheek grass and sage and nodded our heads, knowing that life couldn't get much better.

The shade covered us mid-sentence and that was our cue to get into position. Hot, arid July evenings bring caddisflies. With four-weights in hand, we stand patiently waiting for the fish and insects to become active. "What do you have on, Darren?" I asked.

"A tan Kings River Caddis. You?" he replied.

"Olive Fullback." We knew that we were both mentally recalling our fly box inventories to make sure we had enough of what the other had. I had plenty of K-caddis and I was sure Darren had Fullbacks. We had been here before when one of us would discover the "hot fly" and the other didn't have any with him. Gritting your teeth and begging your buddy for one of his was a real blow to the ego. One or two episodes like that and you carry the country store!

This evening I was lucky; the olive Fullback was the treat. I hooked four to one fish over Darren. While he dug around searching for a size 14 Olive Fullback, I hooked and landed two more 'bows. Out of the corner of my eye I saw his hands begin to shake. I tried to hold back a smile, but it was a hopeless battle I didn't want to win. "So, have any Fullbacks?" I asked. Another fish took. This one was large and jumping, taking line at will. I had to contain my humor and concentrate. Darren of course, was thinking he had to wait another grueling five minutes while I landed the fish before he could get a fly from me. I picked two flies from my box and handed them to Darren. "Take two, you might break one off." As he was tying the fly on, I asked him how many caddisfly imitations he had tried before giving up and asking me for one. He said, "Five, and they were all refused. Isn't it remarkable that in a feeding frenzy trout can tell the difference between color, size, and shape!" We both knew it was the fly rather than fishing ability that had factored the score. Darren was an exemplary fly fisherman.

Caddisflies represent more than half of the aquatic insect life found in most rivers in North America. There are hundreds of species, colors, sizes, and shapes. There is a fifty percent chance or better that fish in these rivers will be keyed on some life-cycle stage of a caddisfly. As a rule, the caddisfly hatch is a big bloom or blanket, providing fish with a plentiful, easy meal. The most difficult part of fishing caddisflies is matching a particular hatch. Due to the overwhelming variations of the species and their four life-cycle stages, the angler needs to put a fair amount of study into imitating them. This book includes many unique caddisfly patterns in each of the life-cycle stages. From the small Beadhead Larva to the giant Cased Caddis, from Twilight Micro Caddis adults to giant October Caddis adults, all have proven successful in front of trout that are feeding on the real thing.

Beadhead Caddis Larva

Color: Brown
Hook: Daiichi 1150
Thread: Brown
  Monocord
Bead: Brass
Body: Dark brown
  rabbit Antron blend
Rib: Gold oval fine
  Mylar
Thorax: Brown long-
  fiber synthetic
  dubbing

Note: The dubbing used here is specially blended to add a realistic appearance. The long-fibers imitate legs and also trap micro bubbles of air that duplicate moving caddis larvae.

Beadhead Caddis Larva

Color: Caddis green
Hook: Daiichi 1150
Thread: Black
  Monocord
Body: Caddis green,
  long-fiber Antron
  dubbing
Rib: Gold fine flax
Thorax: Peacock herl
Note: Caddis larvae
vary in color. Caddis
green is the most popular.

Beadhead Caddis Larva

Color: Gray
Hook: Daiichi 1150
Thread: Black
  Monocord
Bead: Brass
Body: Gray long-fiber
  synthetic dubbing
Rib: Rainbow Krystal
  Flash
Thorax: Black long-
  fiber Antron blend

Note: General rule for bead matching and sizing: 3/32: #16 and below. 1/8: #14 and #12. 5/32: #10 and #8. 3/16: #6 and up.

Beadhead Caddis Larva

Color: Olive
Hook: Daiichi 1150
Thread: Black
  Monocord
Bead: Brass
Body: Olive Antron
  dubbing
Rib: Lime green
  Krystal Flash
Thorax: Dark brown,
  long-fiber Antron
  blend

Note: The color of the body should match that of the insect in your area. Taking a screen sample is beneficial. It is my experience that when the color is matched the success rate increases. You may often get by with whatever color you have, but you wouldn't use a putter to drive a golf ball.

Beadhead Caddis Larva

Color: Peacock
Hook: Daiichi 1150
Thread: Red
  Flymaster
Bead: Brass
Body: Peacock herl
Rib: Copper fine wire,
  cross-wrapped with
  herl
Collar Hackle: White
  speckled partridge
  flank

Beadhead Caddis Larva

Color: Tan/yellow
Hook: Daiichi 1150
Thread: Brown
  Monocord
Bead: Brass
Body: Gold/tan
  synthetic long-fiber
  dubbing
Rib: Copper fine wire
Thorax: Dark brown,
  long-fiber Antron
  blend

Beadhead Flashbody Larva

Color: Dark green
Hook: Daiichi 1150
Thread: Green
  Monocord
Bead: Brass
Body: Olive/peacock
  Sparkle Flash
  Maxibraid
Thorax: Dark brown,
  long-fiber Antron
  blend

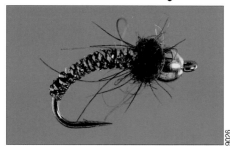

Note: Sparkle Flash Maxibraid is a Tiewell product made with strands of fine nylon thread between pearlescent Mylar. It is durable enough to endure the fine teeth of fish.

Beadhead Flashbody Larva

Color: Green
Hook: Daiichi 1150
Thread: Green
  Monocord
Bead: Brass
Body: Green/olive
  Sparkle Flash
  Maxibraid
Thorax: Peacock herl
Note: Considered an
attractor pattern, but

may imitate the larva molting into the pupa stage. It has the silhouette of the caddis larva, but when water conditions are cloudy, it has flash to attract the fish.

Beadhead Flashbody Larva

Color: Yellow
Hook: Daiichi 1150
Thread: Yellow Monocord
Bead: Brass
Body: Yellow pearl Sparkle Flash Maxibraid
Thorax: Gold, long-fiber Antron blend

Glassy Caddis Larva

Color: Green
Hook: Daiichi 1510
Thread: Olive Flymaster
Body: Olive Antron dubbing and bright green iridescent glass beads
Legs: Wood duck-dyed mallard flank
Head: Brown Antron dubbing
Note: A new "high-tech" pattern for the more discerning fish.

Caddis Larva

Color: Green
Hook: Daiichi 1150
Thread: Black Flymaster
Weight: Small lead wire (thorax area only)
Body: Caddis green, Antron dubbing
Rib: Lime green Krystal Flash
Collar Hackle: Brown ringed-neck pheasant plume fibers
Thorax: Black long-fiber Antron dubbing
Note: The rib is the most important feature of this pattern.

Glassy Caddis Larva

Color: Tan
Hook: Daiichi 1510
Thread: Tan Flymaster
Body: Tan Antron dubbing and tan iridescent glass beads
Legs: Wood duck-dyed mallard flank
Head: Brown Antron dubbing
Note: Each segment of the body is tied separately.

Caddis Larva

Color: Tan
Hook: Daiichi 1150
Thread: Brown Flymaster
Weight: Small lead wire (thorax area only)
Body: Light tan Antron dubbing
Rib: Lime green Krystal Flash
Collar Hackle: Brown ringed-neck pheasant plume fibers
Thorax: Brown long-fiber Antron dubbing

PUPAE

Beadhead Caddis Pupa

Color: Brown
Hook: Daiichi 1560
Thread: Dark brown Flymaster
Bead: Brass
Body: Brown Antron yarn
Thorax: Peacock herl
Wing: Brown ringed-neck pheasant plume fibers

Cased Caddis Larva

Color: Peacock/brown
Hook: Daiichi 2220
Thread: Black Monocord
Weight: Large lead wire
Body: Peacock herl
Rib: Copper medium wire
Body Hackle: Brown saddle hackle, cut short
Throat: Black hackle fibers
Thorax: Light tan and black Antron dubbing
Note: The majority of caddis larvae build body-protecting casings of various available materials in which they mature. This is a great pattern fished in all sizes. I usually fish it on a dropper with a small pupa at the point.

Beadhead Caddis Pupa

Color: Olive
Hook: Daiichi 1560
Thread: Olive Flymaster
Bead: Brass
Body: Olive Antron yarn
Thorax: Peacock herl
Wing: Brown ringed-neck pheasant plume fibers
Note: The body needs to be slightly twisted and wrapped very tightly around hook shank to avoid unraveling and slipping down the bend of the hook.

Beadhead Free-Living Caddis Pupa

Color: Caddis green
Hook: Daiichi 1560
Thread: Brown
  Flymaster
Bead: Brass
Body: Bright green
  Scintilla Caliente
  dubbing
Body Hackle: Natural-
  brown partridge
  plumage

Thorax: Brown Antron dubbing
Wings: 1st: Partridge plumage. 2nd: Ringed-neck pheasant tail
  fibers
Note: Free-living caddis, reside among the rocks without a casing.
They have prominent antennae. The form and silhouette of this pat-
tern imitates the rock worm emerging as the pupa.

Beadhead Free-Living Caddis Pupa

Color: Olive
Hook: Daiichi 1560
Thread: Brown
  Flymaster
Bead: Brass
Body: Olive Scintilla
  Caliente dubbing
Body Hackle: Natural-
  brown partridge
  plumage
Thorax: Brown Antron
  dubbing
Wings: 1st: Partridge plumage. 2nd: Ringed-neck pheasant tail fibers
Note: I like Scintilla because the sparkle imitates the air created by
the insect when emerging to surface.

Beadhead Free-Living Caddis Pupa

Color: Tan
Hook: Daiichi 1560
Thread: Brown
  Flymaster
Bead: Brass
Body: Tan Scintilla
  Caliente dubbing
Body Hackle: Natural-
  brown partridge
  plumage
Thorax: Brown Antron
  dubbing
Wing: 1st: Partridge plumage. 2nd: Ringed-neck pheasant tail fibers

Caddis Pupa, October

Color: Orange
Hook: Daiichi 1560
Thread: Orange
  Monocord
Body: Orange Antron
  dubbing
Rib: Yellow #A Rod
  wrapping thread
Body Hackle: Natural-
  black ringed-neck
  pheasant semi-plume
Thorax: Same as body
Eyes: Tan or black mono eyes
Wing: Bluish green ring-necked pheasant rump, one on each side
Note: The eyes are burned 30-pound monofilament because the
proper size and color is not available. Maxima brand will provide the
best color.

Deep Sparkle Pupa

Color: Black
Hook: Daiichi 1180 or
  1560
Thread: Black
  Flymaster
Body: Black Antron
  dubbing
Legs: Brown ringed-
  neck pheasant plume
  feathers

Thorax: Black Antron
  dubbing
Shellback: Black Antron yarn tied in at bend of hook then pulled
  over to the thorax to create a bubble effect
Note: The bubble and Antron dubbing trap air simulating the bloated
caddis larva shuck. It is important to form an egg shaped symmetrical
bubble. Legs should extend the length of the body.

Deep Sparkle Pupa

Color: Ginger
Hook: Daiichi 1180 or
  1560
Thread: Tan Flymaster
Body: Yellow/tan
  Antron dubbing
Legs: Brown ringed-
  neck pheasant plume
  fibers
Thorax: Light brown
  Antron dubbing
Shellback: Ginger Antron tied in at bend of hook, then pulled over
  to the thorax to create a bubble effect
Note: The Deep Sparkle Pupa is not the same as the Emergent
Sparkle Pupa. The Deep is the first stage of the pupa and lives at the
bottom of the water column. The emerger lives in the upper portion
of the water column.

Deep Sparkle Pupa

Color: Gray
Hook: Daiichi 1180 or
  1560
Thread: Gray
  Flymaster
Body: Gray Antron
  dubbing
Legs: Brown ringed-
  neck pheasant plume
  fibers

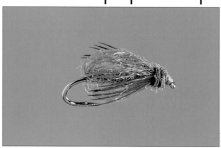

Thorax: Dark gray
  Antron dubbing
Shellback: Light gray Antron yarn tied in at bend of hook, then
  pulled over to the thorax to create bubble effect

Deep Sparkle Pupa

Color: Green
Hook: Daiichi 1180 or
  1560
Thread: Brown
  Flymaster
Body: Light brown
  Antron dubbing
Legs: Brown ringed-
  neck pheasant plume
  fibers
Thorax: Dark reddish
  brown Antron dubbing

Shellback: Green Antron yarn tied in at bend of hook, then pulled
  over to the thorax to create bubble effect

Deep Sparkle Pupa

Color: Yellow/brown
Hook: Daiichi 1180 or 1560
Thread: Brown Flymaster
Body: Light brown Antron dubbing
Legs: Brown ringed-neck pheasant plume fibers
Thorax: Dark reddish brown Antron dubbing
Shellback: Tan Antron yarn tied in at bend of hook, then pulled over to the thorax to create bubble effect
Note: The body should be visible through the Antron bubble. Tying the bubble too heavily will change the effectiveness dramatically.

Glassy Caddis Pupa

Color: Tan
Hook: Daiichi 1510
Thread: Brown Flymaster
Body: Tan transparent glass beads
Rib: Tan combination of Antron, synthetic and long-fiber rabbit dubbing
Head: Brown glass bead with reddish brown dubbing
Wing: Natural deer hair

Glassy Caddis Pupa

Color: Dark green
Hook: Daiichi 1510
Thread: Brown Flymaster
Body: Dark green glass beads
Rib: Olive combination of Antron, synthetic and long-fiber rabbit dubbing
Head: Brown glass bead with reddish brown dubbing
Wing: Natural deer hair
Note: The long fibers of the dubbing are swept back with a toothbrush, creating a bubble shape (pupal shuck).

Net Builder Caddis Pupa

Color: Brown
Hook: Daiichi 1560
Thread: Brown Flymaster
Body: Brown Scintilla Caliente dubbing
Legs: Iridescent pheasant rump plumage
Thorax: Dark brown long-fiber Antron dubbing
Wing: Mallard duck wing
Note: Net-building caddis live in riffles in net houses much like a tent. Their wings and legs are distinct in appearance.

Glassy Caddis Pupa

Color: Gray
Hook: Daiichi 1510
Thread: Black Flymaster
Body: Gray/pearl glass beads
Rib: Gray combination of Antron, synthetic and long-fiber rabbit dubbing
Head: Black glass bead with black dubbing
Wing: Natural deer hair
Note: Wing should extend half of the body length. Body segments are tied separately, not continually.

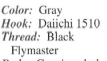

Net Builder Caddis Pupa

Color: Caddis green
Hook: Daiichi 1560
Thread: Brown Flymaster
Body: Bright green Scintilla Caliente dubbing
Legs: Iridescent pheasant rump plumage
Thorax: Brown long-fiber Antron dubbing
Wing: Mallard duck wing

Glassy Caddis Pupa

Color: Green
Hook: Daiichi 1510
Thread: Brown Flymaster
Body: Lime green glass beads
Rib: Olive combination of Antron, synthetic and long-fiber rabbit dubbing
Head: Brown glass bead with reddish brown dubbing
Wing: Natural deer hair

Net Builder Caddis Pupa

Color: Olive
Hook: Daiichi 1560
Thread: Brown Flymaster
Body: Olive Scintilla Caliente dubbing
Legs: Iridescent pheasant rump plumage
Thorax: Dark brown long-fiber Antron dubbing
Wing: Mallard duck wing

EMERGER

Caddis Emerger, Traditional

Color: Orange
Hook: Daiichi 1180
Thread: Orange
  Flymaster
Tail: Natural deer hair
Body: Orange wool
  yarn
Rib: Gold fine wire,
  crossed-wrapped with
  body hackle
Body Hackle: Brown
  webby hackle
Shellback: Natural deer hair

Emergent Sparkle Pupa

Color: Ginger
Hook: Daiichi 1180
Thread: Tan Flymaster
Tail: Ginger Antron
  yarn
Body: Yellow/tan
  Antron dubbing
Thorax: Light brown
  Antron dubbing
Shellback: Ginger
  Antron yarn tied in at
  bend of hook, then pulled over to the thorax to create a bubble
  effect.
Wing: Natural deer hair
Note: The Emergent Sparkle Pupa imitates the life stage just below
or in the water's surface. The pupa is shedding the larval shuck, and
the adult's wings are beginning to protrude from the thorax. Fishing
techniques are described in many publications and should be studied.

Emergent Sparkle Pupa

Color: Gray
Hook: Daiichi 1180
Thread: Gray
  Flymaster
Tail: Gray Antron yarn
Body: Gray Antron
  dubbing
Thorax: Dark gray
  Antron dubbing
Shellback: Gray
  Antron yarn tied in at
  bend of hook, then pulled over to the thorax to create a bubble effect.
Wing: Natural deer hair

Emergent Sparkle Pupa

Color: Green
Hook: Daiichi 1180
Thread: Brown
  Flymaster
Tail: Olive Antron
  yarn
Body: Olive Antron
  yarn
Thorax: Dark reddish
  brown Antron yarn
Shellback: Olive
  Antron yarn tied in at bend of hook, then pulled over to the thorax
  to create a bubble effect
Wing: Natural deer hair

Emergent Sparkle Pupa

Color: Yellow/brown
Hook: Daiichi 1180
Thread: Brown
  Flymaster
Tail: Tan Antron yarn
Body: Light-brown
  Antron dubbing
Thorax: Dark reddish
  brown Antron yarn
Shellback: Tan Antron
  yarn tied in at bend of
  hook, then pulled over to the thorax to create a bubble effect
Wing: Natural deer hair

ADULTS

Caddis CDC Tan

Color: Tan
Hook: Daiichi 1180
Thread: Tan Flymaster
Body: Tan Antron
  dubbing
Body Hackle: Brown
  dry-fly hackle
Wing: Tan CDC
  plumes matched and
  paired with feather
  cups inward

Diving Caddis, Foam Body

Color: Black
Hook: Daiichi 1510
Thread: Black
  Flymaster
Body: Black Ultra
  Chenille or opened-
  cell foam
Thorax: Black Antron
  dubbing
Head: Brown Antron
  dubbing
Wings: 1st: Natural deer hair. 2nd: White Antron yarn
Note: The Antron wing simulates tiny air bubbles trapped along a
diving caddis's back when it breaks the surface of the water trying to
reach the bottom of the riffle to lay its eggs.

Diving Caddis, Foam Body

Color: Olive
Hook: Daiichi 1510
Thread: Brown
  Flymaster
Body: Olive Ultra
  Chenille or opened-
  cell foam
Thorax: Olive Antron
  dubbing
Head: Brown Antron
  dubbing
Wings: 1st: Natural deer hair. 2nd: White Antron yarn

Diving Caddis, Foam Body

Color: Tan
Hook: Daiichi 1510
Thread: Brown
  Flymaster
Body: Tan Ultra
  Chenille or opened-
  cell foam
Thorax: Tan Antron
  dubbing
Head: Brown Antron
  dubbing
Wings: 1st: Natural deer hair. 2nd: White Antron yarn

Twilight Elk Hair Caddis

Color: Brown
Hook: Daiichi 1100
Thread: Brown
  Flymaster
Body: Brown synthetic
  dubbing
Rib: Gold fine wire,
  cross-wrapped with
  body hackle
Body Hackle: Natural-
  brown dry-fly hackle
Wings: 1st: Natural elk hair. 2nd: Chartreuse highly visible Antron
  yarn

Elk Hair Caddis

Color: Black
Hook: Daiichi 1180
Thread: Black
  Flymaster
Body: Black synthetic
  dubbing
Rib: Gold fine wire,
  cross-wrapped with
  body hackle
Body Hackle: Black
  dry-fly hackle
Wing: Natural elk hair
Note: The Elk Hair Caddis is the most well known caddis pattern
throughout the world. A high bushy floater, it can generally be
applied to all caddis hatches.

Elk Hair Caddis

Color: Cream
Hook: Daiichi 1180
Thread: Cream
  Flymaster
Body: Cream synthetic
  dubbing
Rib: Silver fine wire,
  cross-wrapped with
  body hackle
Body Hackle: Ginger
  dry-fly hackle
Wing: Bleached elk hair

Twilight Elk Hair Caddis

Color: Black
Hook: Daiichi 1100
Thread: Black
  Flymaster
Body: Black synthetic
  dubbing
Rib: Gold fine wire,
  cross-wrapped with
  body hackle
Body Hackle: Black
  dry-fly hackle
Wings: 1st: Natural elk hair. 2nd: Pink highly visible Antron yarn
Note: The addition of the Twilight strip not only allows you to see
the fly in very small sizes, but also in low-light conditions which
may include daylight tree shade. Each of the color patterns of Elk
Hair and Slick Water Caddis uses a different color Antron so anglers
can organize their fly box.

Twilight Elk Hair Caddis

Color: Cream
Hook: Daiichi 1180
Thread: Cream
  Flymaster
Body: Cream synthetic
  dubbing
Rib: Silver fine wire,
  cross-wrapped with
  body hackle
Wings: 1st: Bleached
  elk hair. 2nd: Yellow
  highly visible Antron yarn
Body Hackle: Ginger dry-fly hackle

Elk Hair Caddis

Color: Brown
Hook: Daiichi 1180
Thread: Brown
  Flymaster
Body: Brown synthetic
  dubbing
Rib: Gold fine wire,
  cross-wrapped with
  body hackle
Body Hackle: Natural-
  brown dry-fly hackle
Wing: Natural elk hair
Note: The dubbing used for the body should be a semi-coarse
synthetic or Antron blend that is water-repelling.

Elk Hair Caddis

Color: Dun
Hook: Daiichi 1180
Thread: Gray
  Flymaster
Body: Blue dun
  synthetic dubbing
Rib: Silver fine wire,
  cross-wrapped with
  body hackle
Body Hackle: Blue
  dun dry-fly hackle
Wing: Natural elk hair

Brian O'Keefe Photo

Twilight Elk Hair Caddis

Color: Dun
Hook: Daiichi 1100
Thread: Gray Flymaster
Body: Blue dun synthetic dubbing
Rib: Silver fine wire, cross-wrapped with body hackle
Body Hackle: Blue dun dry-fly hackle

Wings: 1st: Natural elk hair. 2nd: Blue highly visible Antron yarn

Twilight Elk Hair Caddis

Color: Orange
Hook: Daiichi 1100
Thread: Orange Flymaster
Body: Orange synthetic dubbing
Rib: Gold fine wire, cross-wrapped with body hackle
Body Hackle: Natural-brown dry-fly hackle

Wings: 1st: Natural elk hair. 2nd: Orange highly visible Antron yarn

Elk Hair Caddis

Color: Olive
Hook: Daiichi 1180
Thread: Olive Flymaster
Body: Olive synthetic dubbing
Rib: Gold fine wire, cross-wrapped with body hackle
Body Hackle: Blue dun dry-fly hackle
Wing: Natural elk hair

Elk Hair Caddis

Color: Tan
Hook: Daiichi 1180
Thread: Tan Flymaster
Body: Tan synthetic dubbing
Rib: Gold fine wire, cross-wrapped with body hackle
Body Hackle: Brown dry-fly hackle
Wing: Natural elk hair

Twilight Elk Hair Caddis

Color: Olive
Hook: Daiichi 1100
Thread: Olive Flymaster
Body: Olive synthetic dubbing
Rib: Gold fine wire, cross-wrapped with body hackle
Body Hackle: Blue dun dry-fly hackle

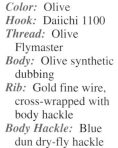

Wings: 1st: Natural elk hair. 2nd: Orange highly visible Antron yarn

Twilight Elk Hair Caddis

Color: Tan
Hook: Daiichi 1100
Thread: Tan Flymaster
Body: Tan synthetic dubbing
Rib: Gold fine wire, cross-wrapped with body hackle
Body Hackle: Brown dry-fly hackle

Wings: 1st: Natural elk hair. 2nd: Yellow highly visible Antron yarn

Elk Hair Caddis

Color: Orange
Hook: Daiichi 1180
Thread: Orange Flymaster
Body: Orange synthetic dubbing
Rib: Gold fine wire, cross-wrapped with body hackle
Body Hackle: Natural-brown dry-fly hackle
Wing: Natural elk hair

Elk Hair Caddis

Color: Yellow
Hook: Daiichi 1180
Thread: Yellow Flymaster
Body: Yellow synthetic dubbing
Rib: Gold fine wire, cross-wrapped with body hackle
Body Hackle: Ginger dry-fly hackle
Wing: Natural elk hair

Goddard Caddis

Color: Tan
Hook: Daiichi 1180
Thread: Brown Flymaster
Body: Natural deer hair, spun
Body Hackle: Brown dry-fly hackle
Antennae: Natural-brown hackle stem
Wing: Body and wing are the same

Note: Spinning the deer hair on a delicate dry-fly hook is difficult; the hook will tend to bend with minimal pressure. Holding the hook with one hand and spinning the hair takes lots of practice, but is the best method to avoid damage to the hook.

Hemingway Caddis

Color: Olive
Hook: Daiichi 1180
Thread: Olive Flymaster
Body: Olive synthetic dubbing
Body Hackle: Blue dun dry-fly hackle
Collar Hackle: Blue dun dry-fly hackle
Thorax: Peacock herl

Wings: 1st: Wood duck-dyed mallard flank fibers. 2nd: Overlapped mallard wing
Note: Treat wings with hair spray to give them durability.

Henryville Caddis

Color: Olive/brown
Hook: Daiichi 1180
Thread: Brown Flymaster
Body: Olive synthetic dubbing
Body Hackle: Grizzly dry-fly hackle
Collar Hackle: Brown dry-fly hackle
Thorax: Light brown Antron dubbing

Wings: 1st: Wood duck-dyed mallard flank fibers. 2nd: Overlapped mallard wing.

October Caddis

Color: Orange
Hook: Daiichi 1710
Thread: Orange Monocord
Body: Orange Antron dubbing
Body Hackle: Brown dry-fly hackle
Antennae: Natural-brown hackle stem
Wing: Natural elk hair tied in three separate sections

Note: A superior October caddis pattern. The three wings add floatation and silhouette. Sits on the water like the real insect.

Parachute Caddis

Color: Tan
Hook: Daiichi 1180
Thread: Tan Flymaster
Body: Natural hare's ear dubbing
Body Hackle: Natural-brown dry-fly hackle
Thorax: Same as body
Wings: 1st: Mottled turkey wing feather. 2nd: Parachute post of white calf body hair

Note: The turkey wing must be coated to prevent splitting.

Slick Water Caddis, Frontier

Color: Black
Hook: Daiichi 1180
Thread: Black Flymaster
Body: Black Ultra Chenille
Rib: Black Flymaster thread for figure-eight around wing
Body Hackle: Black dry-fly hackle

Antennae: Dyed-black hackle stem
Wings: 1st: Natural elk hair. 2nd: White poly yarn
Note: I was being refused by the bigger, smarter fish in slow water where they have more time to inspect their prey, so I developed this pattern to identically imitate a dry non-fluttering caddis. This stroke of luck from my vise is by far the most effective dry caddis pattern available. The body, wing, legs and antennae make a perfect match.

Twilight Slick Water Caddis

Color: Black
Hook: Daiichi 1100
Thread: Black Flymaster
Body: Black Micro Ultra Chenille
Body Hackle: Black dry-fly hackle
Antennae: Dyed black hackle stem
Wings: 1st: Gray poly yarn. 2nd: Pink highly visible Antron yarn

Note: The twilight slick water caddis imitates the abundant micro caddis population. For years, I have been using similar patterns because they are such a huge source of fish food. Once you begin using this pattern, it will become your micro caddis of choice. Incorporated into this pattern is the wide-gapped oversize-eyed 1100 Daiichi hook, wings that you can see, legs, extended body, antennae and durability.

Slick Water Caddis, Frontier

Color: Brown
Hook: Daiichi 1180
Thread: Brown Flymaster
Body: Brown Ultra Chenille
Rib: Brown Flymaster thread for a figure-eight around the wing
Body Hackle: Brown dry-fly hackle
Antennae: Brown hackle stem
Wing: Natural deer hair

Twilight Slick Water Caddis

Color: Brown
Hook: Daiichi 1100
Thread: Brown
  Flymaster
Body: Brown Micro
  Ultra Chenille
Body Hackle: Brown
  dry-fly hackle
Antennae: Brown
  hackle stems
Wings: 1st: Tan poly
  yarn. 2nd: Orange highly visible Antron yarn

Note: The twilight strip enhances the angler's ability to see the fly in low-light conditions. It is also perfect for fishing heavy water or under trees. When the fly sinks or is taken by a fish, the angler instantly knows how to react.

Twilight Slick Water Caddis

Color: Gray
Hook: Daiichi 1100
Thread: Gray
  Flymaster
Body: Gray Micro
  Ultra Chenille
Body Hackle: Blue
  dun dry-fly hackle
Antennae: Blue dun
  hackle stem
Wings: 1st: Gray poly
  yarn. 2nd: Blue highly visible Antron yarn

Slick Water Caddis, Frontier

Color: Cream
Hook: Daiichi 1180
Thread: Cream
  Flymaster
Body: Cream Ultra
  Chenille
Rib: Cream
  Flymaster thread for a
  figure-eight around
  the wing
Body Hackle: Ginger
  dry-fly hackle
Antennae: Ginger hackle stem
Wing: Bleached deer hair

Note: The lighter colors of this pattern have a thread under-wrap on the hook shank to prevent the hook from contrasting against the body material.

Slick Water Caddis, Frontier

Color: Olive
Hook: Daiichi 1180
Thread: Olive
  Flymaster
Body: Olive Ultra
  Chenille
Rib: Olive Flymaster
  thread for a figure-
  eight around the wing
Body Hackle: Blue
  dun dry-fly hackle

Antennae: Blue dun hackle stem
Wings: 1st: Natural deer hair. 2nd: White poly yarn
Note: Wings are anchored down with the figure eight of thread to create a tented wing. The insects tent their wings and tuck their body up inside.

Twilight Slick Water Caddis

Color: Cream
Hook: Daiichi 1100
Thread: Cream
  Flymaster
Body: Cream Micro
  Ultra Chenille
Body Hackle: Ginger
  dry-fly hackle
Antennae: Ginger
  hackle stem
Wings: 1st: Tan poly
  yarn. 2nd: Chartreuse highly visible Antron yarn

Twilight Slick Water Caddis

Color: Olive
Hook: Daiichi 1100
Thread: Olive
  Flymaster
Body: Olive Micro
  Ultra Chenille
Body Hackle: Blue
  dun dry-fly hackle
Antennae: Blue dun
  hackle stem
Wings: 1st: Gray poly
  yarn. 2nd: Orange highly visible Antron yarn

Slick Water Caddis, Frontier

Color: Gray
Hook: Daiichi 1180
Thread: Gray
  Flymaster
Body: Gray Ultra
  Chenille
Rib: Gray Flymaster
  thread for a figure-
  eight around the wing
Body Hackle: Blue
  dun dry-fly hackle
Antennae: Blue dun hackle stem
Wing: Natural deer hair

Slick Water Caddis, Frontier

Color: Tan
Hook: Daiichi 1180
Thread: Tan Flymaster
Body: Tan Ultra
  Chenille
Rib: Tan Flymaster
  thread for a figure-
  eight around the wing
Body Hackle: Brown
  dry-fly hackle
Antennae: Brown
  hackle stem
Wing: Natural elk hair

Twilight Slick Water Caddis

Color: Tan
Hook: Daiichi 1100
Thread: Tan Flymaster
Body: Tan Micro Ultra Chenille
Body Hackle: Brown dry-fly hackle
Antennae: Brown hackle stem
Wings: 1st: Tan poly yarn. 2nd: Orange highly visible Antron yarn

Tied-Down Caddis

Color: Orange
Hook: Daiichi 1720
Thread: Orange Monocord
Tail: Natural elk hair
Collar Hackle: Natural brown dry-fly hackle
Rib: Gold fine wire, crossed wrapped with body hackle
Body: Orange wool yarn
Body Hackle: Natural-brown dry-fly hackle
Shellback: Natural elk hair
Note: An older pattern designed to imitate a caddis emerger suspended in the surface film. Effective fished wet or dry. Body and collar hackles are even in length.

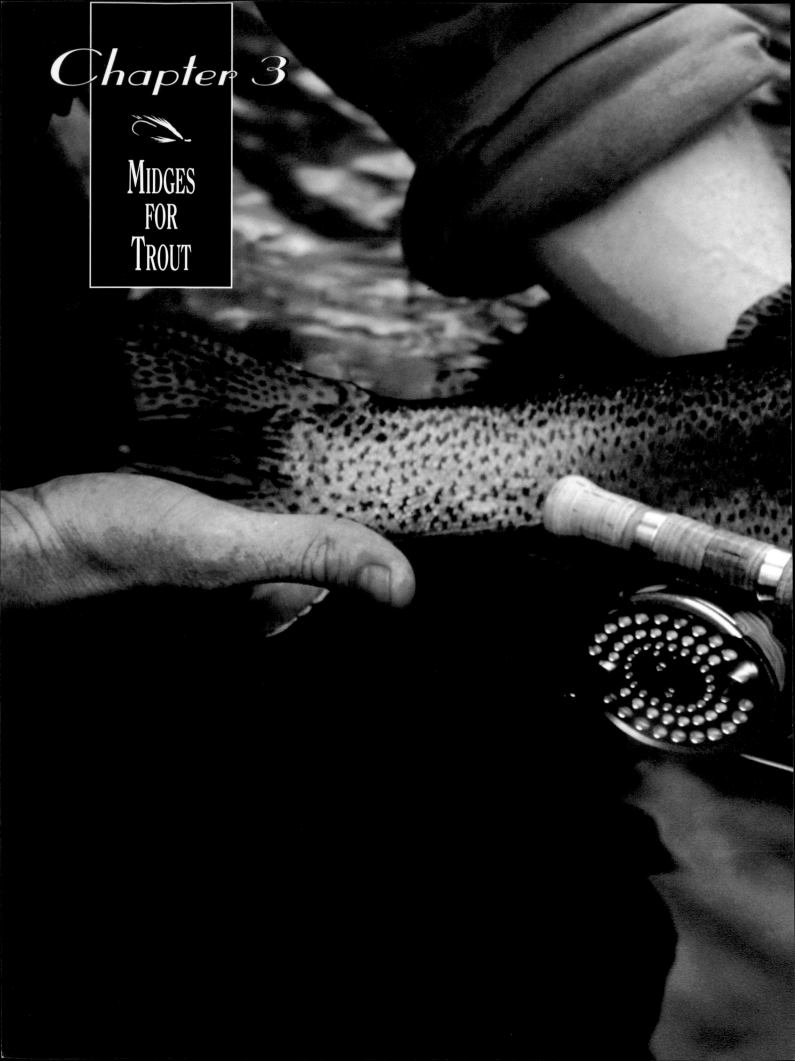

Chapter 3

MIDGES FOR TROUT

Ken Morrish Photo

Beadhead Midge, Shaggy

Color: Black
Hook: Daiichi 1150
Thread: Black
Flymaster
Bead: Brass
Body: Black long-fiber
Scintilla Caliente
dubbing
Rib: Copper fine
wire
Thorax: Gray metallic
glass bead

Note: Form a dubbing loop with copper wire. Twist dubbing inside loop and wrap around hook shank. Once wrapped to glass bead, tie off and dub a small thorax of dubbing to hide thread. Trim excess dubbing to length preferred.

Beadhead Midge, Shaggy

Color: Brown
Hook: Daiichi 1150
Thread: Brown
Flymaster
Bead: Brass
Body: Dark brown,
long-fiber Scintilla
Caliente dubbing
Rib: Copper fine
wire
Thorax: Pearl glass
bead

Note: A versatile pattern that simulates rock worms, midges, aquatic worms and nymphs.

Beadhead Midge, Shaggy

Color: Green
Hook: Daiichi 1150
Thread: Olive
Flymaster
Bead: Brass
Body: Bright green,
long-fiber Scintilla
Caliente dubbing
Rib: Copper fine
wire
Thorax: Dark green
glass bead

Beadhead Midge, Shaggy

Color: Olive
Hook: Daiichi 1150
Thread: Olive
Flymaster
Bead: Brass
Body: Olive, long-fiber
Scintilla Caliente
dubbing
Rib: Copper fine
wire
Thorax: Metallic gray
glass bead

Beadhead Midge, Shaggy

Color: Red
Hook: Daiichi 1150
Thread: Red
Flymaster
Bead: Brass
Body: Red, long-fiber
Scintilla Caliente
dubbing
Rib: Copper fine
wire
Thorax: Metallic gray
glass bead

Midge, Extended Body

Color: Black
Hook: Daiichi 1510
Thread: Black
Flymaster
Body: Black Magic
chenille
Thorax: Black Antron
dubbing, spiky
Shellback: White
Antron yarn cut and
extended over the eye
of hook

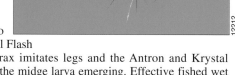

Note: One of the most popular adult midge patterns. It is effective fished wet or dry.

Midge, High Lakes

Color: Black
Hook: Daiichi 1560
Thread: Black
Flymaster
Body: Black Flymaster
thread
Rib: Silver fine wire
Thorax: Black Antron
dubbing, spiky
Shellback: White
Antron yarn and two
strands pearl Krystal Flash

Note: The spiky thorax imitates legs and the Antron and Krystal Flash thorax imitates the midge larva emerging. Effective fished wet or dry.

Midge, High Lakes

Color: Brown
Hook: Daiichi 1560
Thread: Brown
Flymaster
Body: Brown
Flymaster thread
Rib: Gold fine wire
Thorax: Dark brown
Antron dubbing,
spiky
Shellback: White
Antron yarn and two strands pearl Krystal Flash

Note: There are many species of midges of various colors.

Midge, High Lakes

Color: Olive
Hook: Daiichi 1560
Thread: Olive Flymaster
Body: Olive Flymaster thread
Rib: Gold fine wire
Thorax: Olive Antron dubbing, spiky
Shellback: White Antron yarn and two strands pearl Krystal Flash

Note: A great versatile pattern, can be fished wet like a nymph or grease it and fish to rising fish.

Midge, Micro Curved

Color: Red
Hook: Daiichi 1130
Thread: Red Flymaster
Tail: White Antron yarn
Body: Red Flymaster thread
Thorax: Peacock herl
Wing: White Antron yarn

Midge, High Lakes

Color: Red
Hook: Daiichi 1560
Thread: Red Flymaster
Body: Red Flymaster thread
Rib: Silver fine wire
Thorax: Peacock herl
Shellback: White Antron yarn and two strands pearl Krystal Flash

V-Rib Midge

Color: Black
Hook: Daiichi 1560
Thread: Black Flymaster
Tail: White marabou
Body: Dark brown vinyl rib
Thorax: Peacock herl
Antennae: White Antron yarn, split

Note: This is the most anatomically correct midge pattern we carry. It is an effective producer fished wet, but is limited to the lower water column.

Midge, High Lakes

Color: Tan
Hook: Daiichi 1560
Thread: Tan Flymaster
Body: Tan Flymaster thread
Rib: Gold fine wire
Thorax: Tan Antron dubbing, spiky
Shellback: White Antron yarn and two strands pearl Krystal Flash

V-Rib Midge

Color: Blood red
Hook: Daiichi 1560
Thread: Red Flymaster
Tail: White marabou
Body: Blood-red vinyl rib
Thorax: Peacock herl
Antennae: White Antron yarn, split

Midge, Micro Curved

Color: Black
Hook: Daiichi 1130
Thread: Black Flymaster
Tail: White Antron yarn
Body: Black goose biot
Rib: Silver fine wire
Thorax: Peacock herl
Wing: White Antron yarn

Note: Without the fine wire rib, this is a one-fish fly. The curved hook is an adaptation to fishing rivers. Usually midges emerge to the surface of slow water perpendicularly, however in flowing water they ball up until they reach a resting place.

V-Rib Midge

Color: Red
Hook: Daiichi 1560
Thread: Red Flymaster
Tail: White marabou
Body: Red vinyl rib
Thorax: Peacock herl
Antennae: White Antron yarn, split

Midge, Western

Color: Black
Hook: Daiichi 1150
Thread: Black
Flymaster
Body: Lime green
Krystal Flash
Rib: Black, small,
round vinyl rib
Antennae: White
Antron yarn, split
Thorax: Black Antron
dubbing

Note: Tied on an English bent hook that adds movement to attract fish. It is durable, and the vinyl rib segments add character.

Midge, Western

Color: Red
Hook: Daiichi 1150
Thread: Red
Flymaster
Body: Lime green
Krystal Flash
Rib: Red, small, round
vinyl rib
Antennae: White
Antron yarn, split
Thorax: Peacock herl

Note: The red vinyl rib with the Mylar underwrap gives this pattern a brighter glow. This imitates the real insect's iridescent exoskeleton.

Midge, Stripped Quill

Color: Gray
Hook: Daiichi 1130
Thread: Gray
Flymaster
Tail: White Antron
yarn
Body: Peacock herl,
stripped
Thorax: Gray Antron
dubbing
Shellback: White
closed-cell foam

Note: Midges tied on curved hooks are very popular. Normally tied on smaller sizes #20-24. The white foam simulates gills and floats the fly in the surface film. Pull off the foam to fish it deep.

Midge, Suspended Pupa

Color: Black
Hook: Daiichi 1180
Thread: Black
Flymaster
Tail: White Antron
yarn
Body: Black Flymaster
thread
Rib: Lime Krystal
Flash
Thorax: Peacock herl
Shellback: White Antron yarn
Wing: White closed-cell foam

Note: To add thickness, tie the white Antron yarn the length of the hook shank. The lime Krystal Flash rib can make all the difference. I stumbled upon it fishing in eastern Washington State and have used it throughout the Northwest. The rib simulates the air pushed into the midge's larval shuck by the adult when emerging. I believe the air is much like a light, creating an easy target for fish.

Midge, Suspended Pupa

Color: Olive
Hook: Daiichi 1180
Thread: Olive
Flymaster
Tail: White Antron
yarn
Body: Olive Flymaster
thread
Rib: Lime Krystal
Flash
Thorax: Olive Antron
yarn
Shellback: White Antron yarn
Wing: White closed-cell foam

Note: The shellback is tied loosely to simulate midge wings unfolding.

Midge, Suspended Pupa

Color: Tan
Hook: Daiichi 1180
Thread: Tan Flymaster
Tail: White Antron
yarn
Body: Tan Flymaster
thread
Rib: Lime Krystal
Flash
Thorax: Tan Antron
yarn
Shellback: White Antron yarn
Wing: White closed-cell foam

ADULTS

Midge, Century Drive

Color: Black
Hook: Daiichi 1180
Thread: Black
Flymaster
Tail: Dark brown
Antron yarn
Body: Black synthetic
dubbing
Body Hackle: Grizzly
dry-fly hackle
Thorax: Black Antron
dubbing
Shellback: White poly yarn

Note: Silhouette, size and color are most important. The poly yarn shellback imitates the wing of an adult midge, while also adding floatation.

Midge, Century Drive

Color: Olive
Hook: Daiichi 1180
Thread: Olive
Flymaster
Tail: Dark brown
Antron yarn
Body: Olive synthetic
dubbing
Body Hackle: Grizzly
dry-fly hackle
Thorax: Olive synthetic
dubbing
Shellback: White poly yarn

Note: Fishing dry midges is often overlooked. Fish aggressively eat dry or emerging midges, particularly in still water.

Midge, Century Drive

Color: Red
Hook: Daiichi 1180
Thread: Red
 Flymaster
Tail: Dark brown
 Antron yarn
Body: Red thread
Body Hackle: Grizzly
 dry-fly hackle
Thorax: Black thread
Shellback: White poly
 yarn

3056

Midge, Downwing

Color: Gray
Hook: Daiichi 1180
Thread: Black
 Flymaster
Rib: Thread
Collar Hackle: Grizzly
 dry-fly hackle
Wing: Mallard duck
 wing
Note: This small-winged fly, not only imitates a midge, but selective fish will even take it for micro stones, caddis or mayflies.

12211

Chapter 4

STONEFLY DRIES FOR TROUT

Brian O'Keefe Photo

STONEFLIES

Mar Bachmann

The stonefly genera have been around longer than trout or anglers. They are one of the oldest insect orders. Fossil records indicate they have been here for over two hundred million years.

It is because trout can concentrate their feeding activity on stoneflies during all stages of their life cycle that stonefly imitations are very productive fishing flies. Like many other aquatic insects, they live much of their life cycle crawling or slithering on and through the substrate of the riverbed. As they near adulthood, they migrate to the edges of the river where they crawl out, and after a short metamorphosis, become sexually mature, winged adult insects.

Most rivers throughout the West have several very important stonefly families. Different species have diverse lifestyles and exploit different niches within the same environment. Behavioral drift cycles and emergence are often staggered so that one species or another is available as food throughout much of the trout season.

Stonefly nymphs are denizens of the funnels, tunnels, and voids under and between the rocks of the substrate. Here they hide and hunt in relative security from hungry trout. However, this isolation from predation is, in the end, the undoing of many. Population explosions occur to the point that all available food and space is committed. Some species can reach population densities of hundreds per square yard. When an area becomes too crowded or over-harvested, many of the nymphs will leave to find new territory.

Most stonefly nymphs are strong, fast crawlers, but all are very weak swimmers. The easiest form of transportation is simply to drift downstream with the current. This is called a behavioral drift cycle. During the drift, most of the migrating nymphs are exposed, causing mini-feeding frenzies that can be very selective, and can last from a few minutes to several hours. The largest behavioral drift cycles occur from mid-September through May. The drifts can happen daily, usually during low-light hours.

Several weeks before the hatch, nymphs of both salmonflies and golden stones will begin to migrate to staging areas along the banks of the river. Nothing in our rivers produces a feeding frenzy like the annual migration of giant stonefly nymphs. Even the largest trout find it hard to refuse a big stonefly nymph fished deep along the bottom. The activity peaks two weeks before, and one week into, the hatch.

The nymphs of the giant stonefly live in the river for up to three years. They are available to trout in several sizes nearly year-round, however during the migration, the largest nymphs are vulnerable, and appear in big numbers.

In the West, stoneflies hatch from January through August. There are at least two dozen species that are important in the adult stage to the trout angler. These range from the tiny winter blacks (3/8") to the giant salmonfly (over 2").

The salmonfly hatch on Oregon's Deschutes River in late May/June is arguably the best dry-fly fishing the Pacific Northwest has to offer. The hatch starts at the mouth of the river during the first week of May, and by May 25th there are usually a few salmonflies at Warm Springs. The first week in June is peak for the best fifty miles between Maupin and Warm Springs. The hatch trickles off through June, but there are scattered salmonflies around Pelton Dam until nearly the first of July most years. In higher-elevation streams within this region or in the Rocky Mountain states, the peak of all hatches can be as much as a month later.

A dense hatch of golden stones, and several smaller, lesser known but very important species, accompanies the salmonfly hatch. Early in this sequence, fish will be keyed on salmonflies and golden stones. Later in the hatch, especially in places where they have been worked over hard, trout can become very finicky. They often ignore the best-tied and presented large dry patterns. Instead they will select out caddis, alderflies, mayflies and *very often,* smaller stones, usually size #12 to #14 olive stones.

As the salmonfly hatch comes to a close, these smaller stonefly species tend to linger on, and throughout July are replaced with even smaller ones. These summer stoneflies are usually bright yellow size #14 to #16. Small stoneflies have low silhouettes and are very difficult for the angler to see on the water. They are often the prey of trout rising splashily during midday, when there appears to be nothing on the water.

The *Robotic Salmon Fly* and *Robotic Golden Stone* are the products of the fertile mind and exemplary tying skills of my son Troy Bachmann. They were our store's top secret, unsinkable guide flies for a number of years. These foam-body, rubber-legged flies really gave us the edge during the crowded days of the salmonfly hatch. Well, of course the word finally got out. Now they are available to you, and you *will* agree that they are the most realistic giant stone patterns ever produced. They are deadly. So will you be if you can fish them properly.

The *Bullethead Series* were the top-secret guide flies of the late 1980s. In the early 1990s, we added rubber legs and Krystal Flash and they became even more effective. During certain stages of the hatch, such as egg-laying, and in semi-textured water they are still the best you can use.

During the 1980s, as many tiers made their Salmonfly patterns heavier in weight and denser in silhouette, Lee Clark made his flies lighter. His fly is called the *Clark Stone* (Yarn Body Stone). The body is made of coarse, stranded, translucent poly yarn. This pattern floats like a dry feather and will often bring up jaded fish when nothing else will.

Improved Sofa Pillow, Improved Golden Stone, Norm Woods Specials and *Stimulator* type flies were the leading edge patterns of the 1970s and early 1980s. These patterns are still very popular and very productive, especially where the water surface is heavily textured.

The Flint Stones are patterns I created to replicate the low silhouettes of the little olive and yellow stones of summer. Don't be without them from May through August.

Good hunting and good luck.

Bullethead Golden Stone

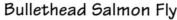

Color: Golden
Hook: Daiichi 1270
Thread: Yellow flat waxed
Tail: Gold-dyed deer hair
Body: Gold wool yarn
Body Hackle: Ginger dry-fly hackle
Head: Gold-dyed deer hair pulled back to form bullet
Legs: Orange round rubber legs
Wing: Naturally light elk hair
Note: One of the most effective golden stone patterns developed. My father and I worked on this pattern for three years, before settling on this variation.

Bullethead Salmon Fly

Color: Orange
Hook: Daiichi 1720
Thread: Flamc flat waxed
Body: Orange macramé cord
Head: Dark elk body hair pulled back to form bullet
Legs: Black round rubber legs
Wings: 1st: Orange Krystal Flash. 2nd: Natural elk hair
Note: My father and I developed The Madam X over ten years ago. This is the latest of many improved patterns developed over the years. It is unique due to the tucked body, large wings, rubber legs and bullethead. Large, but aerodynamic and easy to cast. All of the material is tied within the first 1/4 inch from the eye of the hook. It will look and fish drastically different if not tied correctly.

Flint's Stone

Color: Olive
Hook: Daiichi 1270
Thread: Dark olive Flymaster
Tail: Olive Microfibetts, split with dubbing ball
Body: Olive Super Fine Dubbing
Thorax: Gold Super Fine Dubbing
Collar Hackle: Black dry-fly hackle
Wings: 1st: Pearl Krystal Flash. 2nd: Blue dun plastic fly film
Antennae: Black Microfibetts

Flint's Stone

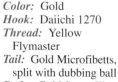

Color: Gold
Hook: Daiichi 1270
Thread: Yellow Flymaster
Tail: Gold Microfibetts, split with dubbing ball
Body: Gold Super Fine Dubbing
Thorax: Yellow Super Fine Dubbing
Collar Hackle: Ginger dry-fly hackle
Wings: 1st: Pearl Krystal Flash. 2nd: Blue dun plastic fly film
Antennae: Black Microfibetts

Flint's Stone

Color: Yellow/red-orange butt
Hook: Daiichi 1270
Thread: Yellow Flymaster
Tail: Gold Microfibetts split with dubbing ball
Butt: 1st: Red. 2nd: Orange synthetic dubbing
Body: Gold Super Fine Dubbing
Thorax: Yellow Super Fine Dubbing
Collar Hackle: Ginger dry-fly hackle
Wing: Pearl Krystal Flash
Antennae: Black Microfibetts

!mproved Golden Stone

Color: Gold
Hook: Daiichi 1270
Thread: Yellow Monocord
Tail: Bleached elk hair
Body: Gold wool yarn
Body Hackle: Ginger dry-fly hackle
Collar Hackle: Ginger dry-fly hackles (2)
Wing: Bleached or light elk hair
Note: This traditional pattern was designed to float high, imitating a flying insect. Fish are selective, and seem to key on fine stages of stonefly hatches. Rarely will one pattern work for all situations.

Improved Sofa Pillow

Color: Orange
Hook: Daiichi 1270
Thread: Flame Flymaster
Tail: Natural elk hair
Body: Orange wool yarn
Body Hackle: Brown dry-fly hackle
Collar Hackle: Brown dry-fly hackles (2)
Wing: Natural elk hair
Note: The body hackle and collar hackle should be exactly the same size. The body hackle is tied in tip-first.

Golden Stone, Calf Tail Wing

Color: Golden/tan
Hook: Daiichi 1270
Thread: Yellow Monocord
Tail: Bleached elk hair
Body: Gold wool yarn
Body Hackle: Ginger dry-fly hackle
Collar Hackle: Ginger dry-fly hackles (2)
Wing: Tan calf tail
Note: The wings are a personal preference. Some fishermen believe calf tail creates the best imitation of the real insect's wings.

Norm Woods Special

Color: Yellow/orange
Hook: Daiichi 1270
Thread: Flame red Flymaster
Tail: Tan calf tail
Body: Gold poly yarn
Body Hackle: Brown dry-fly hackle
Collar Hackle: Brown dry-fly hackle
Thorax: Orange Antron dubbing
Wing: Tan calf tail

Orange Stone, Calf Tail Wing

Color: Orange
Hook: Daiichi 1270
Thread: Flame red Flymaster
Tail: Natural elk hair
Body: Orange wool yarn
Body Hackle: Brown dry-fly hackle
Collar Hackle: Brown dry-fly hackles (2)
Wing: Tan calf tail

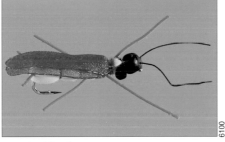

Robotic Stone

Color: Golden
Hook: Daiichi 2220
Thread: Tan flat waxed
Tail: Orange, round rubber legs threaded through body
Body: Gold, medium Rainy's Foam, folded
Rib: Tan flat waxed thread

Legs: Orange, medium, round rubber legs
Antennae: Black, small, round rubber legs
Head: Black or orange, small Rainy's Foam
Wing: Brown nylon wing material
Note: This pattern is unsinkable. It was designed to be realistic enough to fool those "Big Lou's" who have seen everything. Floats flush with the surface, and the legs and antennae move with the current.

Robotic Stone

Color: Orange
Hook: Daiichi 2220
Thread: Orange flat waxed
Tail: Orange, medium, round rubber legs threaded through body
Body: Orange, medium Rainy's Foam, folded
Rib: Orange flat waxed thread

Legs: Black, medium, round rubber legs
Antennae: Black, small, round rubber legs
Head: Black, small Rainy's Foam
Wings: Brown nylon wing material
Note: Wings are made with a burnishing tool. The edges of the nylon must be burned to avoid separation.

Ruling Stone

Color: Black
Hook: Daiichi 1270
Thread: Black Monocord
Tail: Dark dun-dyed deer hair
Body: Black Antron dubbing
Body Hackle: Black dry-fly hackle
Head: Dark dun-dyed deer hair pulled back to form bullet

Wings: 1st: Black rainbow Sparkle Flash. 2nd: Dark dun-dyed deer hair
Note: Tie this pattern to imitate small stone flies. The Sparkle Flash adds the shimmer of moving wings.

Ruling Stone

Color: Gold
Hook: Daiichi 1270
Thread: Yellow Monocord
Tail: Natural elk hair
Body: Yellow Antron dubbing
Body Hackle: Ginger dry-fly hackle
Head: Natural deer hair pulled back to form bullet

Wings: 1st: Gold Sparkle Flash. 2nd: Tan calf tail
Note: The hackle is tied in tip-first to create taper.

Ruling Stone

Color: Olive
Hook: Daiichi 1270
Thread: Olive Monocord
Tail: Natural elk hair
Body: Olive Antron dubbing
Body Hackle: Grizzly dry-fly hackle
Head: Natural deer hair pulled back to form bullet

Wings: 1st: Chartreuse Sparkle Flash. 2nd: Natural elk hair

Yarn-Body Stone

Color: Gold
Hook: Daiichi 1270
Thread: Yellow Monocord
Body: 1st: Gold flat Mylar tinsel. 2nd: Yellow Antron yarn
Collar Hackle: Ginger dry-fly hackles (2)
Wing: Bleached or light elk hair

Yarn-Body Stone

Color: Orange
Hook: Daiichi 1270
Thread: Flame red Flymaster
Body: 1st: Gold flat Mylar tinsel. 2nd: Orange Antron yarn
Collar Hackle: Brown dry-fly hackles (2)
Wing: Natural elk hair

Chapter 5

Terrestrial Dries for Trout

Ant, Antron

Color: Black
Hook: Daiichi 1180
Thread: Black Flymaster
Body: Black Antron dubbing
Body Hackle: Black dry-fly hackle
Thorax: Black Antron dubbing
Wing: White Antron yarn

Note: Use only two or three wraps of hackle, just enough to give the fly legs and floating stability.

Ant, Antron

Color: Brown
Hook: Daiichi 1180
Thread: Brown Flymaster
Body: Brown Antron dubbing
Body Hackle: Brown dry-fly hackle
Thorax: Brown Antron dubbing
Wing: White Antron yarn

Note: The wing provides visibility for the angler, and extra floatation when greased.

Bee, Yellow Jacket

Color: Black/yellow
Hook: Daiichi 1720
Thread: Black Monocord
Body: Black and yellow Antron dubbing, two strips each
Collar Hackle: Brown saddle hackle
Eyes: Black plastic mono eyes
Thorax: Yellow Antron dubbing
Wing: Furnace hen hackle tips

Beetle

Color: Black
Hook: Daiichi 1180
Thread: Black Flymaster
Body: Black Antron dubbing, spiky or peacock herl
Legs: Black deer hair tied back from shellback
Shellback: Black-dyed deer hair, cut over eye of hook to create the head

Beetle, Foam

Color: Black
Hook: Daiichi 1180
Thread: Black Monocord
Body: Black, medium Rainy's Foam
Legs: Black, fine, round rubber legs
Note: It takes an unusual cut to the foam to create the proper look. You will have to experiment.

Bullethead Hopper

Color: Light yellow
Hook: Daiichi 1710
Thread: Yellow Monocord
Tail: Light Yellow extended deer hair belly
Body: Light yellow, extended deer belly hair wrapped around a hackle stem
Rib: Yellow Monocord thread
Legs: Grizzly cut hackle stem tied in a knot to create leg joint
Head: Natural elk hair on top, light-yellow deer belly hair on bottom, pulled back to form bullet
Antennae: Natural-brown stripped hackle stem
Wing: Mottled turkey tail treated with hair spray
Note: Orange poly yarn is used for the strike indicator tied on the top of the head. Optional. The tail and body are tied from same material to form extended body.

Carpenter Ant

Color: Black
Hook: Daiichi 1180
Thread: Black Monocord
Body: Black Antron dubbing
Body Hackle: Brown dry-fly hackle
Thorax: Black Antron dubbing
Shellback: Black Krystal Flash
Wing: Brown hackle tips
Note: In order for this pattern to be fished correctly, trim the underside of the hackle and make sure hackle-tip wings are tied in flat.

Carpenter Ant, Foam Body

Color: Black
Hook: Daiichi 1180
Thread: Black Monocord
Body: Black, small Rainy's Foam
Body Hackle: Black saddle hackle
Thorax: Black, small Rainy's Foam
Wing: Natural-brown saddle hackle tips
Note: The foam body is outstanding; it adds floatation and proper proportions. Cut end of foam at a 45-degree angle and tie in at bend of hook. Fold foam over carefully so you don't squeeze the air out. Tie the head in a similar fashion.

Cicada

Color: Black
Hook: Daiichi 1710
Thread: Black Monocord
Tail: Black-dyed deer hair
Body: Tail material extended to form body
Rib: Cross-wrapped with thread
Legs: Black, medium, round rubber legs
Head: Black-dyed deer hair
Wings: 1st: Black-dyed deer hair. 2nd: Red Antron yarn (indicator)
Note: To maximize floatation, tie in the tail with strong tension, then wrap body portion semi-loosely, and finish body with strong tension. Can also be tied in an olive variation.

Hopper/Stone, Rubber Leg

Color: Yellow
Hook: Daiichi 1710
Thread: Yellow flat waxed
Tail: Natural elk hair
Body: Yellow flat waxed thread wrapped over elk hair underbody
Legs: White, small, round rubber legs
Head: Natural deer hair pulled back to form bullet
Wing: Natural elk hair
Note: This pattern can represent both small hoppers or small dry golden stones. Coloring legs with Pantones® is optional.

Cranefly, Dry, Bachmann's

Color: Tan
Hook: Daiichi 1510
Thread: Tan Flymaster
Tail: Tan-dyed braided nylon
Body: Tan Antron dubbing
Rib: Brown permanent marker
Body Hackle: Large natural brown, slightly-webby hackle
Thorax: Tan Antron dubbing
Shellback: Tan latex
Note: Trim underside of hackle so the fly will lie flat on the water's surface.

Twilight Ant

Color: Black
Hook: Daiichi 1100
Thread: Black Flymaster
Body: Black Antron dubbing
Body Hackle: Black dry-fly hackle
Wing: Pink highly visible Antron yarn looped
Note: Cut hackle so that legs protrude from both sides. The wing and hackle can be treated with dressing to add floatation.

Cricket, Irresistible

Color: Olive
Hook: Daiichi 1710
Thread: Green Monocord
Tail: Olive-dyed deer hair
Body: Olive dyed deer belly hair, spun and cut
Legs: Mottled turkey tail fibers tied in a knot to create leg joint
Head: Same as body. Leave tips of deer hair for a collar
Antennae: Natural-brown stripped hackle stem
Wing: Mottled turkey tail treated with hair spray
Note: This is a very durable fly. The spun deer hair represents a perfect body. Legs, wing and antennae complete the imitation.

Hopper, Parachute

Color: Olive
Hook: Daiichi 1710
Thread: Green Monocord
Body: Olive Antron dubbing
Rib: Red, small round rib
Body Hackle: Grizzly dry-fly hackle
Legs: Mottled turkey tail fibers tied in a knot to create leg joint
Thorax: Same as body
Wings: 1st: Mottled turkey tail. 2nd: Rainbow Krystal Flash. 3rd: White calf body hair

Chapter 6

Nymphs and Wet-Flies for Trout

Brian O'Keefe Photo

THE DIVERSITY OF NYMPHS

Dave Hughes

Once you begin taking a close look at the things that trout eat underwater, a whole new and wonderful world opens up to you. We consider that the aerial world is full of variety: all those mayflies, caddis, stoneflies, midges, and myriad terrestrials flying around. The truth is that all adult mayflies are the same shape; the same is true for caddis, stoneflies, and midges. The species vary in size and color. The shape of each species remains true to the shape of the order. Adult terrestrials arrive in a variety of shapes, but it's truly not a wide variety.

Beneath the water the rules get suspended. Mayflies come in swimmers, clingers, crawlers, and burrowers. Caddis are free-living or cased and some of those that carry cases swim rather than crawl. Some stonefly nymphs are so stout you need to fatten up their imitations with lead wire; others are so slender you need to tie patterns for them with floss or the thinnest yarn. Midges, again, are pretty much midges, but the idea remains valid: the shapes of the aquatic orders of insects vary a lot more beneath the water than they do once they escape it.

It's not necessary to hold your breath and dip your head under water in order to observe this variety of subaquatic insect forms. You should, however, find a way to collect and get a gander at precisely what trout eat during that estimated 80 percent to 90 percent of the time that they feed subsurface. Once you do, you'll have your eyes opened to the need for a broad array of imitations.

Early in my angling career I had a lot of trouble catching trout on nymphs. That was in the days before anybody thought about using split shot to get the things down and strike indicators to report the news about takes. I know that dates me a bit, but when I started fly fishing, nymphing was attempted with floating lines, long leaders, and weighted flies. An upstream cast was used to give the nymph time to sink. In reality, our nymphs rarely got anywhere near the bottom except in the shallowest riffles. Also, in reality we probably got ten strikes for every one we were aware of. On that tenth we usually set the hook just after the trout spit out the fly. A day spent nymphing was frustration built upon misery and the norm was fishlessness.

Even after the split shot and indicator rig got around, I had a difficult time applying it against the trout. The reason, in hindsight, is simple enough; I was rigging right but for the wrong kind of water. I'd put on a light shot or two pinched a couple of feet above the fly, then slide the indicator the same distance up the leader from the shot. I'd fish this rig in six or eight feet of heavy water, and my fly would dangle along three or four feet above the bottom. Let me advise you that suspending a nymph that far above the heads of trout is not going to capture the interest, or even the notice, of very many of them.

One windy but bright day, I slipped the indicator up to the butt of my ten-foot leader and added a couple of extra split shot less than a foot from my fly. I stepped to the head of a

Deschutes River riffle where it was shallow, rather than fishing it farther down where it deepened out and became a run instead of a riffle; the kind of water I'd always fished in my frustrated past. I cast about fifteen feet upstream from the place in that riffle corner where I expected to find trout based on my experience as a dry-fly fisherman on the same types of water. I watched the indicator as it bounced down the heavy water. Just as it reached the place where things began to calm, the indicator disappeared.

In the past I'd always stood and pondered why that might have happened. This time I lifted the rod and gave a yank. Something at the head of the riffle yanked back. It was a redside rainbow about seventeen inches long. Being wise enough even then to repeat what worked, I made the same cast, got the same drift and set the hook with the same yank when the indicator paused as if it suddenly remembered something it had forgotten higher up in the riffle. Another trout of similar size squirted into the air.

I was astonished to hold seven plump trout in my hands before I wore that pod out. It was my moment of epiphany with nymphs. From that day forward nymphs began to work for me, and in a wide variety of situations, not just in Deschutes River riffle corners. I think at that moment I began to have confidence that trout would take nymphs and I would know about it when it happened. But more important, from that emphatic moment forward I began to concentrate on getting rigged right to get my nymphs down on, or very near the bottom. The key to nymphing is to constantly adjust the number of shot on your leader and the position of the strike indicator up or down it as you move from water of one depth and/or current speed to another.

The key to tying a successful nymph selection is to be aware of what trout eat when they're down there where you're going to fish nymphs for them. The first part of that awareness, as I alluded to earlier, is observation. If you don't want to carry any additional gear, you can begin looking at nymphs by simply hoisting rocks off the bottom in various water types. Pick them up and take a close look at what you see crawling around. You'll get a good look at clinger and crawler mayfly nymphs and an occasional swimmer that wasn't quite quick enough to let go its grip. Cased and uncased caddis larvae will both be surprised to find themselves awash in light and the subject of your scrutiny.

Some stonefly nymphs will cling to the stones that you lift, but others that are more agile will swim away and you'll never get a look at them. Midges, of course, are slow thinkers and you'll have no trouble collecting the larval phase this way, though you'll never get so much as a glance at a pupa, which is far more important to your angling.

It's the many forms among the missing that causes me to advise you to get a bit more sophisticated in your collecting. You can simply trot to a biological supply store and order an aquatic sampling net, or you can go to a hardware store and buy a couple of 3/4" dowels and a four-foot section of window screen. Staple the screen to the dowels and with no further construction you have one of the finest kick screen nets you can get, and you're not out ten bucks.

Jam the meshes against the bottom, stand upstream and shuffle your brogues among the bottom rocks. Lift the net and you'll observe all that's down there, including the forms that might have escaped had you merely hoisted the same rocks out of the water. Get your nose close to those wet meshes, and be patient. Some insects are very difficult to see; others remain cryptic in the net until they've been deprived of water for a few minutes. Then they begin to wiggle or crawl, and you notice that there are far more than you thought at first glance.

Don't overdo the collecting; remember that it's the productivity of the bottom that makes for good nymphing. If we all get out there and thrash around, especially in fragile environments, we're likely to damage our own fishing. Collect sparingly, and always release unharmed those specimens you do not want to take back to the tying vise as models for your imitations.

Do take samples from a scattering of water types. If you collect only from riffles, you'll think the stream is full of fast-water types. Collect as well from the bottom of runs, across the tailouts of pools, and even in sandy or muddy sidewaters that look like they would be barren of both insects and trout. They might be, but they also might hold surprises that cause you to find some success where you would never expect it to happen. Be sure to sweep your net through any rooted vegetation and back into all undercuts.

Each of these different environments will show you different nymph forms. That's the reason for the wide variety of shapes I mentioned earlier: each form adapts to a different water and bottom type, and in doing so develops a different way of doing it. These adaptations are reflected in both the shape of each insect and its behavior in its environment.

Let me give you a pleasant assignment before moving on to the next subject: when you've collected, observed, and are about to release your specimens, squat by the water and drop them in and watch the way they escape. Some sink like pebbles; others swim like fish; some struggle as if being in water were foreign to them; others move toward safety with dignity and grace. All of these different movements suggest ways in which you should retrieve or not retrieve the nymphs you fish for each type of insect.

I'll give you another assignment, one that I gave myself long ago and has paid great dividends: go out and buy a special box—make it a big one, as large as your dry-fly box—just for nymphs. I like the kind that have ridges of ripple foam. The reason is simple enough: with these boxes I can line up my nymphs in tidy rows. Now give some thought to the natural nymphs you have seen as most abundant on the waters where you've collected. Then thumb through the pages of this book and observe, just as you did out on the stream, which fly patterns look most like the insects that populate the waters where you fish for trout.

Fill that new nymph box with rows of those patterns, each in at least half a dozen ties of the appropriate range of sizes. Base what you tie on what you've seen, not on what you've read that somebody else has seen. Once you begin doing that, fine-tune your tying and improve not only the focus of what you tie but the quality of each pattern you tie. It's not possible to observe closely and carefully then tie loosely and carelessly.

Honing your observation skills is not an adjunct to honing your tying skills. They're two halves of the same thing, which is tying nymphs that take trout.

THE BIG GRAB: A STREAMER STORY

Ken Morrish

One hot midsummer afternoon on California's lower Hat Creek, I realized what I should have known long ago: that streamers would lead me down the path towards so much of what I wanted.

Even before the day began, I was clear on the principle that big fish would eat a big fly if you fed it to them properly. So, flush with conviction, I spread my crudest earthtoned materials across the picnic table in the state park beneath the bridge. As I began to tie, my thoughts slipped back to Bobby.

I'd met him in the late seventies, long before I could legally drive and at about the same time the leech began its entrance into the American fly box. I bought my first of these webby creations at a shop in Burney because Bobby suggested I should, and he was in my mind the archetypal guide. Like many of the better ones, Bobby was a seriously flawed character. But as an angler and a tier there were few skills he lacked. Of course I was of such a tender age when he showed me a picture of two giant brown trout laid out along a rod, that I lost sleep over the image of their square tails splayed out near the butt and their gnarled heads extending up beyond the first stripping guide. In an instant they became icons for me, symbols of a deeper, darker world where fish were neither pretty or cute, but rather piscivorous monsters with a keen appetite for finned neighbors.

Of course, any fool could tell that the trout in the photo were dead, but for reasons precursory to political correctness and in an effort to prove that Andre Puyans had taught me ethics well, I was compelled to ask: "Did you release them?"

"Hell no," Bobby replied, "I clubbed the big bastards and then did a war dance around them."

If I failed to grasp the significance of that answer, I never forgot that he had caught them on the lower Hat with streamers.

Most anglers approach Northern California's Hat Creek in one of two very predictable ways. The most refined head for the glassy flats armed with light-line weight rods, long leaders sporting 7X tippets, and an assortment of PMD and tiny Trico patterns. The rest shortline nymph the upper riffle, repeatedly lobbing their little shot-laden rigs like a row of angling robots.

It's possible that I might have done the same, but for Bobby's influence, and because of another condition spawned of circumstances beyond my control. Two years earlier, during a drunken beer run in college, my VW van burst into flames, consuming most of my possessions, the most important of which was my tackle. I still remember sifting through

the van's burned-out shell and finding the remains of my five-weight. The tube resembled a four-and-a-half-foot cigarette ash that crumbled upon contact, revealing within a bright white filament of burnt graphite.

Because I was living in Oregon at the time, I had optimistically replaced my deceased five with an eight-weight Scott in hopes of catching steelhead. Or in this case, real big trout. Bobby had told me as a kid, that Fish and Game had electroshocked the lower Hat, revealing a scary old brown that weighed just over 17 pounds. In my mind this registered not as a fish, but rather as *the fish*. I thought about him as I tied in the mottled shade of the picnic table. When done, I had a half dozen variations of a primitive theme; all front weighted #4s, with picked out bodies of Mohair yarn that diffused in a leechy translucence over a long marabou tail. At about three inches long they seemed perfect, their primordial olive-brown tails fluttering in the warm breeze that wafted across the park table.

Typically there are very few anglers beneath the highway bridge on the bank opposite the park. Nonetheless, I was self-conscious as I neared the water. It was more the tackle than the fly—a nine-and-a-half-foot rod, its fighting butt, nine-weight type III head, and dark eight-pound Maxima tippet. "Sacrilegious?" I thought stripping bright running line from the reel. "No," I thought, remembering the wrinkled photo of Bobby's dead fish, "appropriate."

I started fishing well above the lie that I thought might hold the river's largest fish. By the fourth cast I had the desired line length. Retrieving in I would make eight strips, hold the loop, pull six, hold, then four more, hold, then two. With my shooting loops stacked and the head at the tip top, I would roll-cast to the surface, haul back feeding two loops to the backcast, and then haul forward, shooting the lot gently off towards the opposite bank. As the head settled into its swing I made small erratic strips that I imagined creating the vulnerable look of a baitfish.

Now I was truly monster hunting and in fifteen casts my fly would pass beneath the huge overhanging tree where I believed, unquestionably, I would be rewarded. It seemed impossible to fish through the water preceding the lie with any real patience; each cast and swing of my fly reduced my anticipation to an imperative formality. Even so, there came a sudden pulse—a thrashing take—and I pulled tight to a fish. Ten minutes later I cradled it, my best brown to date, twenty-four inches of thick, darkly spotted fish that stared longingly back towards the flowing green weed beds from which it came.

Ken Morrish Photo

For a moment after its release I sat in the tall grass attempting to gloat, waiting for an afterglow of post trophy satisfaction to light me. It was pointless. The hole beneath the tree beckoned. Its dark waters hardly stirred by the brief fight. Surely, the fish I'd just landed was a runt as compared with the one I sought, forced out into the sun-drenched periphery by *him,* the light-loathing beast they had shocked up years before.

I waded out, pulse racing, stripping random lengths of line. The tree was an enormous broad leaf that bent from its base out across half the river. Its canopy grew thick and dark with branches that hung low, some vibrating nervously against the river's surface. A full thirty feet of the far bank was gnarled by the mass of its undercut root wad, where ceaseless current had gnawed earth away from wood. Back then, before silt filled in so much of the Hat, it was hard to figure the depths of the hole I approached.

My cast flew true, landing the fly just off the bank twenty-five feet above the lie. I fed line into the drift, and when it grew taunt, stripped faster than before. In my mind I could see *him* coming, his quarter-sized eye tracking my leech like a laser. Come he did.

I will tell you about the strike in some detail, because that is all there was. It was a strike the likes of which I have never felt again, not by salmon, steelhead or pike; a strike of violent concentration, intent on killing as opposed to mere feeding. While the impact struck my arm, the effect was more like an unexpected blow to the nose—though it left me in more pain.

Afterward I stood midstream, stunned rather than angry, as my line straightened slowly beneath me. The fly was gone I already knew, buried deep within the bony jaw of a dream.

Bobby. I thought of Bobby. Was it possible that had I asked, he might have told me that eight-pound Maxima wasn't enough? I can't imagine he would have, but I will always wonder.

I fished streamers seldom from that time forward. Maybe I was unnerved, or maybe it was the sweet five-weight Pete Woolley gave me soon after that pulled me back towards more "respectable" methods. More than likely though, it was knowing I had blown a rare opportunity and that I lacked within what was needed to rekindle its equal.

Ten years have passed since then, most absorbed by a fetished affair with nymphing that has in some ways left me empty. I rarely fish the Hat. It seems a spoiled stream these days: I know that *the* fish has long since died, and doubt that anything like him has grown to fill his lie. But of late, more and more of my thoughts turn to streamers and how my pulse would race if I were able to fish them with the same faith and skill as the nymph.

I think I am going back soon, not necessarily to the lower Hat, but back to fishing streamers. It's a different world down there, deep amidst the sculpin and dace, in the dark pools where brown trout devour hatchery fish and big rainbows savagely tear the claws from fleeing crayfish. I've decided it is a world I like. . .now that I am somewhat more willing to forego the numbers game for a few fish of exceptional quality; a world where fish and fishermen alike are distilled down to their essential nature as predators.

And if I succeed, perhaps I would even do Bobby's dance, as my prize catches current and swims away.

Baetis Nymph

Color: Tan
Hook: Daiichi 1510
Thread: Black Flymaster
Tail: Blue dun hackle fibers
Body: Black and lime green Krystal Flash twisted and wrapped around hook shank
Thorax: Tan Antron dubbing
Shellback: Mottled turkey tail

Note: Because nymphs ball up as they drift in the water column, the curved hook makes this a very effective pattern. The color of the thorax can be changed to match other small mayfly nymphs.

Beadhead Big Bird, Copper

Color: Brown/partridge
Hook: Daiichi 1560
Thread: Brown Monocord
Weight: Lead wire, large
Tail: Natural-brown partridge plume
Body: Brown synthetic dubbing
Rib: Copper medium wire
Body Hackle: Natural-brown partridge plume
Bead: Copper
Thorax: One or two wraps of dubbing (same as body)

Beadhead Big Bird, Regular

Color: Brown/partridge
Hook: Daiichi 1560
Thread: Brown Monocord
Weight: Lead wire, large
Tail: Natural-brown partridge plume
Body: Light brown synthetic dubbing
Rib: Gold fine oval Mylar
Body Hackle: Natural-brown partridge plume
Bead: Brass
Thorax: One or two wraps of dubbing (same as body)

Beadhead Callibaetis Flashback

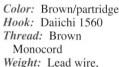

Color: Gray
Hook: Daiichi 1710
Thread: Black Monocord
Bead: Brass
Tail: Natural pheasant rump
Body: Gray wool yarn
Rib: Copper medium wire
Weight: Lead wire, small
Shellback: Pearl flat Mylar extended from tail to head

Beadhead Flash-A-Bugger

Color: Black
Hook: Daiichi 2220
Thread: Black Monocord
Bead: Nickel
Tail: Black marabou with four to six strands of pearl Flashabou
Body: Black chenille
Rib: Silver fine wire
Body Hackle: Black strung saddle hackle
Weight: Lead wire, medium
Lateral Line: Pearl Krystal Flash

Note: The large bead is a great addition, providing action when stripping, weight when swinging, and enabling the hook to ride up to prevent snagging.

Beadhead Flash-A-Bugger

Color: Brown
Hook: Daiichi 2220
Thread: Brown Monocord
Bead: Brass
Tail: Fiery-brown marabou with four to six strands of pearl Flashabou
Body: Brown chenille
Rib: Copper fine wire
Body Hackle: Fiery-brown strung saddle hackle
Weight: Lead wire, medium
Lateral Line: Pearl Flashabou

Beadhead Flash-A-Bugger

Color: Chartreuse/ fuchsia
Hook: Daiichi 2220
Thread: Chartreuse flat waxed
Bead: Nickel
Tail: Fuchsia marabou with four to six strands of pearl Sparkle Flash
Body: Chartreuse chenille
Rib: Silver fine wire
Body Hackle: Fuchsia strung saddle hackle
Weight: Lead wire, medium
Lateral Line: Pearl Sparkle Flash

Note: The reason Sparkle Flash is used on the brighter colored flies, is because they are generally used for steelhead and must be durable.

Beadhead Flash-A-Bugger

Color: Olive
Hook: Daiichi 2220
Thread: Olive Monocord
Bead: Brass
Tail: Olive marabou with four to six strands of pearl Flashabou
Body: Dark olive chenille
Rib: Copper fine wire
Body Hackle: Olive strung saddle hackle
Weight: Lead wire, medium
Lateral Line: Pearl Flashabou

Beadhead Flash-A-Bugger

Color: Orange
Hook: Daiichi 2220
Thread: Orange
    Monocord
Bead: Nickel
Tail: Hot orange
    marabou with four to
    six strands of pearl
    Sparkle Flash
Body: Fluorescent
    orange chenille
Rib: Silver fine wire
Body Hackle: Hot orange strung saddle hackle
Weight: Lead wire, medium
Lateral Line: Pearl Sparkle Flash

Beadhead Flash-A-Bugger

Color: Purple
Hook: Daiichi 2220
Thread: Black
    Monocord
Bead: Copper
Tail: Purple marabou
    with four to six
    strands of purple
    Flashabou
Body: Purple chenille
Rib: Silver medium
    wire
Body Hackle: Purple strung saddle hackle
Weight: Lead wire, large
Lateral Line: Purple Krystal Flash

Beadhead Flash-A-Bugger

Color: Red/hot pink
Hook: Daiichi 2220
Thread: Fluorescent
    pink flat waxed
Bead: Nickel
Tail: Red marabou
    with four to six strands
    of pearl Sparkle Flash
Body: Fluorescent pink
    chenille
Rib: Silver medium
    wire
Body Hackle: Red strung saddle hackle
Weight: Lead wire, large
Lateral Line: Pearl Sparkle Flash

Beadhead Flashbody Nymph

Color: Black/crystal
Hook: Daiichi 1560
Thread: Black
    Monocord
Bead: Brass
Tail: Black hackle
    fibers
Body: Pearl and black
    Krystal Flash, twisted
Weight: Lead wire,
    small
Thorax: Black Antron dubbing, spiky
Shellback: Pearl Flashabou

Beadhead Golden Crawler

Color: Golden
Hook: Daiichi 1150
Thread: Brown
    Flymaster
Bead: Brass
Tail: Brown, fine,
    round rubber legs
Body: Golden synthetic
    dubbing
Rib: Brown, fine,
    round rib
Legs: Brown, fine, round rubber legs
Weight: Lead wire, large
Thorax: Same as body
Note: An excellent imitation, this is a dense, buggy nymph that produces in heavy water.

Beadhead Hare's Ear

Color: Natural hare's
    ear
Hook: Daiichi 1560
Thread: Tan Monocord
Bead: Brass
Tail: Hare's mask
    fibers
Body: Natural hare's
    ear Antron dubbing
Rib: Gold flat Mylar
    #16-18 tinsel
Weight: Lead wire, small
Thorax: Hare's Ear Plus dubbing, spiky
Shellback: Natural-brown mottled turkey tail
Note: The body and thorax are not dubbed with the same materials. Use a dubbing of 50% guard hairs for the thorax. The effect of the spiky thorax simulates legs and adds proportion.

Beadhead Hare's Ear

Color: Flashback
Hook: Daiichi 1560
Thread: Tan Flymaster
Weight: Small lead
    wire
Bead: Brass
Tail: Natural hare's
    mask fibers
Rib: Gold flat #16-#18
    Mylar tinsel
Body: Natural hare's
    ear dubbing
Thorax: Natural Hare's Ear Plus dubbing
Shellback: Pearl Krystal Flash, three strands tied back on each side
    for legs
Note: Hare's Ear Plus dubbing is used for the thorax because it is extra spiky with guard hairs. The added Antron texture gives better definition and simulates leg movement.

Beadhead Hare's Ear

Color: Olive
Hook: Daiichi 1560
Thread: Olive
    Flymaster
Bead: Brass
Tail: Olive hare's mask
    fibers
Body: Olive hare's ear
    Antron dubbing
Rib: Gold flat mylar
    #16-18 tinsel
Weight: Lead wire, small
Thorax: Olive Hare's Ear Plus dubbing, spiky
Shellback: Natural-brown mottled turkey tail

Beadhead Leech, Frontier

Color: Black
Hook: 1720
Thread: Black
  Monocord
Bead: Black
Tail: Black marabou
Body: Black marabou
Note: This pattern is truly ingenious, but difficult to tie. The bead, along with the realistic

flat body formed of marabou make it hard to distinguish from the real thing. When using a stripping technique, the hook rides up and the bead provides the swimming motion of a real leech.

Beadhead Leech, Frontier

Color: Maroon
Hook: Daiichi 1720
Thread: Red
  Monocord
Bead: Black
Tail: Maroon marabou
Body: Maroon
  marabou
Note: Each piece of marabou is tied in at the sides individually

with figure-eights of thread. Try to tie in the marabou in correct proportions and lengths to avoid trimming.

Beadhead Leech, Frontier

Color: Olive
Hook: Daiichi 1720
Thread: Olive
  Monocord
Bead: Black
Tail: Olive marabou
Body: Olive marabou

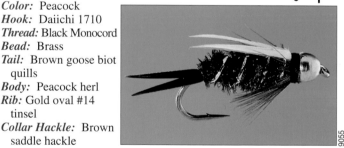

Beadhead Peacock Crawler

Color: Peacock/black
Hook: Daiichi 1150
Thread: Black
  Monocord
Tail: Black, fine, round
  rubber legs
Body: Peacock herl
Rib: Brown 12-pound
  test monofilament
Legs: Black, fine,
  round rubber legs
Weight: Lead wire, large
Thorax: Black long-fiber synthetic dubbing

Beadhead Pheasant Tail

Color: Brown
Hook: Daiichi 1560
Thread: Dark olive
  Flymaster
Bead: Brass
Tail: Ringed-neck
  pheasant tail fibers
Body: Ringed-neck
  pheasant tail fibers,
  wrapped around hook
  shank, tapered

Rib: Copper fine wire, cross-wrapped with pheasant
Legs: Ringed-neck pheasant tail fibers swept and tied back from
  thorax. Cut to length
Thorax: Peacock herl
Shellback: Ringed-neck pheasant tail fibers

Beadhead Pheasant Tail

Color: Flashback
Hook: Daiichi 1560
Thread: Dark olive
  Flymaster
Bead: Brass
Tail: Ringed-neck
  pheasant tail fibers
Body: Ringed-neck
  pheasant tail fibers,
  wrapped around hook
  shank, tapered

Rib: Copper fine wire, cross-wrapped with pheasant
Legs: Pearl Krystal Flash swept and tied back from thorax. Cut to
  length
Thorax: Peacock herl
Shellback: Ringed-neck pheasant tail fibers, Pearl Krystal Flash.
  Legs are the tips of pheasant tied back
Note: Tie in tail using the same piece for body. Create tapered body with bulk of the pheasant tail piece. Krystal Flash imitates the emerger stage of the nymph. When fish are keyed on this phase of the life cycle, this pattern can be deadly.

Beadhead Prince Nymph

Color: Peacock
Hook: Daiichi 1710
Thread: Black Monocord
Bead: Brass
Tail: Brown goose biot
  quills
Body: Peacock herl
Rib: Gold oval #14
  tinsel
Collar Hackle: Brown
  saddle hackle
Weight: Lead wire, medium
Wing: White goose biot quills

Beadhead Rubber Leg Hare's Ear

Color: Brown
Hook: Daiichi 1560
Thread: Brown
  Flymaster
Bead: Brass
Tail: Brown-flake flat
  rubber legs
Body: Brown Antron
  dubbing
Rib: Gold flat #16/18
  Mylar tinsel
Legs: Brown-flake flat rubber legs
Weight: Lead wire, small
Thorax: Brown Hare's Ear Plus dubbing, spiky
Shellback: Natural-brown mottled turkey tail

Beadhead Rubber Leg Hare's Ear

Color: Natural hare's ear
Hook: Daiichi 1560
Thread: Tan Flymaster
Bead: Brass
Tail: Gold-flake flat rubber legs
Body: Natural hare's ear Antron dubbing
Rib: Gold flat #16/18 Mylar tinsel
Legs: Gold flake flat rubber legs
Weight: Lead wire, small
Thorax: Natural Hare's Ear Plus dubbing, spiky
Shellback: Natural-brown mottled turkey tail

Beadhead Shaggy Hare's Ear

Color: Natural hare's ear
Hook: Daiichi 1560
Thread: Tan Flymaster
Body: Tan hare's ear Antron dubbing
Collar Hackle: Gray and white speckled partridge plumage

Beadhead Stone Nymph

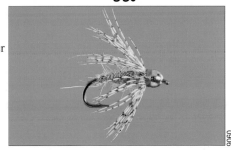

Color: Black
Hook: Daiichi 1270
Thread: Black Monocord
Bead: Black
Tail: Black goose biot quill
Body: Black long-fiber Antron dubbing
Rib: Dark-brown medium vinyl rib
Weight: Lead wire, large
Antennae: Black goose biot quill
Legs: Black, medium, round rubber legs
Thorax: Same as body
Shellback: Three sections of mottled brown turkey tail cut in v-shape
Note: This stonefly nymph has a heavily weighted body. A dubbing ball helps split the tail. The dubbing along the thorax is teased to create a buggy look.

Beadhead Stone Nymph

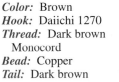

Color: Brown
Hook: Daiichi 1270
Thread: Dark brown Monocord
Bead: Copper
Tail: Dark brown goose biot quills
Body: Dark brown long-fiber Antron dubbing
Rib: Dark-brown medium vinyl rib
Weight: Lead wire, large
Antennae: Dark brown goose biot quills
Legs: Brown, medium, round rubber legs
Thorax: Same as body
Shellback: Three sections of mottled brown turkey tail cut in v-shape

Beadhead Stone Nymph

Color: Golden
Hook: Daiichi 1270
Thread: Gold Monocord
Bead: Brass
Tail: Brown goose biot quills
Body: Golden long-fiber Antron dubbing
Rib: Blood-red small vinyl rib
Weight: Lead wire, large
Antennae: Brown goose biot quills
Legs: Brown, medium, round rubber legs
Thorax: Same as body
Shellback: Three sections of mottled brown turkey tail cut in v-shape
Note: Stone nymphs vary in color. Screen to identify the dominate color and size in your fishing area. This series are those most generally found. The closer the match, the more effective the fly.

Bitch Creek Nymph

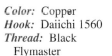

Color: Black and orange
Hook: Daiichi 2220
Thread: Black Monocord
Weight: Lead wire, large
Tail: White, medium, round rubber legs as long as the hook shank
Body: Black and orange variegated chenille
Rib: Copper medium wire, wrapped around thorax only
Body Hackle: Brown webby saddle hackle
Antennae: White, medium, round rubber legs
Thorax: Black chenille

Brassie

Color: Copper
Hook: Daiichi 1560
Thread: Black Flymaster
Body: Copper medium wire
Thorax: Black Antron dubbing, spiky
Note: The color of the wire is optional. Green, red and brown are commonly used.

Callibaetis Epoxyback Nymph

Color: Gray
Hook: Daiichi 1560
Thread: Gray Monocord
Tail: Ringed-neck pheasant tail fibers
Body: Muskrat belly dubbing
Rib: Silver fine wire
Thorax: Natural hare's mask dubbing, looped and trimmed on bottom
Shellback: Ringed-neck pheasant tail fibers, epoxy coated
Note: The epoxyback technique is used to simulate an emerging nymph and to increase durability. This pattern can be fished in lakes and rivers.

Callibaetis Killer

Color: Gray
Hook: Daiichi 1270
Thread: Gray Monocord
Weight: Lead wire, small
Tail: Gray, fine, round rubber legs
Body: Gray Antron dubbing
Rib: Silver fine wire
Body Hackle: Partridge plume
Eyes: Plastic, small mono eyes
Antennae: Gray, fine, round rubber legs
Thorax: Same as body
Shellback: Mottled turkey tail
Note: An extremely buggy pattern that can be tied in various colors.

Carey Special

Color: Black
Hook: Daiichi 1720
Thread: Black Monocord
Weight: Lead wire, medium
Tail: Natural ringed-neck pheasant rump
Body: Black chenille
Rib: Copper medium wire
Collar Hackle: Natural ringed-neck pheasant rump
Note: The collar hackle should be close to even in length with the tail.

Carey Special

Color: Olive
Hook: Daiichi 1720
Thread: Olive Monocord
Weight: Lead wire, medium
Tail: Olive-dyed ringed-neck pheasant rump
Body: Olive chenille
Rib: Copper medium wire
Collar Hackle: Olive-dyed ringed-neck pheasant rump
Note: Ringed-neck pheasant rump varies in color. The general rule is to use green for olive, brown for black, blue for peacock and silver.

Carey Special

Color: Peacock
Hook: Daiichi 1720
Thread: Black Monocord
Weight: Lead wire, medium
Tail: Natural ringed-neck pheasant rump
Body: Peacock herl
Rib: Copper medium wire
Collar Hackle: Natural ringed-neck pheasant rump

Carey Special

Color: Pheasant tail
Hook: Daiichi 1720
Thread: Brown Monocord
Weight: Lead wire, medium
Tail: Brown ringed-neck pheasant plumage
Body: Brown ringed-neck pheasant tail fibers
Rib: Copper medium wire, crossed-wrapped over pheasant
Body Hackle: Natural ringed-neck pheasant rump
Collar Hackle: Gray ringed-neck pheasant after-shaft

Carey Special

Color: Silver
Hook: Daiichi 1720
Thread: Black Monocord
Tail: Natural ringed-neck pheasant rump
Body: Silver flat #12 Mylar tinsel
Collar Hackle: Natural ringed-neck pheasant rump

Crawdad, Bachmann's

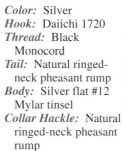

Color: Tan/brown
Hook: Daiichi 2220
Thread: Brown Monocord
Antennae: Root beer Krystal Flash
Throat: Natural red squirrel
Tail: Dark brown marabou
Body: Tan chenille
Rib: Copper medium wire
Body Hackle: Brown webby hen saddle hackle
Pinchers: Lobster rabbit strips
Weight: Lead wire, large
Shellback: Brown mottled turkey tail
Note: This is a spectacular pattern because it is the first crayfish to incorporate movement both in the pinchers and tail. Tied from bend of hook to the eye, starting with the antennae and ending with tail.

Crawdad, Seaweed

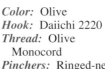

Color: Olive
Hook: Daiichi 2220
Thread: Olive Monocord
Pinchers: Ringed-neck pheasant tail fibers
Tail: Ringed-neck pheasant tail fibers, heavy
Body: Dark olive chenille
Rib: Copper medium wire
Weight: Lead wire, large
Shellback: Ringed-neck pheasant fibers
Note: This simple pattern works on silhouette principles. It is very effective fished in lakes and rivers for trout and bass.

Crawdad, Seaweed

Color: Tan/brown
Hook: Daiichi 2220
Thread: Tan
  Monocord
Pinchers: Ringed-neck
  pheasant tail fibers,
  heavy
Tail: Ringed-neck
  pheasant tail fibers
Body: Tan chenille
Rib: Copper medium
  wire
Weight: Lead wire, large
Shellback: Ringed-neck pheasant tail fibers

Damsel Nymph, Bachmann's

Color: Green
Hook: Daiichi 1710
Thread: Olive
  Flymaster
Tail: Damsel green
  marabou
Body: Damsel green
  marabou wrapped
  around hook shank
Rib: Copper fine wire
Legs/Body Hackle:
  Natural-brown partridge plumage
Thorax: Damsel green marabou wrapped around hook shank
Shellback: Clear or olive latex or plastic
Eyes: Black, small mono eyes
Note: The proportions are everything in tying this pattern successfully. The tail and body are the same piece of marabou. Wrap the rib in the opposite direction than the body. The latex thorax is tied behind and over the eyes to maximize the effect. Legs should be proportionate to size of hook.

Damsel Nymph, Bachmann's

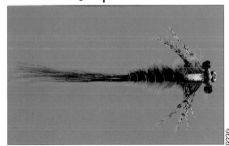

Color: Olive
Hook: Daiichi 1710
Thread: Olive
  Flymaster
Tail: Dark olive
  marabou
Body: Dark olive
  marabou wrapped
  around hook shank
Rib: Copper fine wire
Legs/Body Hackle:
  Natural-brown partridge plumage
Thorax: Dark olive marabou wrapped around hook shank
Shellback: Clear or olive, latex or plastic
Eyes: Black, small mono eyes
Note: The tail provides movement imitating a swimming damsel nymph.

Damsel Nymph, Bachmann's

Color: Tan
Hook: Daiichi 1710
Thread: Tan Flymaster
Tail: Tan grizzly marabou
Body: Tan grizzly
  marabou wrapped
  around hook shank
Rib: Copper fine wire
Legs/Body Hackle:
  Natural-brown
  partridge plume
Thorax: Tan grizzly marabou wrapped around hook shank
Shellback: Brown or clear, latex or plastic
Eyes: Black, small mono eyes
Note: There are many species of damselflies, varying in color.

Damsel, Marabou

Color: Dark olive
Hook: Daiichi 1270
Thread: Olive
  Flymaster
Tail: Dark olive
  marabou
Body: Dark olive
  marabou wrapped
  around hook shank
Rib: Copper fine wire
Wing: Dark olive
  marabou
Note: This is a slender, more general silhouette pattern.

Damsel, Marabou

Color: Olive
Hook: Daiichi 1270
Thread: Olive
  Flymaster
Tail: Olive marabou
Body: Olive marabou
  wrapped around hook
  shank
Rib: Copper fine wire
Wing: Olive marabou
Note: The marabou is
tied in tip-first then wrapped around hook shank to create taper.

Damsel, Marabou

Color: Tan grizzly
Hook: Daiichi 1270
Thread: Tan Flymaster
Tail: Tan grizzly
  marabou
Body: Tan grizzly
  marabou wrapped
  around hook shank
Rib: Copper fine wire
Wing: Tan grizzly
  marabou

Damsel, Ultra

Color: Olive
Hook: Daiichi 1510
Thread: Olive
  Flymaster
Tail: Olive marabou
Body: Olive Ultra
  Chenille
Legs/Body Hackle:
  Natural-brown
  partridge plumage
Thorax: Olive Antron
  dubbing
Shellback: Brown mottled turkey tail
Eyes: Black, mono eyes
Note: A very realistic imitation: eyes, legs, and extended body make it extremely effective. Tie marabou tail on with an extended body tool and trim excess chenille.

Dragonfly Nymph, Rabbit

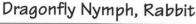

Color: Brown
Hook: Daiichi 1720
Thread: Brown Monocord
Body: Brown rabbit strip wrapped around hook shank
Legs: Black medium, round rubber legs
Thorax: Dark brown Antron dubbing
Shellback: Natural-brown partridge plumage
Eyes: Black metallic hourglass eyes
Note: The rabbit is trimmed to form a triangular shaped abdomen. The eyes and shape of head are also triangular, imitating the real insect.

Dragonfly Nymph, Rabbit

Color: Olive
Hook: Daiichi 1720
Thread: Olive Monocord
Body: Olive rabbitstrip wrapped around hook shank
Legs: Brown medium, round rubber legs
Thorax: Olive Antron dubbing
Shellback: Natural green, ringed-neck pheasant rump plumage
Eyes: Gold hourglass eyes
Note: The eyes not only add weight, but give the fly a unique swimming motion when stripped. Dragonfly nymphs propel themselves by pushing water through special abdominal gills. The rabbit strip simulates that function.

Dragonfly Nymph, Western

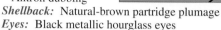

Color: Olive
Hook: Daiichi 1720
Thread: Olive Monocord
Body: Olive Antron dubbing
Weight: Lead wire, medium
Body Hackle: Olive and tan grizzly marabou
Eyes: Black mono eyes
Thorax: Same as body
Shellback: Clear latex
Wing: Brown mottled turkey tail
Note: The grizzly marabou provides lots of action simulating gill movement along the abdomen. The lead in the body gets the fly down with the hook up, and also gives it a swimming action when stripped.

Emergent Nymph, Harrang's

Color: Brown
Hook: Daiichi 1560
Thread: Black Flymaster
Tail: Wood duck-dyed mallard flank or pheasant tail fibers
Body: Pheasant tail fibers wrapped around hook shank
Rib: Silver fine wire
Body Hackle: Peacock herl
Collar Hackle: Peacock herl
Thorax: Pearlescent glass bead
Shellback: Brown mottled turkey tail
Note: John Harrang's idea was to imitate the emerging mayfly nymph as it appeared in the water column; very slender and with a bubble of air. An excellent micro nymph imitation.

FFS Stonefly Nymph

Color: Brown
Hook: Daiichi 2220
Thread: Dark brown Monocord
Tag: Dark brown dubbing ball
Tail: Dark brown goose biots split by dubbing ball
Body: Dark brown synthetic dubbing
Rib: Dark brown, medium vinyl rib
Body Hackle: Dark brown-dyed grizzly saddle hackle
Weight: Lead wire, large
Thorax: Same as body
Antennae: Dark brown goose biot quills
Note: Weighted with .35 lead, the full length of the body, with an additional layer along the thorax.

FFS Stonefly Nymph

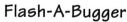

Color: Golden
Hook: Daiichi 2220
Thread: Yellow Monocord
Tag: Golden dubbing ball
Tail: Gold goose biots split by dubbing ball
Body: Golden synthetic dubbing
Rib: Brown medium vinyl rib
Body Hackle: Ginger saddle hackle
Weight: Lead wire, large
Thorax: Same as body
Antennae: Gold goose biot quills

Flashback Hare's Ear

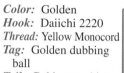

Color: Natural
Hook: Daiichi 1560
Thread: Tan Flymaster
Tail: Natural hare's ear mask fibers
Body: Natural hare's ear Antron dubbing
Rib: Gold flat #16/18 Mylar tinsel
Weight: Lead wire, medium
Thorax: Natural Hare's Ear Plus dubbing, spiky
Shellback: Pearl Krystal Flash. Tie back three stands on each side for legs
Note: I have found that the addition of Krystal Flash increases effectiveness.

Flash-A-Bugger

Color: Black
Hook: Daiichi 1720
Thread: Black Monocord
Tail: Black marabou with four to six strands of pearl Flashabou
Body: Black chenille
Rib: Silver medium wire
Body Hackle: Black strung saddle hackle
Weight: Lead wire, medium
Lateral Line: Pearl Flashabou
Note: The winning combination for tying Flash-A-Buggers: The tail is same length as hook shank, the hackle extends 1/8 inch past hook point and is cross-wrapped with wire rib, the cup of the hackle is webby and faces back, the lateral line of flash.

Flash-A-Bugger

Color: Brown
Hook: Daiichi 1720
Thread: Brown Monocord
Tail: Brown marabou with four to six strands of pearl Flashabou
Body: Brown chenille
Rib: Gold fine wire
Body Hackle: Fiery-brown strung saddle hackle
Weight: Lead wire, medium
Lateral Line: Pearl Flashabou

Flash-A-Bugger

Color: Maroon
Hook: Daiichi 1720
Thread: Maroon Monocord
Tail: Maroon marabou with four to six strands of pearl Flashabou
Body: Maroon chenille
Rib: Copper medium wire
Body Hackle: Wine strung saddle hackle
Weight: Lead wire, medium
Lateral Line: Pearl Krystal Flash

Flash-A-Bugger

Color: Olive
Hook: Daiichi 1720
Thread: Olive Monocord
Tail: Olive marabou with four to six strands of pearl Flashabou
Body: Olive chenille
Rib: Gold fine wire
Body Hackle: Olive strung saddle hackle
Weight: Lead wire, medium
Lateral Line: Pearl Flashabou

Flash-A-Bugger

Color: Peacock
Hook: Daiichi 1720
Thread: Green Monocord
Tail: Forest green marabou with four to six strands of pearl Flashabou
Body: Peacock herl
Rib: Green medium wire
Body Hackle: Olive-dyed grizzly saddle hackle
Weight: Lead wire, medium
Lateral Line: Peacock Flashabou
Note: Found to be a most effective lake pattern for both bass and trout.

Flash-A-Bugger

Color: Purple
Hook: Daiichi 1720
Thread: Black Monocord
Tail: Purple marabou with four to six strands of purple Flashabou
Body: Purple chenille
Rib: Silver fine wire
Body Hackle: Purple strung saddle hackle
Weight: Lead wire, medium
Lateral Line: Purple Flashabou

Flash-A-Bugger

Color: Root beer
Hook: Daiichi 1720
Thread: Brown Monocord
Tail: Root beer brown marabou with four to six strands of pearl Flashabou
Body: Rust brown chenille
Rib: Copper medium wire
Body Hackle: Fiery-brown strung saddle hackle
Weight: Lead wire, medium
Lateral Line: Pearl Krystal Flash

Fry, Alaskan

Color: Multi
Hook: Daiichi 1720
Thread: Clear nylon
Tail: Green Krystal Flash /pearl Sparkle Flash left over from body
Body: Pearl Sparkle Flash wrapped around hook shank, tapered
Coating: Several coats of epoxy
Shellback: Top: Green Krystal Flash. Bottom: Pearl Krystal Flash
Eye: Brass bead with painted black pupils
Note: After twenty unsuccessful attempts to invent an effective fry pattern, the twenty-first was the charm. The key is the combination and color of the body material and the use of epoxy. Fry are slender and almost completely transparent. Oversized eyes are their dominate feature, and the brass bead imitates them perfectly, while helping the fly swim correctly.

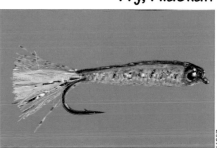

Black Stone Nymph, Kenny's

Color: Black
Hook: Daiichi 1270
Thread: Black Monocord
Tail: Black fine, round rubber legs
Body: Black synthetic dubbing
Rib: Copper medium wire
Legs: Black, fine, round rubber legs
Eyes: Lead hourglass, unpainted
Weight: Lead wire, medium
Thorax: Dubbing, same as body
Shellback: Natural-brown mottled turkey tail
Note: Kenny "Dredgemaster" Morrish developed this style of stonefly nymph to fish heavy waters in Oregon. Many waters around the nation have excessive weight restrictions, and some of these patterns are specifically designed to combat these restrictions.

Golden Stone Nymph, Kenny's

Color: Golden
Hook: Daiichi 1270
Thread: Tan Monocord
Tail: Brown, fine, round rubber legs
Body: Golden Antron dubbing
Rib: Brown, fine, round vinyl rib
Legs: Lead hourglass, unpainted
Eyes: Lead hourglass, unpainted
Weight: Lead wire, medium
Thorax: Dubbing, same as body
Shellback: Natural-brown mottled turkey tail
Note: This is a realistic imitation of any size stone nymph. The eyes and lead force the fly to the bottom where you want it. The legs make it irresistibly buggy.

Golden Stone, Little

Color: Golden
Hook: Daiichi 1560
Thread: Tan Monocord
Tail: Ringed-neck pheasant tail fibers
Body: Golden synthetic dubbing
Rib: Brown monofilament, 6-pound-test
Legs/Body Hackle: Natural-brown partridge plumage
Weight: Lead wire, small
Thorax: Same as body
Shellback: Brown partridge plume

Green Drake Epoxyback Nymph

Color: Olive
Hook: Daiichi 1270
Thread: Green Monocord
Tail: Ringed-neck pheasant tail fibers
Body: Olive Antron dubbing
Rib: Copper fine wire
Abdominal Gills: Olive marabou
Legs: Ringed-neck pheasant plumage
Thorax: Same as body
Shellback: Ringed-neck pheasant tail fibers
Note: The shellback extends the length of the fly. The thorax portion of the shellback has an epoxy coating to imitate the air sack that takes the nymph to the surface. Be careful not to overdress the gills.

Hare's Ear Nymph

Color: Black
Hook: Daiichi 1560
Thread: Black Monocord
Tail: Black hare's mask fibers
Body: Black hare's ear, Antron dubbing
Rib: Gold flat #16/18 Mylar tinsel
Weight: Lead wire, medium
Thorax: Black Hare's Ear Plus dubbing, spiky
Shellback: Peacock herl

Hare's Ear Nymph

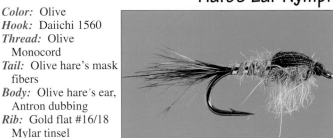

Color: Gold ribbed
Hook: Daiichi 1560
Thread: Tan Monocord
Tail: Natural hare's ear mask fibers
Body: Natural hare's ear, Antron dubbing
Rib: Gold flat #16/18 Mylar tinsel
Weight: Lead wire, medium
Thorax: Natural Hare's Ear Plus dubbing, spiky
Shellback: Brown mottled turkey tail

Hare's Ear Nymph

Color: Olive
Hook: Daiichi 1560
Thread: Olive Monocord
Tail: Olive hare's mask fibers
Body: Olive hare's ear, Antron dubbing
Rib: Gold flat #16/18 Mylar tinsel
Weight: Lead wire, medium
Thorax: Olive Hare's Ear Plus dubbing, spiky
Shellback: Brown mottled turkey tail

Hellgrammite, Bachmann's

Color: Brown
Hook: Daiichi 2220
Thread: Black Monocord
Tail: Brown goose biot quills separated with dubbing ball
Body: Brown, long-fiber synthetic dubbing
Rib: Copper medium wire
Body Hackle: Brown, webby saddle hackle
Weight: Lead wire, medium
Thorax: Brown, long-fiber synthetic dubbing
Shellback: Brown-dyed plastic, tied in several sections
Antennae: Dark brown goose biot quills

Hexagenia Nymph, Bachmann's

Color: Sand/yellow/brown
Hook: Daiichi 1270
Thread: Yellow Monocord
Weight: Lead wire, medium, thorax only
Tail: Yellow-dyed grizzly marabou
Body: Yellow-dyed grizzly marabou
Rib: Copper fine wire
Body Hackle: Yellow-dyed grizzly marabou
Eyes: Black medium, plastic mono eyes
Legs: Wood duck-dyed mallard flank
Thorax: Same as body
Shellback: Clear plastic
Note: This pattern has a small amount of lead under the thorax to give it a realistic swimming action when being striped. The marabou adds motion. Meant to be fished under the surface.

Hexagenia Nymph, Silvey's

Color: Yellow/brown
Hook: Daiichi 1270
Thread: Yellow
  Monocord
Tail: Gray ostrich herl
Body: Gold Antron
  dubbing
Abdominal Gills:
  Brown marabou
Eyes: Black, small
  plastic mono eyes
Thorax: Same as body

Shellback: Ringed-neck pheasant tail fibers, tips tied back for legs
Note: This pattern is not weighted because *Hexagenias* usually hatch during the last hour of daylight or through the night. Therefore, fish are cruising the surface looking for swimming nymphs and emergers.

Hunchback Nymph

Color: Orange/brown
Hook: Daiichi 1130
Thread: Orange
  Flymaster
Tail: Wood duck-dyed
  mallard flank
Body: Brown/orange
  Scintilla Caliente
  dubbing
Rib: Orange Flymaster
  thread
Legs: Wood duck-dyed mallard flank
Thorax: Same as body
Shellback: Brown mottled turkey tail

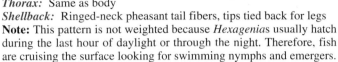

Little Black Nymph

Color: Black/Peacock
Hook: Daiichi 1560
Thread: Black
  Flymaster
Tail: Black-dyed
  golden pheasant crest
  tippet
Body: Peacock herl
Rib: Silver fine wire,
  cross-wrapped
  against fibers
Legs: Tied back from the shellback
Thorax: Peacock herl
Shellback: Black-dyed golden pheasant crest plumage

Marabou Leech

Color: Black
Hook: Daiichi 1270
Thread: Black
  Flymaster
Tail: Black marabou
Body: Black marabou
  wrapped around hook
  shank
Wing: Same as body
Note: Tie in tail tip-first
and use excess marabou

to wrap body. Use the same technique for middle wing. If the tips of the marabou are not thick and full, tear to desired consistency with thumb and forefinger for natural look.

Marabou Leech

Color: Brown
Hook: Daiichi 1270
Thread: Brown
  Flymaster
Tail: Brown marabou
Body: Brown marabou
  wrapped around hook
  shank
Wing: Same as body

Marabou Leech

Color: Olive
Hook: Daiichi 1270
Thread: Olive
  Flymaster
Tail: Olive marabou
Body: Olive marabou
  wrapped around hook
  shank
Wing: Same as body

March Brown Nymph

Color: Peacock/brown
Hook: Daiichi 1560
Thread: Brown
  Flymaster
Weight: Lead wire,
  medium
Tail: Moose hair
  fibers, three split
Body: Brown Antron
  dubbing
Rib: Peacock herl
Body Hackle: Brown, webby saddle hackle
Thorax: Peacock herl
Shellback: Brown mottled turkey tail
Note: March brown nymphs have three distinct tails and prominent gills on their abdomen.

Matt's Fur Nymph

Color: Tan
Hook: Daiichi 1560
Thread: Tan Monocord
Weight: Lead wire,
  medium
Tail: Wood duck-dyed
  mallard flank
Body: Light tan,
  blended opossum
  dubbing
Rib: Gold, medium
  oval tinsel
Thorax: Same as body
Shellback: Wood duck-dyed mallard flank, tie tips back for legs
Note: A standard golden stone nymph, and when tied smaller, a very good mayfly nymph imitation.

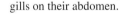

Ken Morrish Photo

Montana Stone

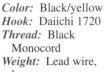

Color: Black/yellow
Hook: Daiichi 1720
Thread: Black Monocord
Weight: Lead wire, large
Body: Black chenille
Body Hackle: Black saddle hackle
Thorax: Yellow chenille
Shellback: Black chenille

Mosquito Larva

Color: Gray
Hook: Daiichi 1180
Thread: Black Flymaster
Tail: Grizzly hackle fibers
Body: Peacock quill, stripped
Rib: Silver fine wire
Thorax: Peacock herl
Antennae: Grizzly hackle fibers

Mysis Shrimp, Eggermyster

Color: White
Hook: Daiichi 1510
Thread: Clear nylon
Tail: White Antron yarn
Body: White Antron yarn twisted with pearl Krystal Flash and wrapped around hook shank
Rib: Clear nylon thread
Body Hackle: Natural grizzly saddle hackle
Eyes: Burned monofilament painted black
Thorax: Cream Antron dubbing
Shellback: White Antron yarn

Note: This is a dead shrimp pattern developed by Rob Eggers, a Colorado native. He explains that during the spring, there is a massive migration of shrimp from the lakes above into the rivers. Many of these shrimp die, and fish frantically feed on them. We studied his collected specimens, and his pattern is a true match. The curved hook imitates the tumbling shrimp.

Mysis Shrimp, Extended Body Eggermyster

Color: White
Hook: Daiichi 1510
Thread: Clear nylon
Tail: White Antron yarn
Body: Cream Antron dubbing
Rib: Clear nylon thread figure-eight around tail
Body Hackle: Natural grizzly saddle hackle
Eyes: Burned monofilament painted black
Shellback: White Antron yarn

Note: You may prefer to use a needle to stiffen the tail in order to rib the extended body if you have difficulty using your fingers. Trim Antron yarn used for shellback slightly long so that it extends over eyes. *Mysis* shrimp have dominant extended body characteristics.

Mysis Shrimp, Live Shrimp

Color: Cream
Hook: Daiichi 1270
Thread: Tan Flymaster
Tail: Natural mallard flank fibers
Body: Clear micro Larva Lace over thread
Rib: Pearl Krystal Flash
Eyes: Clear micro Larva Lace with black yarn
Thorax: White ostrich herl
Shellback: Clear micro Larva Lace

Note: Live *Mysis* shrimp are transparent with a slight iridescent cast. This pattern is an exact match given to me by a guide in Aspen, CO. Finicky fish key on live shrimp, and this realistic pattern does the job.

Pheasant-Tail Emerger

Color: Light brown
Hook: Daiichi 1560
Thread: Brown Flymaster
Tail: Ringed-neck pheasant tail fibers
Body: Ringed-neck pheasant tail fibers wrapped around hook shank
Rib: Copper fine wire
Thorax: Peacock herl
Wing: White poly yarn, pearl Krystal Flash

Note: A great mayfly nymph emerger. Dress the poly to suspend the fly in the surface film, or fish deep.

Pheasant-Tail Nymph

Color: Light brown
Hook: Daiichi 1560
Thread: Brown Flymaster
Tail: Ringed-neck pheasant tail fibers
Body: Ringed-neck pheasant tail fibers wrapped around hook shank
Rib: Copper fine wire
Thorax: Peacock herl
Shellback: Ringed-neck pheasant tail fibers, tips tied back for legs

Pheasant-Tail Nymph, Flashback

Color: Light brown/crystal
Hook: Daiichi 1560
Thread: Brown Flymaster
Tail: Ringed-neck pheasant tail fibers
Body: Ringed-neck pheasant tail fibers wrapped around hook shank
Rib: Copper fine wire
Thorax: Peacock herl
Shellback: 1st: Ringed-neck pheasant tail fibers, tips tied back for legs. 2nd: Several strands of pearl Flashabou

PMD Epoxyback Nymph

Color: Orange/tan
Hook: Daiichi 1270
Thread: Tan Flymaster
Tail: Ringed-neck pheasant tail fibers
Body: Orange/tan Antron dubbing
Rib: Lime green Krystal Flash
Body Hackle: Tan marabou fibers
Thorax: Same as body, spiky
Shellback: Brown mottled turkey tail

Note: The thorax is coated with epoxy to imitate the air sack that the nymph inflates to reach the surface to hatch. The body hackle imitates abdominal gills. Two sparse marabou puffs are tied on both sides of the thorax.

RS2

Color: Beige
Hook: Daiichi 1180
Tail: Wood duck-dyed mallard flank fibers
Body: Beige Super Fine Dubbing
Wings: 1st: Pearl Krystal Flash. 2nd: White poly yarn

Note: Grease the wing of this slender nymph emerger, to suspend it in the surface film. When fish are making dimple rises, there is a good chance they are taking small mayfly emergers. The RS2 can be an effective imitation.

PMD Flashback Nymph

Color: Orange/tan
Hook: Daiichi 1560
Thread: Tan Flymaster
Tail: Ringed-neck pheasant tail fibers
Body: Tannish pink Antron dubbing
Rib: Copper fine wire
Thorax: Same as body, spiky
Shellback: Pearl flat #12 Mylar tinsel

RS2

Color: Gray
Hook: Daiichi 1180
Tail: Natural blue dun hackle fibers
Body: Gray Super Fine Dubbing
Wings: 1st: Pearl Krystal Flash. 2nd: White poly yarn

Prince Nymph

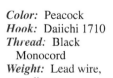

Color: Peacock
Hook: Daiichi 1710
Thread: Black Monocord
Weight: Lead wire, medium
Tail: Brown goose biot quills
Body: Peacock herl
Rib: Gold oval #16/18 Mylar tinsel
Collar Hackle: Brown webby saddle hackle
Wing: White goose biot quills

RS2

Color: Olive
Hook: Daiichi 1180
Tail: Natural blue dun hackle fibers
Body: Olive Super Fine Dubbing
Wings: 1st: Olive Krystal Flash. 2nd: White poly yarn

Prince Nymph, Flashy

Color: Peacock
Hook: Daiichi 1710
Thread: Black Monocord
Weight: Lead wire, medium
Tail: Brown goose biot quills
Body: Peacock herl
Rib: Lime green Krystal Flash
Collar Hackle: Natural-brown partridge plumage
Wing: Pearl Flashabou

Note: The quality of the peacock is important. Thick robust peacock eye sticks are the best to use. Always reverse-wrap the body and rib to ensure durability.

Rubber Leg Hare's Ear

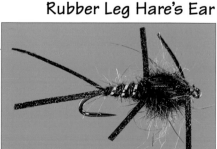

Color: Brown
Hook: Daiichi 1560
Thread: Brown Flymaster
Weight: Lead wire, medium
Tail: Brown-flake flat rubber legs
Body: Brown Antron dubbing
Rib: Gold flat #16/18 Mylar tinsel
Thorax: Brown Hare's Ear Plus dubbing, spiky
Shellback: Brown mottled turkey tail

Note: The legs add a distinctive feature to nymph patterns much like eyes to baitfish patterns. However, the material used is critical. Color must match the real insect, and the texture needs to be supple.

Rubber Leg Hare's Ear

Color: Gold ribbed
Hook: Daiichi 1560
Thread: Tan Flymaster
Weight: Lead wire, medium
Tail: Tan, flat rubber legs
Body: Natural Hare's Antron dubbing
Rib: Gold, flat, #16/18 Mylar tinsel
Thorax: Natural Hare's Ear Plus dubbing, spiky
Shellback: Brown mottled turkey tail

Scud

Color: Orange
Hook: Daiichi 1510
Thread: Orange Flymaster
Tail: Orange hackle fibers
Body: Orange long-fiber Antron and synthetic dubbing blend
Rib: Clear monofilament
Legs: Dubbing pulled down through ribs with a bodkin
Antennae: Orange hackle fibers
Shellback: Four to five strands of orange Krystal Flash /clear plastic

San Juan Worm

Color: Red
Hook: Daiichi 1510
Thread: Red Flymaster
Body: Red Ultra chenille
Note: Aquatic worms live in most river systems and play a large part in a fish's diet. Many entomologists have witnessed migrations and drifts. Migrations and drifts usually occur during the spring or fall runoffs.

Sculpin, Articulated Woolhead

Color: Olive/brown
Hook: 1st: Daiichi 1710. 2nd: Daiichi 1720
Thread: Brown Monocord
Weight: Lead wire, large
Tail: Olive-dyed grizzly marabou
Body: Dark olive/brown synthetic dubbing
Rib: Copper wire, large
Body Hackle: Olive-dyed grizzly marabou, tied Matuka style
Fins: Brown-dyed grizzly marabou
Throat: Red lamb's wool
Thorax: Olive, brown and black lamb's wool
Eyes: Extra large lead hourglass eyes painted white, red and black, and epoxy coated
Note: This pattern has two hooks that are connected with 30-pound-test Dacron backing that allows the two pieces to articulate freely. The grizzly marabou is essential for creating movement. Wool is a strange material that takes some getting used to. Tie wool with a minimum of thread wraps. Thread for the head needs to be strong nylon. The placement and use of lead is critical to achieve proper balance. Some experimenting should be expected.

San Juan Worm

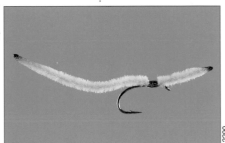

Color: Tan
Hook: Daiichi 1510
Thread: Tan Flymaster
Body: Tan Ultra chenille
Note: Burn both ends of chenille with a lighter to achieve proper look.

Scud

Color: Gray/olive
Hook: Daiichi 1510
Thread: Olive Flymaster
Tail: Natural blue dun hackle fibers
Body: Gray/olive long-fiber Antron and synthetic dubbing blend
Rib: Clear nylon thread
Legs: Dubbing pulled down through ribs with a bodkin
Antennae: Natural blue dun hackle fibers
Shellback: Two or three strands of pearl Flashabou/clear latex strip

Sculpin, Big Eye

Color: Tan/brown
Hook: Daiichi 2220
Thread: Brown Monocord
Weight: Lead wire, medium
Tail: Brown-dyed grizzly hen hackle splayed outward/root beer Krystal Flash
Body: Tan synthetic dubbing
Body Hackle: Brown-dyed grizzly saddle hackle
Eyes: Lead hourglass painted black, with white irises and red and black pupils
Thorax: Dubbing, same as body
Lateral Line: Root beer Krystal Flash
Note: The tail has two large webby hackles on the outside of two small hackles in the middle. When wrapping the body hackle, be sure to wrap the bottom fluffy part as the collar hackle.

Serendipity

Color: Green
Hook: Daiichi 1510
Thread: Olive Monocord
Body: Green Antron yarn twisted and wrapped around hook shank
Head: Natural deer hair spun and cut to shape

Note: The head is wedge shaped and atop the hook shank. Personal preference may differ as to how to cut the head and wing.

Serendipity

Color: Red
Hook: Daiichi 1510
Thread: Red Monocord
Body: Red Antron yarn twisted and wrapped around hook shank
Head: Natural deer hair spun and cut to shape

Serendipity

Color: Tan
Hook: Daiichi 1510
Thread: Tan Monocord
Body: Tan Antron yarn twisted and wrapped around hook shank
Head: Natural deer hair spun and cut to shape

Soft Hackle

Color: Partridge/gray
Hook: Daiichi 1560
Thread: Gray Monocord
Tail: Gray-speckled partridge plumage
Body: Gray Antron dubbing
Rib: Gold flat #16/18 Mylar tinsel
Collar Hackle: Gray-speckled partridge plumage

Note: Tie partridge hackle in tip-first making sure the cup of the feather is sweeping back. Hackle should reach to the bend of the hook.

Soft Hackle

Color: Green
Hook: Daiichi 1560
Thread: Tan Flymaster
Tail: Gray-speckled partridge plume
Body: Green rayon floss
Collar Hackle: Tan-speckled partridge plumage
Thorax: Natural hare's ear dubbing

Soft Hackle

Color: Partridge/hare's ear
Hook: Daiichi 1560
Thread: Tan Flymaster
Tail: Brown-speckled partridge plumage
Body: Natural hare's ear Antron dubbing
Rib: Gold flat #16/18 Mylar tinsel
Collar Hackle: Brown-speckled partridge plumage

Soft Hackle

Color: Partridge/yellow
Hook: Daiichi 1560
Thread: Yellow Flymaster
Tail: Tan-speckled partridge plumage
Body: Yellow rayon floss
Thorax: Natural hare's ear dubbing
Collar Hackle: Tan-speckled partridge plumage

Soft Hackle

Color: Pheasant tail
Hook: Daiichi 1560
Thread: Brown Flymaster
Tail: Ringed-neck pheasant tail fibers
Body: Ringed-neck pheasant tail fibers wrapped around hook shank
Rib: Copper, medium wire
Thorax: Peacock herl
Collar Hackle: Brown-speckled partridge plumage

Soft Hackle

Color: Starling
Hook: Daiichi 1560
Thread: Black Flymaster
Tail: Male starling plumage
Body: Peacock herl
Rib: Gold fine wire
Collar Hackle: Male starling plumage

Woolly Worm

Color: Black
Hook: Daiichi 1720
Thread: Black Monocord
Weight: Lead wire, medium
Tail: Red poly yarn
Body: Black chenille
Rib: Gold fine wire
Body Hackle: Black webby saddle hackle, cross-wrapped with wire

Ugly Bug Nymph

Color: Black
Hook: Daiichi 2220
Thread: Black Monocord
Tail: Black, medium, round rubber legs
Body: Black chenille
Body Hackle: Six black, medium, round rubber legs
Thorax: Black chenille
Antennae: Two black, medium rubber legs
Weight: Lead wire, large. Double-wrapped in thorax area to create proper taper.

Woolly Worm

Color: Brown
Hook: Daiichi 1720
Thread: Brown Monocord
Weight: Lead wire, medium
Tail: Flame poly yarn
Body: Brown chenille
Rib: Gold fine wire
Body Hackle: Brown, webby saddle hackle, cross-wrapped with wire

WD-40

Color: Brown
Hook: Daiichi 1130
Thread: Brown Flymaster
Tail: Wood duck-dyed mallard flank feathers
Body: Thread
Thorax: Tan Scintilla Caliente dubbing
Shellback: Same as tail

Note: The current trend in nymphing techniques is to use small or micro nymphs, and WD-40s are some of the most productive.

Woolly Worm

Color: Olive
Hook: Daiichi 1720
Thread: Olive Monocord
Weight: Lead wire, medium
Tail: Flame poly yarn
Body: Olive chenille
Rib: Gold fine wire
Body Hackle: Brown, webby saddle hackle, cross-wrapped with wire

WD-40

Color: Olive
Hook: Daiichi 1130
Thread: Dark olive Flymaster
Tail: Wood duck-dyed mallard flank feathers
Body: Thread
Thorax: Olive Scintilla Caliente dubbing
Shellback: Same as tail

Whiz Banger Leech

Color: Black/ chartreuse
Hook: Daiichi 2220
Thread: Chartreuse flat waxed
Weight: Lead wire, medium
Tail: Black rabbit strip
Body: Black rabbit strip
Eyes: Chrome hour glass inset eyes, with plastic lure eyes, epoxy coated
Thorax: Chartreuse chenille

Whiz Banger Leech

Color: Black/pink
Hook: Daiichi 2220
Thread: Black Monocord
Weight: Lead wire, medium
Tail: Black rabbit strip
Body: Black rabbit strip
Eyes: Chrome hour glass inset eyes, with plastic lure eyes, epoxy coated
Thorax: Fluorescent pink chenille

Note: This is a very versatile pattern. Used in Alaska for all species. Steelhead, lake trout and bass find it hard to resist the lifelike effect of the rabbit. The lead eyes add a lot of action.

Zonker

Color: Black
Hook: Daiichi 2220
Thread: Black Monocord
Tail: Black rabbit strip
Body: Aluminum tape overlapped, cut to shape and covered with silver Mylar tubing
Collar Hackle: Black strung saddle hackle
Shellback: Black rabbit strip
Eyes: Painted yellow irises with black pupils, epoxy coated

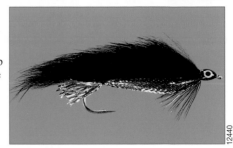

Whiz Banger Leech

Color: Chartreuse/ fluorescent pink
Hook: Daiichi 2220
Thread: Fluorescent pink, flat waxed
Weight: Lead wire, medium
Tail: Chartreuse rabbit strip
Body: Chartreuse rabbit strip
Eyes: Chrome hourglass inset eyes, with plastic lure eyes, epoxy coated
Thorax: Fluorescent pink chenille

Zug Bug

Color: Peacock
Hook: Daiichi 1710
Thread: Black Monocord
Weight: Lead wire, medium
Tail: Peacock sword
Body: Peacock herl
Rib: Copper medium wire
Collar Hackle: Brown ringed-neck pheasant plume
Wing: Wood duck-dyed mallard flank

Note: The wing extends half the length of the hook shank and the legs reach the point of the hook.

Whiz Banger Leech

Color: Orange/red
Hook: Daiichi 2220
Thread: Fluorescent red flat waxed
Weight: Lead wire, medium
Tail: Orange rabbit strip
Body: Orange rabbit strip
Eyes: Chrome hour glass inset eyes, with plastic lure eyes, epoxy coated
Thorax: Fluorescent red chenille

Whiz Banger Leech

Color: Red/orange
Hook: Daiichi 2220
Thread: Hot orange flat waxed
Weight: Lead wire, medium
Tail: Red rabbit strip
Body: Red rabbit strip
Eyes: Chrome hour glass inset eyes, with plastic lure eyes, epoxy coated
Thorax: Hot orange chenille

Chapter 7

STEELHEAD AND SALMON FLIES

THE HISTORY AND THE ROMANCE OF STEELHEAD FLY TYING

Bill McMillan

In 1961 there were relatively few established steelhead fly patterns. That was the year I began both steelhead fly fishing and steelhead fly tying. For example, my 1962 edition of Ray Bergman's *Trout* had 16 steelhead flies in its colored plate of "steelhead and streamer patterns." Nine more steelhead patterns could be found among the plate of "new wet flies"— 25 steelhead flies in all. *Trout* was the most complete source book on American fly fishing at the time with colored plates of 687 fly patterns.

However, Bergman's *Trout* did not provide a complete picture of steelhead fly fishing or of steelhead flies. No book did. His only steelhead experiences were on Oregon's Umpqua River. It did not portray the more diverse methods of steelhead fly fishing in differing West Coast regions, nor of the steelhead fly pattern developments that had been taking place in pockets of geographic and social isolation.

The available steelhead fly fishing literature of the early 1960s was limited. The first book solely on steelhead fishing was Claude Kreider's *Steelhead* (1948). Clark Van Fleet's *Steelhead to a Fly* (1954) was the first book entirely on steelhead fly fishing. Both authors were from California. By their very titles, these two books had considerable influence on the direction of steelhead fly fishing in the 1950s and 1960s.

The Kreider book pictured and described 20 steelhead flies and three Atlantic salmon flies that he considered "proven patterns." Van Fleet suggested about a dozen flies which were broken into color-types with minimal emphasis on specific patterns. Most of the patterns in both books dated to the 1930s or older, and most were included in Bergman's *Trout* (first printing in 1938).

It is known that steelhead fly fishing was being practiced at least as early as 1890 on California's Eel River. Trey Combs quotes a surprisingly sophisticated discussion about California steelhead and steelhead fly fishing from the August, 1899 issue of *Forest and Stream* magazine in *The Steelhead Trout* (1973).

In that same book, Combs includes two fly patterns specifically designed for steelhead, the Soule and the Van Zandt, that date to 1890. They may have been the first. Benn's Coachman, the Martha and the Carson followed within the next ten years. But there were probably others—anonymous flies that died with their similarly anonymous inventors. History is like that: a puny record of the knowns.

The perception of steelhead fly fishing remained little changed, other than the gradual spread to more rivers, from 1890 until the 1970s. It was considered a peculiarly "Western" form of fly fishing using bright-colored wet flies (attractor patterns) that was never quite legitimate by East Coast standards.

Perhaps it was too connected to Zane Grey, an author who made a fortune from his novels of the West and on the writings of his exotic adventures as a sportsman, but who eluded consideration as an important example of American literature or intellect.

But steelhead fly fishing did change in those 80 years. The problem was that there was very little communication among the isolated niches of steelhead anglers. No single steelhead fly fisherman knew the breadth of his own sport.

That changed in the latter 1960s when West Coast anglers began to have a local periodical. *Salmon Trout Steelheader*, a magazine published in Portland, Oregon, was the vehicle that launched many West Coast angling authors who wrote articles and later books that suddenly illuminated the breadth of what steelhead fly fishing had become. And in the exchange of angling ideals, favored tackle, novel fly patterns, and angling methods initiated in *Salmon Trout Steelheader*, the sport of steelhead fly fishing would come to bloom with an increasingly articulate literature that has since brought it to the legitimate equal of Atlantic salmon fishing.

However, as far as I knew, in the early 1960s I was the only steelhead fly fisherman in the Camas/Washougal area of southwest Washington. I had no contact with other steelhead fly fishermen excepting for two brief exchanges: A Seattle man in his 60s whom I watched fishing lower Wind River in a painfully slow use of a sinking line; and a man in his 30s who lived in the little town of Bingen and who told me he filled his punchcard each summer fishing the Klickitat River with a Muddler. Both encounters had a lasting impact—profound disinterest in the former and eventual emulation of the latter.

Throughout the West there were similar pockets of lone anglers learning the craft of steelhead fly fishing. And it was often in those pockets of angling isolation from which came unique fly patterns and the methods to fish them. From isolation came anglers such as Tommy Brayshaw on the Coquihalla, Syd Glasso on the Sol Duc and Roderick Haig-Brown on the Campbell.

I came to love and to nurture isolation. What was learned came through sheer trial and error—no limitations in the emulation of a teacher whose every movement, tackle, flies, methods, ethics and even clothing were mimicked. And yet, teachers I had. They came to me in books. But unlike a mentor in person, they were easy to sample, test, judge and eventually keep or discard. And from it came a wonderful freedom in my steelhead fly fishing. The freedom to find my own plodding way—and to create the flies that fit the methods I enjoyed to fish.

So, that July morning in 1961 when a steelhead rose from a maelstrom of white-water pockets in Wind River Canyon to take a #8 Red Ant with a deliberate head and tail rise marked the beginning. I was 16 years old. Most of my life thereafter would be spent in a solitary wandering of steelhead rivers. And nights would be spent in the yellow glow of dim light hunched over a fly tying vise, reading books, or writing in journals. Little else mattered. Life was elemental. . .a seeking of life at its simplest, deepest, most basic level. A level far removed from the trivial distractions of human self-consciousness. And steelhead took me there. To the steelhead level.

Flies became my medium of progression in steelhead fishing. And initially the available steelhead fly patterns were a frustrating limitation. The local sports shop where I lived in Camas, Washington had only three or four boxes of steelhead flies tied by the Golden West Company. Each box had a half dozen flies.

Only two of the patterns appealed to me: #8 Red Ant and #4 Golden Demon. That first summer in 1961, I bought two of each. My rod was a nine-foot Wright and McGill "Sweetheart"; the reel was a 1495 1/2 Pfleugar Medalist; and the silk line was a GAF that my father had purchased shortly after World War II. I was off and running into a life that became a long romance with everything associated with steelhead—including fly tying.

I had tied trout flies since the age of eleven. They weren't much. Good tying materials were hard to come by in those days, and as in all my endeavors, books were my teachers. It was slow progression. But with the new interest in steelhead fly fishing, my fly tying leaped ahead. As often happens, "necessity became the mother of invention." I couldn't buy steelhead flies locally beyond the three or four boxes at the Camas Sports Center. So I had to tie my own if there were to be any real selection.

But what to tie? Kreider's book was unknown to me, and I hadn't seen Van Fleet since reading it in weekly "installments" as a nine-year-old in a Portland department store where my parents shopped for family necessities every other Friday night.

But the Camas Public Library had *Northwest Angling* by Bradner (1950) with its wonderful fly plates that included 15 steelhead patterns; *Western Trout* by Macdowell (1948) with a colored plate that included nine steelhead patterns; *The Wise Fisherman's Encyclopedia* (1953) had a plate with 13 steelhead flies; and, most important in the long term, *Fisherman's Summer* by Haig-Brown (1959) with its dry-fly revelations and a description of the Steelhead Bee as first used in 1951. And of course, in 1962, I purchased *Trout* with its 25 steelhead flies.

I quickly memorized the materials for the limited number of steelhead patterns and read about their uses, histories, and the stories of the fish they caught. But despite the best of intentions, as I would begin to tie a steelhead pattern that attracted me, somehow my mind would deviate, and something very different would appear in my fly tying vise.

I don't remember, now, where I got the idea to fish a nymph for steelhead. I do know that the big stonefly nymph I tied in the winter of 1961 or 1962 was suggested by an article on nymph fishing for trout by Ted Trueblood in *Outdoor Life* or *Field & Stream*.

As was common, I didn't have exactly the right materials he suggested for the pattern. I improvised to come up with something similar. It was tied on a #4, 4XL hook. The body was wrapped with lead. The tail and hackle I made of guinea. And the body was brown, fuzzy, Mohair wool.

In early March of 1963 I hooked three winter steelhead on the big nymph. It wasn't pretty. It wasn't inventive. But it was my own tie, and it caught steelhead. This simple nymph pattern tied in several variations caught a lot of steelhead and trout for me through the mid-1970s (including more than 100 steelhead hooked on it in 1972 alone). At that point I decided it was time to move on to other methods of fishing. Pursuing it further could only have reduced the sport to mindless habit, although I still keep one or two with me for just-in-case situations.

By 1964 it was becoming clear that the commercially tied steelhead flies of the era were not well designed for the way I preferred to fish. Most had bulky chenille bodies, buoyant bucktail wings, and relatively light-wired hooks. They fished well enough on the sinking lines that had come to be the standard choice for steelhead fly fishing, but quickly skidded to the surface when fished in the faster runs with my preferred floating line choice—all the more so in peak winter flows when fly depth was critical.

I liked the color simplicity of the old Thor pattern. By replacing the red chenille body with fluorescent red wool, exchanging the white bucktail wing for one of white calf tail, by substituting a red calftail beard for the brown hackle, and by using red calf tail instead of the orange hacklefiber tail of the original, I found that the pattern fished very well on a floating line when tied on a 3 extra stout hook. I called it a Fluorescent Thor and the first day of use in March 1964, a very large winter steelhead visibly took the fly as it swung across a favorite tailout slick.

It became clear that there was room for change in the way steelhead flies were tied, particularly if I were going to continue to use a floating line in winter conditions. In the years that followed, I developed a number of my own steelhead fly patterns, or adapted existing patterns, using hooks and materials that would fish effectively using the tackle and methods I preferred.

It often seemed that the most creative time of year for steelhead fly tying occurred with the transition of winter to spring. Of the many patterns that came out of those February and March nights, only a few lasted long enough to stay on the end of my leader the necessary hours to eventually hook steelhead. And several of those seemed charmed only once or twice and vanished from my fly wallets or boxes in the years that followed. I simply lost faith in them. But some 10 or 12 of those patterns remain the core around which my steelhead fly fishing has built.

However, I explored with more patterns than just my own. I found a number of the Atlantic salmon patterns both attractive and effective for steelhead as well as some of the beautifully designed steelhead flies that others created. And now, after 36 years of steelhead fly fishing, I have hooked steelhead on 83 different fly patterns (not counting color variations of the same patterns) in 43 rivers from southern Oregon to northern British Columbia, and from the Kamchatka Peninsula to central Idaho.

This is not particularly remarkable. I know steelhead anglers who have fished more rivers. There are probably others who have hooked steelhead on more patterns. I only like to use it as an example to dispel myths: that only certain flies will catch steelhead; or that steelhead will only take flies in certain ways on some rivers.

Perhaps the most important lesson in steelhead fly fishing is to always distrust the words "never" and "only." It's a lesson that may have been easier to learn in the freedom of fly fishing isolation where trial and error were the primary teachers. *Any* fly pattern an angler has enough faith in to use the 6 to 20 hours often needed to hook a single steelhead will work if fished in a manner that brings out the best attributes of the chosen pattern. The key word is faith.

No pattern, no matter how famous or well tied, will catch steelhead unless the angler has faith enough to use it persistently. No pattern catches steelhead unless it is in the water.

What stirs faith in a fly? Faith, like beauty, is stirred differently in each beholder. When choosing a fly, faith is often determined through an alchemy of visual appeal, reputation, past experiences, and conditions of water, weather and light at the moment. It's a silent, intuitive and sometimes elusive power that can make or break angling success.

Choosing a steelhead fly is now more difficult than it was in 1961. Steelhead fly patterns were then minor variations on a single theme. The choice was primarily one of color variations in bodies of wool or chenille beneath bucktail wings ... or so it seemed from the available selection in tackle shops or in the available literature.

But with the rise of a local magazine in the late 1960s, it became apparent that steelhead fly fishing was more complex than previously imagined. So, too, were the fly patterns— Spey flies, dry flies, damp flies, and colors and materials that blew steelhead fly fishing wide open.

Trey Combs' three important books on steelhead fishing well document the progression of the sport through the increasing numbers of steelhead fly patterns. In *The Steelhead Trout* (1971), 142 steelhead fly patterns were listed. That was nearly a six-fold increase from the 25 patterns in *Trout* (1962).

Just five years after *The Steelhead Trout*, Combs' *Steelhead Fly Fishing and Flies* (1976) was published with 320 listed steelhead patterns. It included the 142 previous patterns, but it remains that in five years the number of steelhead fly patterns had more than doubled.

With *Steelhead Fly Fishing* (1991), Combs expanded the steelhead pattern list further with descriptions of 338 flies, most differing from those in *Steelhead Fly Fishing and Flies*. Again, the number of flies had more than doubled.

So today steelhead fly fishermen have nearly 700 patterns to choose from. There are presently as many steelhead fly patterns as the 1962 edition of *Trout* listed in the combined fly patterns for all species!

For the experienced angler this remarkable range of fly choices helps to spur experimentation, but for the beginning fly fisherman it can be a daunting choice filled with confusion. It was easier to become a steelhead fly fisherman in 1960 with choice limited to 25 flies. And it was even more so in 1890 with a choice between only two.

Generally steelhead fly fishing success is not dependent on fly pattern, but rather is dependent on learning to distinguish the type of water steelhead prefer for a lie; developing the tenacity of character to keep casting any chosen fly for the weeks, months, or even years it may take to eventually hook that first steelhead; and in learning the angle of the cast to the water that will make the chosen flies work effectively.

Initially, the fewer the fly choices the better. Minimize the variables. Pick a fly that is personally appealing and then learn the method(s) that can make it effective.

But as the angler progresses, experimentation with presentation options and matching them to fly patterns that bring out the best in the differing methods is what makes steelhead fly fishing a vital, provocative, lifetime sport. The angler learns to look for specific qualities in the differing patterns.

Long, soft, pliable hackles and wings that will not trap air tied combined with a stout hook are needed if the fly is meant to fish deep while fished through heavy water with a floating line. But neither the size/weight of the hook nor the air-trapping qualities of the materials are limitations when fishing a sinking-tip line. For instance, marabou may be a wonderfully supple choice for a fly on a sinking line, but it holds too much air to be effective on a pattern to be fished deep on a floating line.

By contrast, flies fished on the surface need to be tied on light-wired hooks combined with buoyant materials that can keep relatively large-sized steelhead patterns floating. Bushy, stiff hackles are necessary for skaters that will bounce across the surface like thistledown in the wind; softer, sparser hackles are for dry flies designed to drift *in* the surface film or "riffle hitched" against it; and stiff protruding wings carefully figure-eighted into place allow the fly to effectively paddle about when dragged across the surface.

This is why experienced steelhead anglers so often turn to tying their own patterns: so that they can incorporate their vision of fishing method into the fly pattern that only they themselves can create. Only they know their own vision. Colors, hairs, hackles and hooks—all are lifeless. Only the angler can bring the inanimate variables to life with a fishing method that completes the creation of the vision. And the vision is recreated each time the angler casts and fishes the fly.

This is the art of fly fishing—the final elusive skill that is the creation of a vision that becomes the common meeting ground between man and fish. And the creation of that vision may take place 500 times, through 500 casts, in a full day's fishing.

This is the endless romance that takes place in the fly tier's mind in those long, creative, contemplative hours in the dim, yellow glow of a lamp on February nights. The romance of creating a meeting ground between man and steelhead through the ploy of a fly-tying vision.

Agitator

Color: Black
Hook: Daiichi 2451
Thread: Black Monocord
Tail: 1st: Blood red marabou. 2nd: Red Krystal Flash. 3rd: Black marabou
Body Hackle: Black strung saddle hackle
Thorax: Black chenille
Eyes: Large nickel hourglass

Note: One red and one black marabou feather are tied twice the length of hook shank, and additional black marabou feathers are tied half that length, one on the top and two on the bottom.

Agitator

Color: Purple/flame
Hook: Daiichi 2451
Thread: Black Monocord
Tail: 1st: Fluorescent orange marabou. 2nd: Purple Krystal Flash. 3rd: Purple marabou.
Body Hackle: Purple strung saddle hackle
Thorax: Purple chenille
Eyes: Large nickel hourglass

Note: A great steelhead fly that is not difficult to tie. The eyes are tied on top of the hook, which causes it to ride up when fished. The head is medium chenille tied in a figure-eight around the eyes using strong tension to make it round and durable.

Agitator, Sandy Candy

Color: Pink/red
Hook: Daiichi 2451
Thread: Shell pink flat waxed
Tail: 1st: Two shell pink marabou. 2nd: Gold Flashabou
Body Hackle: Hot orange and hot pink strung saddle hackle
Thorax: Fluorescent shell pink chenille
Eyes: Large nickel hourglass

Alaskan Roe Bug

Color: Chartreuse
Hook: Eagle Claw L1197N
Thread: Fluorescent chartreuse flat waxed
Body: Pearl Sparkle Flash
Body Hackle: Chartreuse strung saddle hackle
Eyes: Stainless bead chain, large

Wings: 1st: Pearl Sparkle Flash. 2nd: Chartreuse poly yarn. 3rd: Pearl Sparkle Flash.
Note: An effective salmon pattern. The bulk of the poly yarn and the flash imitates a large roe cluster.

Alaskan Roe Bug

Color: Orange
Hook: Eagle Claw L1197N
Thread: Fluorescent orange flat waxed
Body: Pearl Sparkle Flash
Body Hackle: Hot orange strung saddle hackle
Eyes: Stainless bead chain, large

Wings: 1st: Pearl Sparkle Flash. 2nd: Flame poly yarn. 3rd: Pearl Sparkle Flash

Alaskan Roe Bug

Color: Pink
Hook: Eagle Claw L1197N
Thread: Fluorescent pink flat waxcd
Body: Pearl Sparkle Flash
Body Hackle: Hot pink strung saddle hackle
Eyes: Stainless bead chain, large
Wings: 1st: Pearl Sparkle Flash. 2nd: Hot pink poly yarn. 3rd: Pearl Sparkle Flash

Articulated Leech

Color: Black
Hook: Daiichi 2220
Thread: Black flat waxed
Body: Black rabbit strip
Rib: 1st hook: Hook shank. 2nd hook: Silver, medium flat Mylar
Loop: 30-pound Dacron backing
Eyes: Large nickel hourglass
Wing: Pearl Krystal Flash

Note: Two flies tied separately. Each tail and body are the same piece of rabbit strip. Make sure the rabbit is tied in so the hair sweeps back naturally. The loop is tied the entire length of the second hook and glued with head cement. The rabbit strips are less than 1/8" thick and are wrapped tightly around hook shank to avoid slipping while exposing shank as rib.

Articulated Leech

Color: Purple
Hook: Daiichi 2220
Thread: Black flat waxed
Body: Purple rabbit strip
Rib: 1st hook: Hook shank. 2nd hook: Silver medium flat Mylar
Loop: 30-pound Dacron backing
Eyes: Large nickel hourglass
Wing: Purple Flashabou

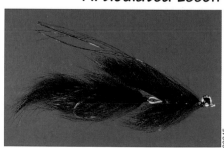

Big Black Bunny Leech

Color: Black
Hook: Daiichi 2220
Thread: Black flat waxed
Bead: Nickel 3/16
Body: Black rabbit strip
Note: It is surprising how effective this pattern can be with all species of fish. Secure bead with super glue.

Big Flesh Bunny Leech

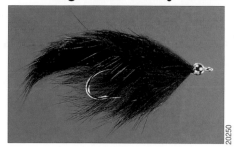

Color: Flesh
Hook: Daiichi 2220
Thread: White flat waxed
Bead: Nickel 3/16
Tail: Pearl Krystal Flash
Body: Flesh rabbit strip
Note: By far the best flesh fly. The bead and rabbit work together, to create a realistic imitation.

Big Purple Bunny Leech

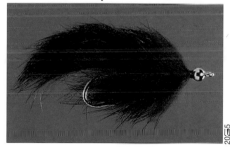

Color: Purple
Hook: Daiichi 2220
Thread: Black flat waxed
Bead: Nickel 3/16
Body: Purple rabbit strip

Big Red Bunny Leech

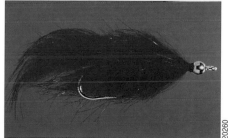

Color: Red
Hook: Daiichi 2220
Thread: Red flat waxed
Bead: Brass 3/16
Body: Red rabbit strip

Blue Mack's Canyon

Color: Multi
Hook: Daiichi 2441
Thread: Black Monocord
Tag: Copper fine wire
Body: Orange wool, one-third of body length
Rib: Copper fine wire
Thorax: Black chenille, two-thirds of body length
Collar Hackle: Fluorescent sky blue strung saddle hackle
Wings: 1st: Black kid goat. 2nd: Hot orange kid goat
Note: Steelhead are often fished with sparse, low-water styled flies. This is a modification of the Mack's Canyon developed by Mark Melody, an avid steelheader on the famed Deschutes River. Big, loud fly patterns are often ineffective in clear-water streams. Instead, unobtrusive, natural patterns can be winners.

Bomber, Martini

Color: Olive/red
Hook: Daiichi 2421
Thread: Black flat waxed
Tail: Natural moose body hair
Body: Red and olive deer hair, spun and cut
Rib: Silver fine wire
Body Hackle: Olive-dyed, grizzly saddle hackle
Wing: White calf tail
Note: Tied on a light wire hook with the deer hair packed tightly for better floatation, this is a favorite grease line style steelhead fly. Deer hair is cut to preferred length in cigar shape. The hackle is tied in butt-first, wrapped back to tail and secured with wire that is cross-wrapped forward.

Bomber, Martini

Color: Purple/black
Hook: Daiichi 2421
Thread: Black flat waxed
Tail: Natural moose body hair
Body: Black and purple deer hair spun and cut
Rib: Silver fine wire
Body Hackle: Purple strung saddle hackle
Wing: White calf tail
Note: Saddle hackle adds movement and floatation to the fly on the water's surface. The wing must be tied slightly behind the eye of the hook at a 30° angle to provide maximum skating. White calf tail is used because of its visibility and stiffness.

Bomber, Martini

Color: Red/black
Hook: Daiichi 2421
Thread: Black flat waxed
Tail: Natural moose body hair
Body: Black and red deer hair spun and cut
Rib: Silver fine wire
Body Hackle: Black strung saddle hackle
Wing: White calf tail

Bomber, Regular

Color: Natural/chartreuse
Hook: Daiichi 2421
Thread: Black flat waxed
Tail: Chartreuse calf tail
Body: Natural deer body hair spun and cut
Rib: Silver fine wire
Body Hackle: Natural grizzly saddle hackle
Wing: Chartreuse calf tail

Note: The chartreuse calf tail increases visibility for the fisherman, while keeping it attractive to the fish. Wire adds important durability, so that when the fly is struck by the fish's teeth it doesn't unravel the fly.

Bomber, Regular

Color: Natural/white
Hook: Daiichi 2421
Thread: Black flat waxed
Tail: White calf tail
Body: Natural deer hair
Rib: Silver fine wire
Body Hackle: Natural grizzly saddle hackle
Wing: White calf tail

Note: The stiffer the hackle, the better the fly will skate.

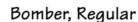

Boss

Color: Black/orange
Hook: Daiichi 2441
Thread: Black Monocord
Tail: Black kid goat hair
Body: Black chenille
Rib: Silver flat #14 Mylar
Body Hackle: Orange strung saddle hackle
Eyes: Stainless bead chain, large

Note: The tail is equal length of the body, and tied up with a few wraps of thread. Hackle should be webby and swept back.

Comet

Color: Silver /orange
Hook: Eagle Claw L1197N
Thread: Orange flat waxed
Tag: Silver diamond-braid Mylar
Tail: Orange kid goat hair
Body: Silver diamond-braid Mylar
Body Hackle: Orange strung saddle hackle
Eyes: Stainless bead chain, large

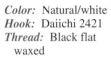

Conrad

Color: Black/green
Hook: Daiichi 2441
Thread: Black Monocord
Tag: Silver, fine French oval tinsel
Body: Chartreuse rayon floss butt (1/3)/black synthetic dubbing (2/3)
Rib: Silver, fine French oval tinsel
Butt: Silver, fine French oval tinsel
Body: Silver flat #14 Mylar tinsel
Wing: Black-dyed squirrel tail

Coppertop

Color: Bronze/black
Hook: Daiichi 2441
Thread: Black Monocord
Tail: Copper Krystal Flash
Body: Copper wire, large 1/2
Body Hackle: Black strung saddle hackle
Thorax: Black medium chenille, 1/2
Wing: Copper Krystal Flash

Note: Pay attention to where the hackle is tied into the fly. Some are before the wing while others follow. The placement dramatically effects the overall appearance.

Cosseboom

Color: Green
Hook: Daiichi 2441
Thread: Fluorescent red Flymaster
Tag: Silver small oval tinsel
Tail: Kelly green floss
Body: Kelly green floss
Rib: Silver flat #14 Mylar tinsel
Collar Hackle: Chartreuse strung saddle hackle
Wing: Natural silver, gray squirrel tail

Cotton Candy

Color: Pink
Hook: Daiichi 1710
Thread: Pink flat waxed
Tail: Pink Lady Glo Bug yarn
Body: Fluorescent shell pink, medium chenille
Wing: Same as tail

Note: A terrific roe pattern for rainbows and steelhead anywhere. Developed by the guide staff at Rainbow King Lodge, it simulates flesh from decaying salmon carcasses or their roe.

Dan's Favorite

Color: Silver/blue
Hook: Daiichi 2441
Thread: Black
Monocord
Tail: Navy blue calf
tail
Body: Silver flat #14
Mylar tinsel
Rib: Gold, small oval
tinsel
Collar Hackle: Navy
blue strung saddle hackle
Wing: Navy blue calf tail

Dark Mack's Canyon

Color: Black/orange
Hook: Daiichi 2441
Thread: Black
Monocord
Tag: Gold, oval small
tinsel
Body: Orange and
black wool yarn,
equal portions
Rib: Gold oval small
tinsel
Collar Hackle: Black strung saddle hackle
Wings: 1st: Black kid goat hair. 2nd: Orange kid goat hair
Note: The correct proportions make a steelhead fly charismatic. The
body should be perfectly smooth. The wing is equal to the bend of
the hook and not too heavy.

Deep-Eyed Wog

Color: Pink
Hook: Daiichi 2722
Thread: Hot pink flat
waxed
Tail: 1st: Pink Pearl
Krystal Flash. 2nd:
Hot pink marabou.
3rd: Pearl Flashabou
Rib: Hot pink strung
saddle hackle
wrapped between
body material
Body: 1/8" hot pink rabbit strip wrapped around hook shank
Eyes: Chrome hourglass, extra-large
Weight: Lead wire, large
Note: The Pink Pollywog has been very effective on the surface, but
there are ten times the fish under the surface that will take the Deep
Wog. The colder the water, the less active the fish. This irresistible
fly gets right in their face.

Doc Spratley

Color: Brown/black
Hook: Daiichi 2441
Thread: Black
Monocord
Tail: Natural mallard
flank
Body: Black Antron
dubbing
Rib: Silver, flat #14
Mylar tinsel
Collar Hackle: Grizzly
saddle hackle
Wing: Ringed-neck pheasant tail fibers

Egg, Frontier Natural

Color: Chinook
Hook: Daiichi 1510
Thread: Yellow
Monocord
Tail: Golden-nugget
Glo Bug yarn
Body: Chinook-orange
epoxy
Note: The colors of
these egg patterns are
identical to the real
thing. An effective substitute for fishing beads, considered immoral
because of the high mortality of wild fish with their use.

Egg, Frontier Natural

Color: Salmon
Hook: Daiichi 1510
Thread: Orange
Monocord
Tail: Orange marabou
Body: Salmon-orange
epoxy
Note: The density of
the epoxy enables the
fly to sink at a medium
rate.

Egg, Frontier Natural

Color: Sockeye
Hook: Daiichi 1510
Thread: White
Monocord
Tail: White marabou
Body: Pink epoxy
Note: The tail imitates
the egg sac membrane
and helps the fly ride
hook first, which produces
more solid hook ups.

Egg, Frontier Natural

Color: Steelhead
Hook: Daiichi 1510
Thread: White
Monocord
Tail: White marabou
Body: Steelhead
orange epoxy

Egg, Frontier Natural "Double Egg"

Color: All
Hook: Daiichi 1510
Thread: White Monocord
Tail: White marabou
Body: Epoxy

Egg Sucking Leech

Color: Purple/pink
Hook: Daiichi 2220
Thread: Black Monocord
Weight: Lead wire, large
Tail: Purple rabbit strip tied in for both tail and wing
Body: Purple chenille
Body Hackle: Purple schlappen hackle
Thorax: Fluorescent shell pink chenille
Wing: Purple pearl Krystal Flash

Eggo

Color: Pink
Hook: Daiichi 1130
Thread: Pink flat waxed
Body: Shell pink chenille
Eyes: Nickel inset hourglass, with plastic lure eyes, pink irises and black pupils.

Note: The combination of the hourglass eyes and the especially heavy wire hook, puts this egg on the bottom in any water. Mainly designed to reach places with swift deep current or fly-fishing waters that prohibit excess use of lead weight.

Euphausid

Color: Pearlescent
Hook: Eagle Claw L1197N
Thread: White flat waxed
Tail: Pearl Flashabou
Body: Pearl Flashabou
Wing: Pearl Flashabou
Note: A small shrimp pattern.

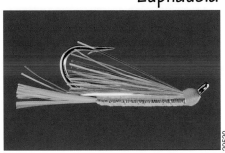

Eggo

Color: Red
Hook: Daiichi 1130
Thread: Fluorescent red flat waxed
Body: Fluorescent red chenille
Eyes: Nickel inset hourglass, with plastic lure eyes, red irises and black pupils.

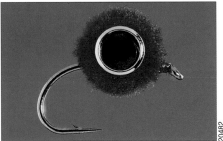

Eyed Shrimp

Color: Chartreuse
Hook: Eagle Claw L1197N
Thread: Chartreuse flat waxed
Tail: Red marabou
Body: Chartreuse poly yarn
Rib: Gold French oval #14 tinsel
Eyes: Painted yellow irises with black pupils, epoxy coated
Wing: White kid goat hair tied upside-down to bend of hook
Note: A fantastic fall steelhead and salmon pattern that fishes upside-down to prevent snagging.

Egg Sucking Leech

Color: Black/red
Hook: Daiichi 2220
Thread: Red Monocord
Weight: Lead wire, large
Tail: Black rabbit strip tied in at both tail and wing
Body: Black chenille
Body Hackle: Black schlappen hackle
Thorax: Fluorescent red chenille
Wing: Black Krystal Flash

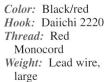

Note: Not a Woolly Bugger with an egg tied onto the end of it. This pattern incorporates much more movement. Having fished both patterns, I found that the rabbit, Krystal Flash and hackle attract fish better.

Eyed Shrimp

Color: Orange/white
Hook: Eagle Claw L1197N
Thread: Flame flat waxed
Tail: Red marabou
Body: Flame poly yarn
Rib: Gold French oval #14 tinsel
Eyes: Painted yellow irises with black pupils, epoxy coated
Wing: White kid goat hair tied upside-down to bend of hook

Ferry Canyon

Color: Purple/orange
Hook: Daiichi 2441
Thread: Black Monocord
Tail: Purple strung saddle hackle fibers
Body: Flame acrylic Sparkle Yarn 1/3
Rib: Silver flat #16/18 Mylar tinsel
Collar Hackle: Purple strung saddle hackle
Thorax: Purple chenille 2/3
Wings: 1st: Mulberry Sparkle Flash. 2nd: Purple marabou

Fly Dejour

Color: Bluish purple/pink
Hook: Daiichi 2441
Thread: Burgundy Flymaster
Tag: Silver fine, round #12 tinsel under-wrapped through butt section to create underbody
Butt: Pink Edge Bright
Body: Bluish purple synthetic dubbing
Rib: Silver flat #14 Mylar tinsel
Body Hackle: Purple strung saddle hackle
Wing: White kid goat hair with four strands pearl/pink Krystal Flash

Freight Train

Color: Multi
Hook: Daiichi 2441
Thread: Black Monocord
Tail: Purple strung saddle hackle fibers
Body: Equal portions of orange and pink rayon floss for butts, 1/2 of total length
Rib: Silver fine wire
Body Hackle: Purple strung saddle hackle
Thorax: Purple chenille, 1/2
Wing: White kid goat hair with four strands pearl Krystal Flash

General Practitioner

Color: Black
Hook: Daiichi 2441
Thread: Black Monocord
Tag: Gold flat #14 Mylar tinsel
Tail: Black kid goat hair/red Krystal Flash
Body: Black salmon/steelhead dubbing
Body Hackle: Black schlappen hackle, three sections
Eyes: Fluorescent pink-dyed, golden pheasant crest tippets
Wings: Middle: Black-dyed golden pheasant rump. Regular: Black-dyed golden pheasant rump plumes, two paired

General Practitioner

Color: Orange
Hook: Daiichi 2441
Thread: Orange flat waxed
Tail: Orange kid goat hair. Dyed hot orange pheasant rump
Body: Hot orange salmon/steelhead dubbing
Rib: Gold French oval #14 tinsel
Body Hackle: Orange schlappen hackle
Eyes: Fluorescent orange-dyed golden pheasant crest tippets
Wings: 1st: One hot orange-dyed golden pheasant plume. 2nd: One of the same in the middle. 3rd: Two of the same at head.

General Practitioner

Color: Purple
Hook: Daiichi 2441
Thread: Black Monocord
Tag: Gold flat #14 Mylar tinsel
Tail: Purple kid goat hair
Body: Purple salmon/steelhead dubbing
Rib: Gold French oval #14 tinsel
Body Hackle: Purple schlappen hackle
Eyes: Fluorescent pink-dyed golden pheasant crest tippets
Wings: 1st: One purple-dyed golden pheasant tippet. 2nd: One of the same in the middle. 3rd: Two of the same at head

Glo Bug

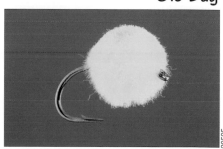

Color: Orange/flame
Hook: Daiichi 1510
Thread: Yellow Kevlar
Body: Steelhead orange with flame dot Glo Bug yarn

Glo Bug

Color: Orange/orange
Hook: Daiichi 1510
Thread: Orange Kevlar
Body: Golden nugget with steelhead orange dot Glo Bug yarn

Glo Bug

Color: Peach/flame
Hook: Daiichi 1510
Thread: Orange Kevlar
Body: Peach with flame dot Glo Bug yarn

Grease Liner

Color: Orange
Hook: Daiichi 2421
Thread: Orange Monocord
Tail: Natural elk hair
Body: Orange salmon/steelhead dubbing
Collar Hackle: Natural-brown strung saddle hackle
Wing: Natural elk hair
Note: Use a dubbing loop for best results dubbing the body.

Glo Bug

Color: Pink/flame
Hook: Daiichi 1510
Thread: Orange Kevlar
Body: Bright pink with flame dot Glo Bug yarn

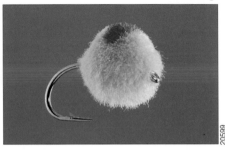

Grease Liner

Color: Peacock
Hook: Daiichi 2421
Thread: Black Monocord
Tail: Red deer hair
Body: Peacock herl
Rib: Green medium wire
Collar Hackle: Natural grizzly saddle hackle
Wing: Natural elk hair

Golden Demon

Color: Gold Mylar
Hook: Daiichi 2441
Thread: Black Monocord
Tail: Golden pheasant crest
Body: Gold French oval #12 tinsel
Collar Hackle: Orange strung saddle hackle
Wing: Natural red squirrel tail

Green Butt Skunk

Color: Black/green
Hook: Daiichi 2441
Thread: Black Monocord
Tail: Red strung saddle hackle fibers
Body: Chartreuse chenille butt, 1/4
Rib: Silver flat #14 Mylar tinsel
Thorax: Black chenille
Collar Hackle: Black strung saddle hackle
Wing: White kid goat hair with four strands pearl of Flashabou
Note: Steelhead flies are different than trout flies, and so are the fishermen who fish them. A steelhead fly has its own spirit; they are chosen with artful skill, searching for quality, proportion, materials used and charisma.

Grease Liner

Color: Black
Hook: Daiichi 2421
Thread: Black Monocord
Tail: Natural moose body hair
Body: Black wool yarn
Collar Hackle: Black strung saddle hackle
Wing: Natural moose body hair
Note: Treat front foil of wing with head cement so fly skates easily.

Juicy Bug

Color: Black/bright red
Hook: Daiichi 2441
Thread: Black Monocord
Tail: Red strung saddle hackle fibers
Body: Black chenille butt, 1/4
Rib: Silver flat #14 Mylar tinsel
Thorax: Fluorescent red chenille
Wing: Double wing, white kid goat hair
Note: Tie in one clump wing material, pull straight up and split in half with bodkin. Figure-eight with two turns of thread.

Kenai Special

Color: Pink/silver
Hook: Mustad 34007
Thread: Cerise flat waxed
Tail: Pearlescent Mylar tubing
Body: Pearlescent Mylar tubing
Weight: Lead wire, large
Collar Hackle: Silver Mylar tubing
Wing: Fluorescent pink rabbit strip

Note: This pattern was designed on the Kenai River in Alaska to fish for the five species of pacific salmon. It is heavily weighted and tied on a stainless steel hook so that it can be fished in virtually all waters.

Krystal Bugger

Color: Chartreuse
Hook: Daiichi 2220
Thread: Chartreuse flat waxed
Weight: Lead wire, large
Tail: Chartreuse marabou with three strands chartreuse Krystal Flash
Body: Chartreuse Ice Chenille, large
Body Hackle: Chartreuse strung saddle hackle
Bead: Nickel 3/16

Krystal Bugger

Color: Pink
Hook: Daiichi 2220
Thread: Orange flat waxed
Weight: Lead wire, large
Tail: Orange marabou with three strands orange Krystal Flash
Body: Orange Ice Chenille, large
Body Hackle: Orange strung saddle hackle
Bead: Nickel 3/16

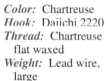

Krystal Bugger

Color: Orange
Hook: Daiichi 2220
Thread: Pink flat waxed
Weight: Lead wire, large
Tail: Pink marabou with three strands pink Krystal Flash
Body: Pink Ice Chenille, large
Body Hackle: Pink strung saddle hackle
Bead: Nickel 3/16

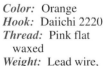

Krystal Bugger

Color: Red
Hook: Daiichi 2220
Thread: Red flat waxed
Weight: Lead wire, large
Tail: Red marabou with three strands red Krystal Flash
Body: Red Ice Chenille, large
Body Hackle: Red strung saddle hackle
Bead: Nickel 3/16

Limit Lander

Color: Orange/purple
Hook: Daiichi 2441
Thread: Black Monocord
Tail: Orange Krystal Flash
Body: Orange acrylic Sparkle Yarn butt 1/3
Rib: Fine silver wire
Thorax: Purple chenille 2/3
Collar Hackle: Purple strung saddle hackle
Wings: 1st: Black Krystal Flash between butt and body. 2nd: Purple Krystal Flash

Mack's Canyon

Color: Orange/white/black
Hook: Daiichi 2441
Thread: Black Monocord
Tail: Orange and white strung hackle fibers (equal portions)
Body: Orange and black wool (equal portions)
Rib: Silver flat #14 Mylar tinsel
Body Hackle: Black strung saddle hackle
Wing: Orange and white kid goat hair (equal portions)

Muddler After-Dinner Mint

Color: Green
Hook: Daiichi 2220
Thread: Black flat waxed
Body: Green Diamond Braid Mylar
Head: Natural deer hair, spun and trimmed
Wings: 1st: Green-dyed squirrel tail. 2nd: Brown-dyed turkey biot quill

Note: This Muddler series has been the choice of some of the greatest steelhead fishermen in the Northwest for many years. Some would avow that these three patterns are all you need to fish top water steelhead. Colors match fishing conditions and fish mood. Many fishermen fish them on sink tips and praise their effectiveness.

Muddler After-Dinner Mint

Color: Purple
Hook: Daiichi 2220
Thread: Black flat waxed
Body: Purple Diamond Braid Mylar
Head: Black-dyed deer hair, spun and trimmed
Wings: 1st: Purple-dyed squirrel tail. 2nd: Black-dyed turkey biot quill

Patriot

Color: Yellow/white
Hook: Daiichi 2441
Thread: Black Monocord
Tail: Red strung saddle hackle fibers
Body: Yellow rayon floss
Rib: Silver flat #14 Mylar tinsel
Collar Hackle: Blue strung saddle hackle
Wing: White kid goat hair

Muddler After-Dinner Mint

Color: Red
Hook: Daiichi 2220
Thread: Red flat waxed
Body: Red Diamond Braid Mylar
Head: Red-dyed deer hair, spun and trimmed
Wings: 1st: Red-dyed squirrel tail. 2nd: Red-dyed turkey biot quill

Polar Shrimp

Color: Hot orange/ white
Hook: Daiichi 2441
Thread: Black Monocord
Tail: Red strung saddle hackle fibers
Body: Fluorescent orange chenille
Collar Hackle: Hot orange strung saddle hackle
Wing: White kid goat hair with four strands pearl Flashabou

October Caddis

Color: Orange
Hook: Daiichi 2421
Thread: Black Monocord
Tail: Natural red squirrel tail
Body: Orange wool yarn
Collar Hackle: Brown strung saddle hackle
Wing: Natural red squirrel tail, split

Note: The positioning of the wings is critical for the fly to skate. Wings need to be heavy and canted at 35 degrees. Body should be taped as shown.

Pollywog

Color: Pink
Hook: Daiichi 2722
Thread: Fluorescent pink flat waxed
Tail: 1st: Pink Krystal Flash. 2nd: Hot pink marabou. 3rd: Pearl Flashabou
Body: Hot pink deer hair, spun and trimmed

Note: Cut and shape the body, so that the top is flat and the bottom is rounded to insure proper swimming. If cut correctly, under tension the fly should ride hook up and skip on the water's surface without snagging debris.

Paint Brush

Color: Multi
Hook: Eagle Claw L1197N
Thread: Burgundy Flymaster
Body: Gold flat #12 Mylar tinsel
Body Hackle: Hot orange strung saddle hackle, palmered
Collar Hackle: Purple strung saddle hackle/light blue schlappen

Popsickle

Color: Multi
Hook: Daiichi 2441
Thread: Fluorescent orange flat waxed
Body: Hot orange/red marabou
Wing: Purple and gold Flashabou
Collar Hackle: Purple marabou
Note: The materials are tied on the first third of the hook shank. Wrap marabou tip-first around hook shank for best swimming.

Prawn, Silvey's Super

Color: Black
Hook: Daiichi 1750
Thread: Black flat waxed
Eyes: Black large bead chain
Tail: Red Super Hair, split
Body: Black rabbit strip
Body Hackle: Orange-dyed golden pheasant crest tippets
Collar Hackle: Orange-dyed golden pheasant crest tippets
Wing: Black-dyed golden pheasant plumage
Note: The Super Hair should be tied in under and above the eyes to split the tentacles and make them appear fanned out. Bead chain or plastic eyes can be used. Crossed-cut rabbit strip is used so that hair lies back naturally. Some fishermen prefer the rabbit tied in the opposite direction to prevent collapsing under water pressure. The density of the rabbit is important. If tied too dense, the rabbit will hinder the desired swimming motion.

Prawn, Silvey's Super

Color: Orange
Hook: Daiichi 1750
Thread: Fluorescent orange flat waxed
Eyes: Black large bead chain
Tail: Red Super Hair, split
Body: Orange rabbit strip
Body Hackle: Hot orange-dyed golden pheasant crest tippets
Collar Hackle: Hot orange-dyed golden pheasant crest tippets
Wing: Hot orange-dyed golden pheasant plumage

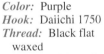

Prawn, Silvey's Super

Color: Purple
Hook: Daiichi 1750
Thread: Black flat waxed
Eyes: Black large bead chain
Tail: Red Super Hair, split
Body: Purple rabbit strip
Body Hackle: Purple-dyed golden pheasant crest tippets
Collar Hackle: Purple-dyed golden pheasant crest tippets
Wing: Purple-dyed golden pheasant plumage
Note: Colors of material are interchangeable to build desired contrast.

Prawn, Silvey's Super

Color: Red
Hook: Daiichi 1750
Thread: Fluorescent orange flat waxed
Eyes: Black large bead chain
Tail: Red Super Hair, split
Body: Red rabbit strip
Body Hackle: Hot pink-dyed golden pheasant crest tippets
Collar Hackle: Hot pink-dyed golden pheasant crest tippets
Wing: Hot red-dyed golden pheasant plumage

Prawn, Silvey's Super

Color: Salmon
Hook: Daiichi 1750
Thread: Fluorescent shell pink flat waxed
Eyes: Black large bead chain
Tail: Red Super Hair, split
Body: Salmon pink rabbit strip
Body Hackle: Hot pink-dyed golden pheasant crest tippets
Collar Hackle: Hot pink-dyed golden pheasant crest tippets
Wing: Hot red-dyed golden pheasant plumage

Prawn, Silvey's Super

Color: White
Hook: Daiichi 1750
Thread: White flat waxed
Eyes: Black large bead chain
Tail: White Super Hair, split
Body: White rabbit strip
Body Hackle: Natural guinea, jumbo
Collar Hackle: Natural mallard flank, large
Wing: Natural mallard flank, large
Note: Closest match to the natural. Many anglers use this pattern in the estuaries, bays and surf.

Prism

Color: Peacock
Hook: Daiichi 2441
Thread: Green Monocord
Tag: Copper, medium wire
Tail: Natural pheasant crest tippet fibers
Body: Peacock herl
Rib: Copper, medium wire
Body Hackle: Grizzly strung saddle hackle
Wing: Natural red squirrel tail fibers

Purple Angel

Color: Pink/purple
Hook: Daiichi 2441
Thread: Black Monocord
Tail: Purple strung saddle hackle fibers
Body: Fluorescent pink chenille butt, 1/4
Rib: Silver flat #14 Mylar tinsel. Thorax only.
Thorax: Purple chenille
Collar Hackle: Purple strung saddle hackle
Wing: White kid goat hair with four strands pearl Flashabou

Purple Peril

Color: Purple
Hook: Daiichi 2441
Thread: Black Monocord
Tail: Purple strung saddle hackle fibers
Body: Purple chenille
Rib: Silver flat #14 Mylar tinsel
Collar Hackle: Purple strung saddle hackle
Wing: Natural red squirrel tail

Sand Shrimp

Color: Multi
Hook: Mustad 37160
Thread: Orange Monocord
Weight: Lead wire, large
Tail: Hot orange marabou
Body: White chenille
Rib: Yellow flat waxed thread

Body Hackle: Hot orange strung saddle hackle. Under thorax only.
Thorax: White chenille
Shellback: Clear plastic strip over two outside strands of orange chenille. One center strand fluorescent pink chenille.
Note: Many steelhead and salmon feed on ghost shrimp. This is the best imitation I have seen. It is designed to be fished in heavy water and deep pools.

Red Ant

Color: Red/brown
Hook: Daiichi 2441
Thread: Black Monocord
Tail: Natural golden pheasant tippets
Body: Peacock herl/red rayon floss
Collar Hackle: Fiery-brown strung saddle hackle
Wing: Brown-dyed bucktail

Note: This traditional pattern is purposely tied sleek, low-water style. It has been proven that drab and discreet patterns are very effective in all types of water, and at all times of the year.

Sandy Candy

Color: Pink
Hook: Daiichi 2441
Thread: Red Flymaster
Body: Hot pink and hot orange marabou
Collar Hackle: Hot pink and hot orange schlappen hackle
Wing: Gold Flashabou

Red Butt Skunk

Color: Red/black/white
Hook: Daiichi 2441
Thread: Black Monocord
Tail: Red strung saddle hackle fibers
Body: Fluorescent red chenille butt, 1/4
Rib: Silver flat #14 Mylar tinsel. Thorax only
Thorax: Black chenille
Collar Hackle: Black strung saddle hackle
Wing: White kid goat hair with four strands of pearl Flashabou

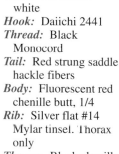

Sandy Spider

Color: Orange
Hook: Daiichi 2441
Thread: Burgundy Flymaster
Tag: Silver small oval tinsel
Body: Silver flat #12 Mylar tinsel for underbody. Hot orange Edge Bright
Thorax: Hot orange Antron dubbing
Body Hackle: Fluorescent yellow strung saddle hackle
Collar Hackle: Natural mallard flank, Spey style

Signal Light

Color: Multi
Hook: Daiichi 2441
Thread: Black Monocord
Tail: Purple strung saddle hackle
Body: Flame, 1/4 Chartreuse acrylic Sparkle Yarn
Rib: Silver fine oval tinsel

Red Wing Black Bird

Color: Red/black
Hook: Daiichi 2441
Thread: Black Monocord
Tail: Red strung saddle hackle fibers
Body: Black chenille
Rib: Silver flat #14 Mylar tinsel
Collar Hackle: Red-dyed guinea plumage
Wing: Red kid goat hair or calf tail

Thorax: Black chenille, 1/2
Collar Hackle: Purple strung saddle hackle
Wings: 1st: Mulberry Sparkle Flash. 2nd: Black marabou
Note: Most steelhead patterns shown here are with the collar hackle tied in before the wing, but be careful, there are a few exceptions.

Silver Hilton

Color: Black/grizzly
Hook: Daiichi 2441
Thread: Black Monocord
Tail: Natural mallard flank
Body: Black chenille
Rib: Silver flat #14 Mylar tinsel
Collar Hackle: Natural grizzly saddle hackle

Wing: Grizzly neck hackle tips, matched and paired, tied with cups of feathers outward

Skunk

Color: Black/white
Hook: Daiichi 2441
Thread: Black Monocord
Tail: Red strung saddle hackle fibers
Body: Black chenille
Rib: Silver flat #14 Mylar tinsel
Collar Hackle: Black strung saddle hackle

Wing: White kid goat hair with four strands of pearl Flashabou

Skykomish Sunrise

Color: Deep red
Hook: Daiichi 2441
Thread: Red Flymaster
Tail: Red and yellow strung saddle hackle fibers (equal portions)
Body: Deep red rabbit and opossum dubbing blend

Rib: Silver flat #14 Mylar tinsel
Collar Hackle: Yellow, then red strung saddle hackle
Wing: White kid goat hair
Note: Many steelhead fly tiers prefer to use dubbing instead of chenille. A dubbed body tends to be more lifelike and fluid. Any of the patterns presented here with chenille, can be substituted with dubbing.

Spey, Summer Deep Purple

Color: Purple
Hook: Daiichi 2441
Thread: Black Monocord
Body: Purple Diamond Braid Mylar tinsel, 1/2
Rib: Silver fine oval tinsel
Body Hackle: Purple-dyed golden pheasant semi-plume
Thorax: Purple chenille

Collar Hackle: 1st: Purple-dyed pheasant semi-plume. 2nd: Purple-dyed golden pheasant rump feather.

Spey, Summer Frontier

Color: Multi
Hook: Daiichi 2441
Thread: Burgundy Flymaster
Body: Red rayon floss, 1/2
Rib: Silver flat #14 Mylar and silver fine oval tinsel
Body Hackle: Purple schlappen hackle stripped on one side

Thorax: Purple opossum dubbing, 1/2
Collar Hackle: Natural guinea plume
Wings: 1st: Two matched and paired purple hackle tips in the center. 2nd: Two matched and paired red hackle tips on the outside
Note: Spey flies have their own unique look and style.

Spey, Summer Lady Caroline

Color: Brown
Hook: Daiichi 2050
Thread: Brown Flymaster
Tail: Burnt-orange strung saddle hackle fibers
Body: Brown synthetic dubbing
Rib: Gold small oval tinsel cross-wrapped with silver fine oval tinsel
Body Hackle: Gray-dyed large Chinese chicken hackle, thorax area only
Collar Hackle: Burnt-orange strung saddle hackle stripped on one side
Wing: Wood duck-dyed mallard flank

Spey, Summer Midnight Express

Color: Black/purple
Hook: Daiichi 2441
Thread: Black Flymaster
Body: Purple braided Mylar tinsel, 1/2
Rib: Silver fine oval tinsel
Body Hackle: Black-dyed golden pheasant semi-plume

Thorax: Black chenille, 1/2
Collar Hackle: 1st: Black-dyed golden pheasant semi-plume. 2nd: Purple dyed golden pheasant rump feather
Wing: Purple Sparkle Flash

Spey, Summer Sunrise

Color: Orange
Hook: Daiichi 2441
Thread: Red Flymaster
Body: Red braided Mylar tinsel, 1/2
Rib: Silver fine oval tinsel
Body Hackle: Orange-dyed golden pheasant semi-plume

Thorax: Shell pink chenille, 1/2
Collar Hackle: 1st: Orange-dyed golden pheasant semi-plume. 2nd: Orange-dyed golden pheasant rump feather

Spey, Winter Candlelight

Color: Yellow/black
Hook: Daiichi 2051
Thread: Orange Monocord
Tag: One wrap silver fine oval tinsel
Body: Fluorescent orange rayon floss, 1/2
Rib: Silver fine oval tinsel
Body Hackle: Yellow-dyed large Chinese hackle stripped on one side
Thorax: Medium dark-orange synthetic dubbing, 1/2
Collar Hackle: Black marabou
Wing: Orange goose

Note: Wing feathers should be tented and married at the top. The angle and width of the rib can change the appearance of the fly significantly.

Spey, Winter Expression

Color: Purple
Hook: Daiichi 2051
Thread: Black Monocord
Body: Fuchsia rayon floss, 1/2
Rib: Silver flat #14 Mylar tinsel
Body Hackle: Purple marabou
Thorax: Purple opossum dubbing, 1/2
Collar Hackle: Natural guinea plume
Wing: White goose

Spey, Winter Green Butt Skunk

Color: Green/black
Hook: Daiichi 2051
Thread: Black Monocord
Tail: Red strung saddle hackle fibers
Body: Fluorescent chartreuse rayon floss, 1/3
Rib: Silver flat #14 Mylar tinsel
Body Hackle: Black marabou
Thorax: Black Antron dubbing, 2/3
Collar Hackle: Natural guinea plume
Wing: White goose

Note: One wrap of tinsel behind tail to prop it up.

Spey, Winter Jack O' Lantern

Color: Orange/black
Hook: Daiichi 2051
Thread: Orange Monocord
Body: Gold rayon floss 1/3/Orange rayon floss 2/3
Rib: Gold flat #12 Mylar tinsel and gold fine oval tinsel
Body Hackle: Orange-dyed large Chinese chicken hackle
Collar Hackle: Black marabou and natural guinea
Wing: Orange goose

Spey, Winter Punch

Color: Pink/chartreuse
Hook: Daiichi 2051
Thread: Black Monocord
Body: Fuchsia rayon floss, 1/2
Rib: Silver flat #14 Mylar tinsel
Body Hackle: Hot pink-dyed large Chinese chicken hackle
Thorax: Lime green synthetic dubbing, 1/2
Collar Hackle: Lime green-dyed large Chinese chicken hackle
Wing: Wood duck-dyed mallard flank feather

Note: The two hackles, should be tapered from back to front and match the same angle. The hackle wrapped around the body has one side stripped.

Spey, Winter Sunkist

Color: Orange
Hook: Daiichi 2051
Thread: Orange Monocord
Body: Hot orange rayon floss, 1/2
Rib: Gold flat #14 Mylar tinsel
Body Hackle: Orange marabou
Thorax: Red opossum dubbing, 1/2
Collar Hackle: Red-dyed guinea plume
Wing: White goose

Steelhead Caddis

Color: Ginger
Hook: Daiichi 2421
Thread: Tan Monocord
Body: Ginger Antron dubbing
Head: Light natural elk hair, spun and trimmed
Wing: Natural mottled turkey tail

Note: For the fly to skate freely, the angle and amount of deer hair trimmed for the head is critical. Trim and build the head for desired action. Coat wing with hair spray for added durability.

Steelhead Caddis

Color: Orange
Hook: Daiichi 2421
Thread: Orange Monocord
Body: Orange Antron dubbing
Head: Natural elk hair, spun and trimmed
Wing: Natural mottled turkey tail

Street Walker

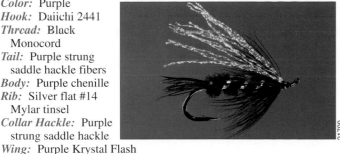

Color: Purple
Hook: Daiichi 2441
Thread: Black Monocord
Tail: Purple strung saddle hackle fibers
Body: Purple chenille
Rib: Silver flat #14 Mylar tinsel
Collar Hackle: Purple strung saddle hackle
Wing: Purple Krystal Flash

Wally Waker

Color: Moth
Hook: Daiichi 2421
Thread: Black flat waxed
Tail: Natural moose body hair
Body: Black-dyed with natural middle stripe spun deer hair
Throat: Natural moose body hair
Wing: Chartreuse calf tail split into two wings

Tied-Down Caddis

Color: Orange
Hook: Eagle Claw L1197N
Thread: Fluorescent orange flat waxed
Tail: Natural elk hair tips
Body: Orange wool yarn
Rib: Gold fine wire
Body Hackle: Natural-brown furnace saddle hackle
Collar Hackle: Natural-brown furnace saddle hackle
Shellback: Natural elk hair extended from tail

Wally Waker

Color: Standard
Hook: Daiichi 2421
Thread: Black flat waxed
Tail: Natural moose body hair
Body: Black, natural black striped spun deer hair
Throat: Natural moose body hair
Wing: White calf tail split into two wings
Note: A surface skater, excellent in big water. Can be varied in size and density to adapt to river conditions.

Undertaker

Color: Multi/black
Hook: Daiichi 2441
Thread: Black Monocord
Tag: Silver #14 Mylar tinsel
Tail: Chartreuse rayon floss
Butt: Silver tinsel underwrap, chartreuse rayon floss overwrap
Body: Orange marabou, 1/4
Thorax: Black chenille
Collar Hackle: Black strung saddle hackle
Wing: Black-dyed squirrel tail

Winters Hope

Color: Multi
Hook: Daiichi 2441
Thread: Burgundy Flymaster
Body: Silver flat #12 Mylar tinsel
Collar Hackle: 1st: Blue. 2nd: Purple schlappen
Wings: 1st: Two yellow neck hackles matched and paired together. 2nd: Two orange neck hackle tips matched and cupped to outside of yellow. 3rd wing: Olive calf tail, above and centered
Note: Many long time steelhead fly anglers prefer using dry lines to catch steelhead. There is a level of zen or Valhala, if you will, that accompanies the technique. Bill McMillan's book *Dry Line Steelhead* (out of print) shares these unique qualities.

Wally Waker

Color: Bee
Hook: Daiichi 2421
Thread: Black flat waxed
Tail: Natural moose body hair
Body: Black with rusty-brown middle stripe deer hair, spun and trimmed
Throat: Natural moose body hair
Wing: Natural elk body hair split into two wings

Chapter 8

SALTWATER FLIES

Brian O'Keefe Photo

BONEFISH ARE BONEFISH, NO MATTER WHERE THEY ARE

Brian O'Keefe

Several times a year I must wade into bonefish flats somewhere in the world. The need to replenish my senses with aqua green water and cloudless skies directs me there. I have also developed a passion for the abundant wide-open spaces and plentiful fish, which come with their own unique challenges. These fish and their environment have their own sets of rules and regulations.

Bonefish, in particular, can be found in a broad variety of warm-water landscapes all over the world. Their diet is very diverse. They eat worm-like creatures and many kinds of shrimp, crabs, clams and minnows. There are numerous flies available that have been specifically designed to match their diet.

Bonefish have the reputation of being selective, scrupulous, unpredictable and of course powerful; and where they live adds an even greater challenge. To meet all of the requirements for a successful bonefish mission, one must be prepared. The angler is required to carry a variety of lines and flies to match the demanding conditions. The right equipment and the correct fly patterns are critical. You need to study the area that you will be fishing in general and specific terms. Often, if it is my first experience in new water, I go armed to the gills. I look like a traveling salesman, but I have the confidence of finding the right combination for a commendable trip.

I remember a beautiful day in April 1997 when I had the honor of being the first outsider to fly fish the bonefish flats of Bikini Atoll in the western Pacific. Used as a strategic naval outpost during World War II, the island had been isolated from the public for the last 50 years. I was anxious to arrive, expecting to feast on the unsuspecting prey.

The flats and the bonefish were what I had imagined. I assumed it was going to be extremely easy to catch them, so I loaded my rod without thinking about methodology. I cast to the first pod of fish in immediate range. The first five fish followed the fly but wouldn't eat. I started changing flies frantically in disbelief. The Gotcha, Deep Eyed Minnow, and Christmas Island Specials all proved ineffective.

In my newly encountered anxiety, "bonefish are bonefish" surfaced in my mind, and I stepped back to calm myself. Without rhyme or reason, I had approached the bonefish on these flats as if they were fish in a hatchery. When all else fails, use the proper methodology. I began to dissect the elements—water type, depth, current, tidal flow, and fish cover. What line and leader should I be using? What food types are the fish feeding on? Being able to read the water and then understand how the combined elements dictate your approach and fishing technique is a process of study that will greatly reward you.

The tide was flowing out and the bonefish were bunched up in pods, rooting around the sand and turtle grass for shrimp. They were in an average depth of two feet and bucking the strong current. The fish were in a feeding frenzy and spooking them with a fly's surface splash wasn't going to scare them. I decided to go with a floating line, long leader, and a heavy pink Frontier Marabou Shrimp. At last a six-pound bone inhaled the fly. This strategy proved to be very effective in the area's daily recurring conditions. That was my hot fly that week and I was glad I had a dozen.

Christmas Island has an all-together different disposition. It is famous for its accommodations and experienced guides, and for taking bonefish on the fly. The first year Christmas Island opened for bonefishing, the "hot fly" was whatever you had on. The fishing conditions were obliging to beginners. However, it wasn't long before the fish were educated and a perfect cast with the right fly and your best sneaky approach was essential. Every night at dinner the conversation invariably turned to the "hot fly of the day." The fish would feed very selectively, keying on a particular size, color, and silhouette.

The Christmas Island Special series was designed to match particular colors, shapes, and weights to the island's bonefish dietary requirements. This pattern series is well known to be the most effective on Christmas Island, but the flies are slightly overdressed so they can be fished in a variety of water types in the Bahamas, Belize, and Venezuela.

I am from the old school when it comes to fly size: big fly, big fish. A thirty-inch individual bonefish cruising through debris, such as mangrove roots, turtle grass or mud mounds, first needs to see the fly. It also must be big enough, resemble something edible, and be worth the effort of pursuit.

Many of the larger bonefish patterns also work on permit, patrolling bar jack, trevally, mutton snapper, etc. Many different fish species may attack the same prey simultaneously. I recall one such episode off a small island near Placencia, Belize. There were small tarpon in four feet of water and bonefish in one to two feet, both hammering on the same bait-ball. I used the same Glass Minnow fly to catch them both.

The moral of these stories is that a successful fishing trip favors the prepared angler. There is such a diversity of fish species utilizing the same area in saltwater, that it is nearly impossible to be prepared for them all. However, if you do your homework, you will have the main half a dozen staples covered. Don't forget that diversity of fly patterns with a good range in size is just as important, if not of greater importance, then your fancy rod and reel.

A Dash of Salt and Passion

Tom Earnhardt

From the poling tower over my outboard motor I could see two small pods of fish working the edge of the flat about 150 feet from the boat. I yelled to my angling companion when one of the pods suddenly turned and began heading directly for us on the port side. The fish were in less than two feet of water over a light sand bottom as they closed rapidly. At 80 feet the tight pod of about six fish moved into a patch of grass and suddenly baitfish began to shower around them.

"Take 'em now," I hollered. "They're at two o'clock, 70 feet. Drop the fly on them."

With only one false cast, my partner delivered a small olive Clouser Minnow to a spot just in front of the moving fish. After only one strip, I saw several flashes of silver. Almost simultaneously I heard the screams of my friend and his reel as a green torpedo sped away toward the nearest deep water several hundred yards away. In an instant the fish had taken 100 yards of backing. Seconds later it was over 150 yards away and still taking line.

In the scenario above, you have probably assumed that the water was warm and that there were palm trees and mangroves on the horizon. You probably also guessed that my angler was tethered to a bonefish, or perhaps a permit or tarpon.

Good guesses, but you couldn't be more wrong. In the situation above the water temperature was in the mid-50s and the fall air was brisk. Both of us wore slickers over several layers of warm clothes. The nearest bonefish was almost a thousand miles to the south.

The fish in this story were false albacore, and the flats were in North Carolina. The tackle, the excitement, and the adrenaline rush, however, are the same for saltwater anglers in Florida, Christmas Island, or Cape Cod.

I have been an avid fly fisherman for over 40 years now and although I still love fly fishing for trout, salmon, smallmouth bass, and bluegill, my angling heart and soul resides in saltwater. Since the early 70s fly fishing has taken me to some of the most beautiful spots on earth. In saltwater I have taken fish on flies from lava cliffs in New Zealand, ankle deep water in the Bahamas, crashing surf near Montauk, and thick spartina marsh grass near Charleston. Much of what I know about fishing the salt was learned over numerous trips to the Keys in the 70s and 80s.

In recent years I have come to grips with two major myths surrounding saltwater fly fishing. The first is that, unlike freshwater fly fishing, saltwater fly rodding is done with big rods, big flies, and long casts by strong, well-coordinated angler/athletes. Nothing could be further from the truth. If you seek a variety of species in saltwater, you will need to develop a complete flyfishing game. Some fish do require heavy rods (10-, 12- and 14-weights) and reels with lots of backing. Most of the saltwater fishing I do, however, is done with lighter rods (6-, 7-, and 8-weights) and requires the same delicacy and accuracy as required in freshwater fishing. Stripers in shallow water can be just as skittish as any brown trout, and a determined redfish rooting for crabs will demand the same pinpoint accuracy that you had to develop trying to take rainbow trout holding in a feeding lane. Saltwater fishing often does require fast casting at a greater distance. Although long casters do have the ability to cover more water, a substantial portion of the fish I catch in the salt are inside of 40 feet. Many fish, such as school stripers and bluefish, can be caught by anglers new to the sport. Saltwater fly rodding has fish for all skill levels.

Even though fish in saltwater are often larger and stronger, large flies are not always called for. Good saltwater anglers must learn to read the water and know the feeding habits of their quarry. Along with baitfish imitations, a good fly box also contains a variety of patterns imitating shrimp, crabs, squid, and eels. I regularly carry patterns as small as size 8 and as large as 6/0. "Matching the hatch" can be just as important in saltwater. Even though the large variety of patterns available may seem daunting, a few basic patterns, such as Deceivers and Clouser Minnows, will take fish almost anywhere.

The other myth that I have confronted in recent years is that the best saltwater fishing is in tropical destinations requiring a plane ticket and a large bank account. It is only in the last decade that I have begun to fully appreciate how exciting saltwater fly fishing can be in almost every coastal area. Who can say that catching striped bass, bonito, false albacore, and bluefish in the Northeast is not just as exciting as anything that the tropics have to offer. I have lived most of my life in North Carolina, but I have had the privilege of traveling around the world in search of various fish. I have now come to realize that my home waters hold more secrets and more types of fish than I will ever master in my lifetime. Almost year round I have access to what I believe is some of the finest fishing in the world. In protected sounds and bays I catch weakfish, redfish, Spanish mackerel, and even flounder. In the inlets and nearshore waters of my home state I catch stripers, cobia, king mackerel, and albacore. Just offshore yellowfin tuna, barracuda, dolphin, amberjack, and even billfish are available.

Although I now appreciate the saltwater fish available to me in North Carolina, many angler friends from other states have now told me that they, too, have begun to explore the fisheries near their homes. Whether they live in Texas, Louisiana, Alabama, Florida, Georgia, Virginia, Massachusetts, or Washington state, there is great saltwater fishing for anglers willing to break out of their envelopes and explore the possibilities.

Thirty years ago I was a happy, contented angler. However, when placed with a fly rod next to water into which God had added a liberal dash of salt, the quality and excitement of my angling life changed forever.

Anchovy, Frontier

Color: Baitfish
Hook: Mustad 34011
Thread: Clear nylon
Body: Rainbow Krystal Flash wrapped around hook shank
Wings: 1st: (bottom) White FisHair. 2nd: (top of hook) White FisHair. 3rd: Green FisHair. 4th: Gold holographic Flashabou. 5th: Green FisHair. 6th: Green holographic Flashabou. 7th: Peacock herl
Lateral Line: Silver holographic Flashabou/silver Krystal Flash
Throat: Red Krystal Flash
Head: Wedge-shaped clear epoxy over Pantone® coloring
Eyes: Silver lure eyes with black pupils
Note: Tying baitfish patterns like the Anchovy can be very challenging due to the number of steps and materials involved. You will need a keen eye to understand how some of the patterns are pieced together. I have described each material and each step in the order they are tied. For example: wing one is the first wing tied onto the hook. One of the most important aspects when tying baitfish patterns is that both sides of the fly are identical in color and density. Symmetry is critical to ensure that the fly looks and swims like the real fish, is easy to cast and doesn't twist in the water when being retrieved.

Antron Crab

Color: Blue/tan
Hook: Mustad 34007
Thread: White flat waxed
Tag: Tan marabou/green Krystal Flash tied in the middle
Tail: Two pairs of natural grizzly hackle tips on each side for pinchers
Body: White and blue Antron rug yarn
Eyes: Lead hourglass painted silver with black pupils. Epoxy coated
Note: It is important to imitate the shape as well as the color and size. Often dominant features such as eyes, gills, shape, movement and color will trigger feeding in the preying fish.

Antron Crab

Color: Brown
Hook: Mustad 34007
Thread: Brown Monocord
Tag: Tan marabou/green Krystal Flash tied in the middle
Tail: Two pairs of dark brown-dyed grizzly hackle tips on each side for pinchers
Body: Brown Antron yarn
Legs: Black, medium, round rubber legs
Eyes: Lead hourglass painted brown with white irises and black pupils. Epoxy coated
Note: The Antron rug yarn is tied on top of the hook with figure-eights of thread and trimmed to size. Density and location of the yarn is important for proper swimming and sinking. The bigger the size, the more yarn and the heavier the eyes.

Antron Crab

Color: Green
Hook: Mustad 34007
Thread: Green Monocord
Tag: Green marabou/green Krystal Flash tied in the middle
Tail: Two pairs of green-dyed grizzly hackle tips on each side for pinchers
Body: Green Antron yarn
Legs: Brown, medium, round rubber legs
Eyes: Lead hourglass painted black with pale green irises and black pupils. Epoxy coated
Note: The positioning and weight of the eyes is important. They need to be heavy enough to sink and swim the Antron. They are tied on top of the hook so that it rides upward to prevent snagging.

Antron Crab

Color: Sand
Hook: Mustad 34007
Thread: Tan Monocord
Tag: Tan marabou/pearl Krystal Flash tied in the middle
Tail: Two pairs of natural grizzly hackle tips on each side for pinchers
Body: Tan Antron yarn
Legs: Brown, medium, round rubber legs
Eyes: Lead hourglass painted yellow with brown pupils. Epoxy coated
Note: There are hundreds of species of crabs, and a color to match each one. Many permit and bonefish guides will tell you, "you can never have enough crabs."

Antron Murkin Crab

Color: Tan/brown
Hook: Mustad 34007
Thread: Fluorescent green flat waxed
Tag: Tan marabou/pearl Krystal Flash tied in the middle
Tail: Two pairs of natural grizzly hackle tips on each side for pinchers
Body: Tan and brown striped Antron yarn
Legs: White with red tips, medium, round rubber legs
Eyes: Lead hourglass painted red with black pupils. Epoxy coated
Note: Epoxy coating the eyes and head is essential for use in saltwater. Crabs are often fished and retrieved over sand and coral substrate and without epoxy the paint scrapes off within the first few casts, thus losing a very effective element.

Bachmann's Sea Urchin

Color: Brown/black
Hook: Mustad 34007
Thread: Black Kevlar
Tag: 30-pound clear mono weed guard
Body: Brown and black, medium, round rubber legs, spun
Eyes: One 3/16 brass bead
Note: The bead helps the fly sink, and ride and land hook-up.

Ballyhoo, Frontier

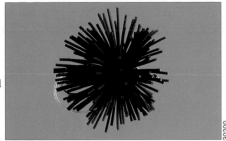

Color: Multi
Hook: Mustad 34011
Thread: Green Monocord
Tail: 1st: Four to six white saddle hackles paired and matched on both sides. 2nd: Green Chinese saddle hackles paired and laid over white, one on each side
Body: White Neer Hair
Above Lateral Line: Emerald green Sparkle Flash
Head: Green with red tips Monocord, epoxy coated
Eyes: Painted white and green irises with black pupils
Wings: 1st: Blue bucktail. 2nd: Peacock herl
Note: There has been much debate about the significance of eyes on baitfish patterns. I believe that the effectiveness of a pattern with eyes is twice what it is without eyes. Placing the pupil at the back of the iris is believed to imitate a frightened fry.

Belize

Color: Black/red
Hook: Mustad 34007
Thread: Flame flat waxed
Tail: 50-pound mono burned at end, 1" extensions past bend of hook
Body: Black rabbit strips wrapped around tail and hook
Collar Hackle: Red guinea plume
Head: Flame flat waxed thread. Epoxy coated
Note: The extended body of monofilament allows a greater swimming action, while preventing fouling around the hook.

Black Death

Color: Black/red
Hook: Mustad 34007
Thread: Red Monocord
Tag: 30-pound clear mono loop tail guard
Tail: 1st: Pearl Krystal Flash. 2nd: Black rabbit strip
Collar Hackle: Red-dyed gray fox squirrel tail
Eyes: Large, with painted white irises with black pupils
Head: Red Monocord thread. Epoxy coated

Bonafide Crab

Color: Brown
Hook: Mustad 34007
Thread: Brown Monocord
Legs: Eight black, small, round rubber legs. Tie knot in middle of leg
Body: Top: Brown Furry Foam. Bottom: Tan felt
Pinchers: Dyed-olive grizzly saddle hackle
Eyes: Burned monofilament painted black
Weight: Lead hourglass eye
Antennae: Green pearl Krystal Flash
Note: The functional design of crab patterns is extremely important. The fly needs to sink, fish, swim and look just like a real crab. The Furry Foam is the key to successfully landing the crab correctly. The foam has trapped air cells that keep the top floating upward, while the felt bottom soaks up water, becoming denser. The lead eyes are tied so the hook rides up to prevent snagging. The pinchers, eyes, weight and legs are assembled with thread. Hot glue patches the body material together on both sides of the hook.

Bonafide Crab

Color: Tan
Hook: Mustad 34007
Thread: Brown Monocord
Legs: Eight black, small, round rubber legs. Tie knot in middle of leg
Body: Top: Tan Furry Foam. Bottom: Tan felt
Pinchers: Dyed-olive grizzly saddle hackle
Eyes: Burned monofilament painted black
Weight: Lead hourglass eyes
Antennae: Pearl Krystal Flash

Bonefish Bitters

Color: Amber
Hook: Mustad 34007
Thread: Brown Monocord
Tail: Brown Antron yarn/bronze Sparkle Flash
Legs: Tan with bronze-flake rubber legs
Eyes: Stainless bead chain
Head: Amber epoxy
Wing: Natural elk hair
Note: Many fly manufacturers use hot glue to form the heads which can melt in your fly box on a hot day, rendering all of your flies useless. Epoxy is foolproof and also looks, sinks and swims better.

Bonefish Bitters

Color: Olive
Hook: Mustad 34007
Thread: Green Monocord
Tail: Green Antron yarn/chartreuse Sparkle Flash
Legs: Green with black-flake rubber legs
Eyes: Stainless bead chain
Head: Green epoxy
Wing: Natural elk hair

Charley, Bonefish Mud

Color: Gold
Hook: Mustad 34007
Thread: Brown Monocord
Tail: Gold Krystal Flash
Body: Gold Krystal Flash under clear medium Larva Lace
Eyes: Brass medium bead chain
Wing: Natural-brown bucktail

Bonefish Interceptor

Color: Pearl/wine
Hook: Mustad 34007
Thread: White flat waxed
Tail: Pearl Krystal Flash/silver Sparkle Flash/burgundy Sparkle Flash
Body: Pearl Krystal Flash spun into yarn
Eyes: Lead hourglass painted white with pink irises and white and black pupils
Wing: Same as tail
Note: Tied long and wispy to imitate shrimp. Bonefish can be extremely spooky, and the splash of the weight can scatter the school. I recommend having various patterns and weights.

Charley, Dead Coral

Color: Tan
Hook: Mustad 34007
Thread: Tan Flymaster
Body: Mixed root beer and pearl Krystal Flash under body. Clear Larva Lace overwrap
Eyes: Stainless small bead chain
Wing: Light tan calf tail with four strands of pearl Krystal Flash

Bonefish Special

Color: Gold
Hook: Mustad 34007
Thread: Black Monocord
Tail: Orange marabou, thick and short
Body: Gold, flat #14 Mylar tinsel under clear large Larva Lace
Wing: White calf tail with a pair of grizzly neck hackles cupped to the outside
Head: Black Monocord thread with white stripe, epoxy coated

Charley, Grass Shrimp

Color: Green
Hook: Mustad 34007
Thread: Green Monocord
Body: Green Flashabou tinsel underwrap, with grass green Larva Lace overwrap
Eyes: Stainless small bead chain
Wing: Green-dyed gray squirrel tail/two strands lime green Flashabou on each side

Caribbean Lobster

Color: Rust
Hook: Mustad 34007
Thread: Fluorescent orange flat waxed
Tail: 50-pound mono burned at end. 1" extensions past bend of hook
Body: Lobster rabbit strips wrapped around tail and hook
Collar Hackle: Orange strung saddle hackle, heavy
Head: Fluorescent orange, 1/2 inch flat waxed thread, epoxy coated

Charley, Honey Shrimp

Color: Root beer
Hook: Mustad 34007
Thread: Tan Monocord
Body: Root beer Krystal Flash under wrap, with tan Larva Lace overwrap
Eyes: Stainless small bead chain
Wing: Tan-dyed calf tail/two strands root beer Krystal Flash on each side

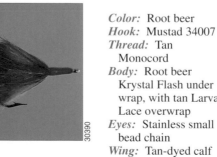

Charley, Krystal Shrimp

Color: Hot pink
Hook: Mustad 34007
Thread: Pink Monocord
Tail: Pink Krystal Flash
Body: Pink Krystal Flash only on back part. Clear Larva Lace overwrap
Eyes: Stainless bead chain
Wing: Pink Krystal Flash/hot pink-dyed grizzly neck hackle, one on each side

Charley, Rabid

Color: Pearl/tan
Hook: Mustad 34007
Thread: Yellow Monocord
Body: Green pearl flat #12 tinsel underwrap, with clear 20-pound monofilament over wrap
Eyes: Stainless bead chain
Wing: Flesh rabbit hair/tan calf tail

Christmas Island Special

Color: Chartreuse
Hook: Mustad 34007
Thread: Tan Monocord
Tail: Chartreuse Krystal Flash
Body: Chartreuse Krystal Flash
Eyes: Gold extra-small hourglass eyes painted green with white irises and black pupils
Wings: 1st: Chartreuse Krystal Flash. 2nd: Tan Antron yarn

Christmas Island Special

Color: Orange
Hook: Mustad 34007
Thread: Flame Flymaster
Tail: Orange Krystal Flash
Body: Orange Krystal Flash
Eyes: Gold extra-small hourglass eyes painted orange with white irises and black pupils
Wings: 1st: Orange Krystal Flash. 2nd: Tan Antron yarn

Christmas Island Special

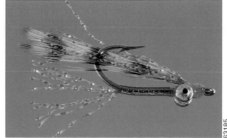

Color: Pink
Hook: Mustad 34007
Thread: White Monocord
Tail: Pink Krystal Flash
Body: Pink Krystal Flash
Eyes: Gold extra-small hourglass eyes painted pink with white irises and black pupils
Wings: 1st: Pink Krystal Flash. 2nd: Tan Antron yarn

Christmas Island Special

Color: Tan
Hook: Mustad 34007
Thread: Tan Flymaster
Tail: Root beer Krystal Flash
Body: Root beer Krystal Flash
Eyes: Gold extra-small hourglass eyes painted brown with tan irises and black pupils
Wings: 1st: Root beer Krystal Flash. 2nd: Tan Antron yarn

Christmas Island Special

Color: Yellow
Hook: Mustad 34007
Thread: Yellow Flymaster
Tail: Yellow Krystal Flash
Body: Yellow Krystal Flash
Eyes: Gold extra-small hourglass eyes painted yellow with white irises and black pupils
Wings: 1st: Yellow Krystal Flash. 2nd: Tan Antron yarn

Cockroach

Color: Brown
Hook: Mustad 34011
Thread: Brown Monocord
Tail: Four grizzly saddle feathers flared, and four strands silver Flashabou on each side
Body: Silver Diamond Braid Mylar tinsel
Wing: Natural-brown bucktail
Head: Brown Monocord thread, epoxy coated
Note: A sleek tarpon fly. The design allows long, easy casting. Can be tied with a cupped together tail, or splayed to increase the action.

Darting Coral Shrimp

Color: Orange/pearl
Hook: Mustad 34007
Thread: Orange Flymaster
Body: Orange Flashabou
Eyes: Black small mono eyes
Wings: 1st: Orange Flashabou. 2nd: Fluorescent orange Antron yarn

Note: A popular pattern for fishing shallow flats because there is no lead to splash. Destination resorts with a following of bonefish anglers have announced that the fish are becoming very selective. A large variety of sizes and weights are recommended.

Darting Coral Shrimp

Color: Pink/pearl
Hook: Mustad 34007
Thread: Fluorescent pink Flymaster
Body: Pink Krystal Flash
Eyes: Black small mono eyes
Wings: 1st: Pink Krystal Flash. 2nd: Fluorescent pink Antron yarn. 3rd: White Antron yarn

Darting Coral Shrimp

Color: Tan/pearl
Hook: Mustad 34007
Thread: Tan Flymaster
Body: Root beer Krystal Flash
Eyes: Black small mono eyes
Wings: 1st: Root beer Krystal Flash. 2nd: Tan Antron yarn

Darting Coral Shrimp

Color: White/pearl
Hook: Mustad 34007
Thread: White Flymaster
Body: Pearl Krystal Flash
Eyes: Black small mono eyes
Wings: 1st: Pearl Krystal Flash. 2nd: Fluorescent white Antron yarn

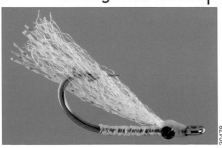

Darting Coral Shrimp

Color: Yellow/tan
Hook: Mustad 34007
Thread: Tan Flymaster
Body: Yellow Krystal Flash
Eyes: Black small mono eyes
Wings: 1st: Yellow Krystal Flash. 2nd: Fluorescent yellow Antron yarn. 3rd: Tan Antron yarn

Deceiver

Color: Blue/white
Hook: Mustad 34011
Thread: Blue flat waxed
Tail: Four to six white saddle hackles paired and matched on both sides/large Day-Glo™ tubing
Collar Hackle: Top 1/2: Blue bucktail/blue Sparkle Flash/peacock herl. Bottom 1/2: White bucktail
Head: Blue flat waxed thread, epoxy coated
Eyes: Painted yellow irises with black pupils

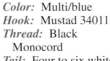

Note: Pay close attention to the proportions and shape. It is difficult to find matching pairs of feathers that naturally lie together for the tail so you will need a large amount to pick through. The large Day-Glo™ tubing really makes this fly look realistic in the water. The bucktail is hand-stacked for a natural look. The fly should look like a baitfish when collapsed.

Deceiver, Flash Dance

Color: Multi/blue
Hook: Mustad 34011
Thread: Black Monocord
Tail: Four to six white saddle hackles paired and matched on both sides/large pearlescent tubing
Body: Pearlescent tubing
Lateral Line: Silver Sparkle Flash
Collar Hackle: Top 1/2: Blue bucktail/green Sparkle Flash. Bottom 1/2: White bucktail
Throat: Red Krystal Flash
Head: Black flat waxed thread, epoxy coated
Eyes: Painted white irises with black pupils

Note: A small, slender, more translucent baitfish imitation. Some baitfish are transparent and schooling fish key on those qualities.

Deceiver

Color: Green/white
Hook: Mustad 34011
Thread: Olive flat waxed
Tail: Four to six white saddle hackles paired and matched on both sides/large Day-Glo™ tubing
Collar Hackle: Top 1/2: Green bucktail/green Sparkle Flash/peacock herl. Bottom 1/2: White bucktail
Head: Olive flat waxed thread, epoxy coated
Eyes: Painted yellow irises with black pupils

Deceiver, Margarita

Color: Green/chartreuse/white
Hook: Mustad 34011
Thread: Black Monocord
Tail: Four to six white saddle hackles paired and matched on both sides/silver Sparkle Flash
Body: Pearl Sparkle Flash
Collar Hackle: Top 1/2: White and yellow Neer Hair/silver and green Sparkle Flash. Bottom 1/2: White Neer Hair
Throat: Red and yellow pearl Krystal Flash
Head: Black flat waxed thread, epoxy coated
Eyes: Painted white irises with black pupils
Note: A thicker more robust pattern. The Neer Hair adds bulk, but when casting, the water is instantly thrown from the fly making it light.

Deceiver

Color: White
Hook: Mustad 34011
Thread: White flat waxed
Tail: Four to six saddle hackles paired and matched on both sides/large Day-Glo™ tubing
Collar Hackle: Top 1/2: White bucktail. Bottom 1/2: White bucktail
Lateral Line: Silver Sparkle Flash
Head: White with red band flat waxed thread, epoxy coated

Deceiver

Color: Red/white
Hook: Mustad 34011
Thread: Red flat waxed
Tail: Four to six saddle hackles paired and matched on both sides/large Day-Glo™ tubing
Collar Hackle: Top 1/2: Red bucktail. Bottom 1/2: Red bucktail
Lateral Line: Red rainbow Sparkle Flash
Head: Red flat waxed thread, epoxy coated
Eyes: Painted white with black pupils

Deceiver, Wild Bill

Color: Multi
Hook: Mustad 34011
Thread: Blue flat waxed
Tail: White bucktail with grape Flashabou on top
Body: Grape Flashabou
Collar Hackle: Top 1/2: Peacock herl/paired peacock swords/mulberry Sparkle Flash/root beer Krystal Flash
Throat: Bottom 1/2: White bucktail
Eyes: Painted white irises with black pupils
Head: Blue flat waxed thread, epoxy coated
Note: This Deceiver pattern is flashy and active. It is often difficult to discover what will stimulate a fish's attack response; it is good to have a Deceiver for every purpose.

Deceiver, Streaker

Color: Large baitfish
Hook: Mustad 34011
Thread: Green flat waxed
Tail: Four to six saddle hackles paired and matched on both sides
Body: White Chinese hackle wrapped around hook shank to improve girth
Lateral Line: Silver flash tape/peacock herl
Collar Hackle: Top 1/2: Peacock herl/paired peacock swords/ chartreuse bucktail. Bottom 1/2: White bucktail
Head: Green flat waxed thread, glitter and epoxy coated
Eyes: Painted white irises with black pupils
Note: The largest baitfish available without a stinger setup. Can be tied up to 11 inches. A very productive blue-water pattern for big fish. The materials can be difficult to locate, especially the paired swords. Make sure the chartreuse bucktail is parted so that the peacock sword is between the two sections and on top.

Deep-Eyed Baitfish

Color: Anchovy
Hook: Mustad 34007
Thread: Clear nylon
Body Hackle: Top 1/2: Lime green and silver Krystal Flash/white and sea foam green Super Hair
Collar Hackle: Bottom 1/2: White Super Hair
Eyes: Chrome hourglass with black pupils, epoxy coated
Note: Designed by Tom Earnhardt, this is a great small baitfish pattern tied any size. The synthetic material is both durable and imitating. Can be trolled or fished around rocks. Another advantage of fishing this synthetic pattern versus one of natural materials is when fishing in a pod that are feeding on a different size of fish than what your fly imitates, you can simply trim it with your pocket knife to match the hatch. Very easy to cut and taper to any length.

Deep-Eyed Baitfish

Color: Herring
Hook: Mustad 34007
Thread: Clear nylon
Body Hackle: Top 1/2:
    Sea foam green Super
    Hair/gold Sparkle
    Flash/lime green
    Super Hair
Collar Hackle: Bottom
    1/2:White Super Hair
Eyes: Chrome hour-
    glass with black pupils, epoxy coated

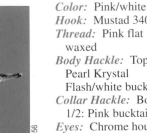

Note: Be sure the fly is tied symmetrically. That is, if it were cut in half, both sides are identical. You don't want a fly that spins. The somewhat-long head is epoxy coated to blend the body materials. A perfect baitfish imitation that is extremely durable.

Deep-Eyed Baitfish

Color: Silver shiner
Hook: Mustad 34007
Thread: Clear nylon
Body Hackle: Top 1/2:
    Gray Super Hair/lime
    green and silver
    Krystal Flash/white
    Super Hair
Collar Hackle: Bottom
    1/2: White Super Hair
Eyes: Chrome hour-
    glass with black pupils, epoxy coated

Deep-Eyed Minnow

Color: Chartreuse/
    white
Hook: Mustad 34007
Thread: Chartreuse
    flat waxed
Body Hackle: Top 1/2:
    White bucktail/
    chartreuse pearl
    Krystal Flash/
    chartreuse bucktail
Collar Hackle: Bottom
    1/2: White bucktail
Eyes: Lead hourglass painted white with red pupils, epoxy coated

Deep-Eyed Minnow

Color: Olive
Hook: Mustad 34007
Thread: Olive
    Monocord
Body Hackle: Top 1/2:
    Olive bucktail
Collar Hackle: Bottom
    1/2:White bucktail
Lateral Line: Silver
    Flashabou
Eyes: Brass hourglass
    with black pupils, epoxy coated

Note: Bucktail should come together to naturally taper and resemble a fish form; not fanned like a broom.

Deep-Eyed Minnow

Color: Pink/white
Hook: Mustad 34007
Thread: Pink flat
    waxed
Body Hackle: Top 1/2:
    Pearl Krystal
    Flash/white bucktail
Collar Hackle: Bottom
    1/2: Pink bucktail
Eyes: Chrome hour
    glass with black
    pupils, epoxy coated

Deep-Eyed Minnow

Color: Sculpin
Hook: Mustad 34007
Thread: Red
    Flymaster
Body Hackle: Top 1/2:
    Metallic orange
    Krystal Flash/natural
    brown bucktail
Collar Hackle: Bottom
    1/2: Orange bucktail
Eyes: Lead hourglass
    painted red with black pupils, epoxy coated

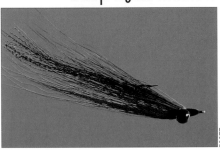

Deep-Eyed Minnow

Color: Silver shiner
Hook: Mustad 34007
Thread: Gray flat
    waxed
Body Hackle: Top 1/2:
    Rainbow
    Flashabou/gray
    bucktail
Collar Hackle: Bottom
    1/2: White bucktail
Eyes: Lead hourglass
    painted white with black pupils, epoxy coated

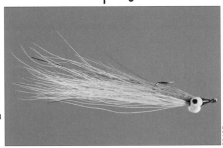

Deep Shrimp

Color: Brown
Hook: Mustad 34007
Thread: Tan Flymaster
Tail: 1st: Natural
    mallard flank. 2nd:
    Red squirrel tail
Body: Clear 20-pound
    monofilament
Body Hackle: Natural-
    brown saddle hackle
Antennae: Pearl
    Krystal Flash
Eyes: Lead hourglass painted brown with black irises and yellow
    pupils, epoxy coated

Note: Shrimp make up the largest part of the diet of saltwater fish. Like crabs, shrimp have hundreds of shapes, sizes and colors. There are a few universal patterns and many region-specific patterns. The Deep Shrimp are designed to be fished in three to six feet of water for medium-size game fish such as snook, tarpon and permit.

Deep Shrimp

Color: Gray/white
Hook: Mustad 34007
Thread: Black Flymaster
Tail: 1st: Silver Krystal Flash. 2nd: Flesh rabbit strip
Body: Gray acrylic yarn
Antennae: Black Krystal Flash
Eyes: Lead hourglass painted black with white pupils

Glass Minnow

Color: Blue back
Hook: Mustad 34011
Thread: White flat waxed
Body: Silver, flat #12 Mylar tinsel under body, clear 20-pound mono overwrap
Wing: White, light blue, and dark blue FisHair
Lateral Line: Silver prism tape
Head: White flat waxed thread top painted blue, epoxy coated
Eyes: Painted yellow irises with black pupils
Note: Small baitfish patterns as these are standard flies fished in rivers, lagoons, estuaries, flats and reefs. Generally tied on size 1, 4XL hook.

Epoxy Mini Puff

Color: Pink
Hook: Mustad 34007
Thread: Pink flat waxed
Tail: White calf tail/six strands of pink Krystal Flash
Body Hackle: Hot pink strung saddle hackle
Head: Clear hot glue over eyes
Eyes: Stainless bead chain

Glass Minnow

Color: Blue/green back
Hook: Mustad 34011
Thread: White flat waxed
Body: Pearl, flat #12 tinsel underwrap and clear 20-pound monofilament over wrap
Wing: White, green and blue bucktail
Lateral Line: Silver Sparkle Flash
Head: White flat waxed thread, epoxy coated
Eyes: Painted red irises with black pupils
Note: Should be tied so that the wing is wedge-shaped and somewhat flared to prevent collapsing while being fished.

Epoxy Mini Puff

Color: White
Hook: Mustad 34007
Thread: White flat waxed
Tail: White calf tail/one grizzly neck hackle on both sides
Body Hackle: White strung saddle hackle
Head: Clear hot glue over eyes
Eyes: Stainless bead chain

Glass Minnow

Color: Brown back
Hook: Mustad 34011
Thread: Red flat waxed
Body: Silver, flat #12 Mylar tinsel under wrap and clear 20-pound monofilament overwrap
Wing: White bucktail/ silver Sparkle Flash/natural brown bucktail
Head: Deep red flat waxed thread, epoxy coated
Eyes: Painted white irises with black pupils

Epoxy Shrimp

Color: Tan
Hook: Mustad 34007
Thread: Tan Monocord
Tail: Tan Super Hair/gold Krystal Flash
Body: Tan Monocord thread
Body Hackle: Tan strung saddle hackle
Eyes: Burned monofilament, painted black and epoxy coated
Shellback: Tan Super Hair epoxy coated

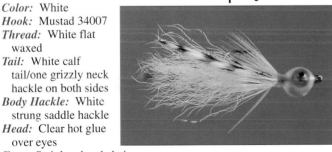

Glass Minnow

Color: Gray back
Hook: Mustad 34011
Thread: White flat waxed
Body: Pearl, flat #12 Mylar tinsel under wrap and clear 20-pound monofilament overwrap
Wing: White, black and gray bucktail
Lateral Line: Silver Sparkle Flash
Head: White flat waxed thread, epoxy coated
Eyes: Painted yellow irises with black pupils

Glass Minnow

Color: Green
Hook: Mustad 34011
Thread: Olive Monocord
Body: Silver, flat #12 Mylar tinsel under wrap and clear 20-pound monofilament overwrap
Wings: 1st: Polar bear white Super Hair. 2nd: Green Super Hair
Lateral Line: Silver prism tape
Head: Olive monocord thread, epoxy coated
Eyes: Painted yellow irises with black pupils

Glass Minnow

Color: Olive back
Hook: Mustad 34011
Thread: White flat waxed
Body: Pearl, flat #12 Mylar tinsel under wrap and clear 20-pound monofilament overwrap
Wings: 1st: White bucktail. 2nd: Olive bucktail
Lateral Line: Silver Sparkle Flash
Head: White flat waxed thread, epoxy coated
Eyes: Painted yellow irises with black pupils

Glory Shrimp

Color: Pearl/tan
Hook: Mustad 34007
Thread: Tan Flymaster
Tail: Pearl Sparkle Flash
Body: Tan chenille
Eyes: Gold bead chain
Wing: Pearl Sparkle Flash

Gotcha

Color: Green/pearl
Hook: Mustad 34007
Thread: Pink flat waxed
Tail: Green Sparkle Flash
Body: Green Sparkle Flash
Eyes: Stainless bead chain
Wing: Tan Neer Hair with two strands of pearl Krystal Flash on each side

Gotcha

Color: Pink
Hook: Mustad 34007
Thread: Pink flat waxed
Tail: Pink Krystal Flash
Body: Pink Krystal Flash
Eyes: Stainless bead chain
Wing: Tan Neer Hair with two strands of pink Krystal Flash on each side

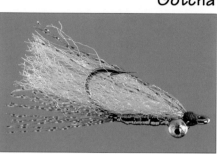

Gotcha

Color: Root beer
Hook: Mustad 34007
Thread: Orange Flymaster
Tail: Root beer Krystal Flash
Body: Root beer Krystal Flash
Eyes: Stainless bead chain
Wing: Tan Neer Hair with two strands of root beer Krystal Flash on each side

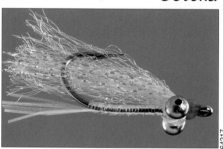

Gotcha

Color: Tan/pearl
Hook: Mustad 34007
Thread: Pink flat waxed
Tail: Pearl Flashabou
Body: Pearl Flashabou
Eyes: Stainless bead chain
Wing: Tan Neer Hair with two strands of pearl Krystal Flash on each side

Gotcha

Color: Yellow/tan
Hook: Mustad 34007
Thread: Yellow Flymaster
Tail: Yellow Krystal Flash
Body: Yellow Krystal Flash
Eyes: Stainless bead chain
Wing: Tan and yellow Neer Hair with two strands of yellow Krystal Flash on each side

Hair Shrimp

Color: Tan
Hook: 34007
Thread: Tan flat waxed
Tail: Gold Krystal Flash
Body: Gold Krystal Flash wrapped around hook shank
Wings: 1st: White calf tail. 2nd: Two natural grizzly neck hackles, one on each side splayed outwards
Eyes: Lead hourglass with painted white irises and black pupils
Head: Natural deer hair, spun and trimmed

Marabou Shrimp

Color: Pink
Hook: Mustad 34007
Thread: Fluorescent pink flat waxed
Body: Gold, flat #12 Mylar tinsel under wrap, with clear Larva Lace overwrap
Eyes: Lead hourglass eyes painted pink with white irises and black pupils

Wing: Fluorescent pink marabou with two natural grizzly neck hackles

Note: Many saltwater fish like pulsating action. Marabou is hard to beat if you desire this behavior. One of the secrets of a good bonefish fly is the density of the material. You can dress this pattern slightly heavy, and when on location, pull or cut the marabou if needed.

Marabou Shrimp

Color: Tan
Hook: Mustad 34007
Thread: Yellow Monocord
Body: Gold, flat Mylar tinsel #12 underwrap, with clear Larva Lace overwrap
Eyes: Lead hourglass eyes painted yellow with brown pupils

Wing: Tan marabou with two natural grizzly neck hackles

Marabou Shrimp

Color: White
Hook: Mustad 34007
Thread: White flat waxed
Body: Gold, flat #12 Mylar tinsel under wrap, with clear Larva Lace overwrap
Eyes: Lead hourglass eyes painted white with white irises and black pupils

Wing: Tan marabou with two natural grizzly neck hackles

Marabou Shrimp

Color: Yellow
Hook: Mustad 34007
Thread: Yellow flat waxed
Body: Gold flat #12 Mylar tinsel under wrap, with clear Larva Lace overwrap
Eyes: Lead hourglass eyes painted yellow with white irises and black pupils

Wing: White and fluorescent yellow marabou with two dyed-tan grizzly neck hackles

Mic's Crab

Color: Tan
Hook: Mustad 34007
Thread: Tan flat waxed
Tail: Tan marabou/lime green Krystal Flash/two natural brown hackle tips
Body: Natural elk hair, spun and cut to shape and dotted with brown permanent marker

Eyes: Burned 40-pound monofilament painted black at ends
Head: Lead hourglass painted brown
Pinchers and Legs: Tan rubber bands, knotted and cut, and glued to the bottom

Note: A nice option with this crab is that when you are on location it is easy to change the color and design pattern with Pantone® markers to fit the local quarry.

Missing-Link Shrimp

Color: Tan
Hook: Mustad 34007
Thread: White flat waxed
Tail: 1st: Tan Neer Hair. 2nd: Natural grizzly neck hackles, one on each side. 3rd: Pearl Krystal Flash
Body: Tan Ultra Chenille

Body Hackle: Natural grizzly saddle hackle, trimmed
Eyes: Gold bead chain

Needle Fish, Frontier

Color: Multi
Hook: Mustad 34007, two
Thread: Clear nylon
Tail: Pearlescent Day Glo™ Mylar tubing, frayed
Body: Pearlescent Day-Glo™ Mylar tubing over leader to connect the two hooks

Wings: Layered. Polar bear white Super Hair/chartreuse Krystal Flash/green Super Hair/dark green Super Hair/green holographic Flashabou
Throat: Red Krystal Flash
Head: Pearlescent Mylar tubing colored with Pantone® markers. Epoxy coated
Eyes: Plastic lure eyes with yellow irises and black pupils

Note: The hooks are connected with 50-pound wire leader. Double the leader, loop through both eyes of the hooks and tie down with thread. The second hook is detachable allowing the tubing to be tied to the first hook. This pattern is designed to be trolled, but if you wish to cast it, connect the wings to the second hook with clear nylon thread so the wing will move freely, but not tangle with the hook.

Brian O'Keefe Photo

Orange Grizzly

Color: Orange
Hook: Mustad 34007
Thread: Fluorescent orange flat waxed
Tag: Fluorescent red chenille tied in a ball to help split wings (optional)
Tail: Two orange and two grizzly saddle hackles matched, paired and splayed outward
Body Hackle: Orange and grizzly strung saddle hackles, mixed
Head: Fluorescent orange flat waxed thread heavily wrapped æ" and epoxy coated
Note: The head of the fly is heavily coated with epoxy to prevent coming apart when snelled.

Puff Shrimp

Color: Orange
Hook: Mustad 34007
Thread: Shell pink flat waxed
Eyes: Stainless bead chain
Wings: 1st: White calf tail. 2nd: Pearl Krystal Flash. 3rd: Natural grizzly neck hackles, one on each side
Thorax: Shell pink Ultra Chenille
Note: The wing is tied up to hide the hook point. Take one wrap of Ultra Chenille under the wing and around hook shank. Eyes are tied on top of the hook so it rides up.

Pacific Big Eye Baitfish, Frontier

Color: Multi
Hook: Mustad 34007
Thread: Chartreuse flat waxed
Eyes: Silver deep sea eyes/silver lure eyes with black pupils, epoxy coated
Gills: Red Krystal Flash
Head: High-melt clear hot glue
Wing Bottom: 1st: White Antron yarn. 2nd: Large Everglo tubing
Wing Top: 1st: White Antron yarn. 2nd: Green Super Hair dubbing, 3rd: Green holographic Flashabou. 4th: Peacock herl

Puff Shrimp

Color: Pink
Hook: Mustad 34007
Thread: Fluorescent pink flat waxed
Eyes: Stainless bead chain
Wings: 1st: Pink calf tail. 2nd: Pearl Krystal Flash. 3rd: Pink-dyed grizzly neck hackles, one on each side
Thorax: Pink Ultra Chenille
Note: The amount of flash tied into a bonefish pattern is subjective, often depending on the mood of the fish.

Placencia Emerald Crab

Color: Green
Hook: Mustad 34007, keeled
Thread: Olive flat waxed
Pinchers and Legs: Ten green, small, round rubber legs, four tied into two pinchers
Body: Green and olive deer hair spun and cut to shape
Weight: Large hourglass eyes hot glued to the bottom
Note: The crab is weighted with one large lead hourglass eye glued to the bottom with hot glue. Spread glue evenly across the bottom for protection. The hook must be keeled to improve hook gap and swimming.

Puff Shrimp

Color: Pink/white
Hook: Mustad 34007
Thread: Fluorescent pink flat waxed
Eyes: Stainless bead chain
Wings: 1st: White calf tail. 2nd: Pearl Krystal Flash. 3rd: Pink-dyed grizzly neck hackles, one on each side
Thorax: Hot pink Ultra Chenille

Placencia Mud Crab

Color: Brown
Hook: Mustad 34007, keeled
Thread: Brown flat waxed
Tail: Five strands green Krystal Flash
Pinchers and Legs: Rubber band cut into two pinchers and legs. Color with black marker
Body: Brown and natural deer hair spun and cut to shape
Weight: Large hourglass eyes hot glued to the bottom

Puff Shrimp

Color: Tan/orange
Hook: Mustad 34007
Thread: Tan Monocord
Eyes: Stainless bead chain
Wings: 1st: Tan calf tail. 2nd: Pearl Krystal Flash. 3rd: Orange-dyed grizzly neck hackles, one on each side
Thorax: Tan Ultra Chenille

Puff Shrimp

Color: White
Hook: Mustad 34007
Thread: White Monocord
Eyes: Stainless bead chain
Wings: 1st: White calf tail. 2nd: Pearl Krystal Flash. 3rd: Natural grizzly neck hackles, one on each side
Thorax: Cream Ultra Chenille

Reef Shrimp

Color: Orange
Hook: Mustad 34007
Thread: Flame flat waxed
Tag: Flame flat waxed thread
Eyes: Stainless bead chain
Body: Epoxy with glitter
Wing: 1st: Red buck tail. 2nd: Pearl Flashabou/gold Krystal Flash. 3rd: Orange-dyed grizzly neck hackle splayed out

Note: The body is formed by wrapping 30-pound monofilament into a heart shape around eyes and filling it with 5-minute Epoxy. A sample is necessary to approach tying this pattern.

Russian Bullet Baitfish

Color: Black/white/ silver
Hook: Mustad 34011
Thread: Red flat waxed
Body: Silver braided Mylar tinsel
Weight: Lead wire, large
Head: Bullet is formed with black and white bucktail
Wing: Silver Flashabou, bullet material tied black

Note: The top and bottom wing is formed with the same bucktail used for the bullethead. Do not stack hair. For desired baitfish form, leave hair uneven.

Sand Crab

Color: Bleached
Hook: Mustad 34007
Thread: Tan flat waxed
Tail: Tan marabou with six strands of pearl Krystal Flash
Body: Bleached elk hair spun and cut
Eyes: Large lead hour glass
Pinchers and Legs: Rubber bands
Weight: Lead hourglass eye

Note: Legs and pinchers are glued to the bottom with white hot glue.

Snapping Shrimp

Color: Olive
Hook: Mustad 34007
Thread: Black Monocord
Body: Olive wool yarn
Wings: 1st: Brown Fis-Hair. 2nd: Natural grizzly hackles splayed. 3rd: Four strands of bronze Krystal Flash

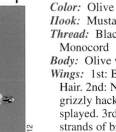

Snapping Shrimp

Color: Tan/orange
Hook: Mustad 34007
Thread: Black Monocord
Body: Orange (butt) Antron dubbing
Thorax: Tan Antron dubbing
Wing: Brown FisHair

Splayed Tarpon Fly

Color: Black/red
Hook: L067M Billy Pate
Thread: Black flat waxed
Wing: Three black, matched and paired saddle hackles splayed outward/gold Sparkle Flash
Collar Hackle: Red marabou

Head: Black flat waxed thread, epoxy coated
Eyes: Painted white irises with black pupils
Note: Splayed Tarpon flies are among some of the most difficult to tie due to the lack of good round-tipped hackles that can be matched and paired, and the ability to apply them symmetrically. If you find good hackle, half of the battle is over. If the fly is not tied correctly, count on spinning and darting when it's being fished.

Splayed Tarpon Fly, Forest Fire

Color: Brown/orange
Hook: L067M Billy Pate
Thread: Orange Monocord
Wing: Three fiery brown-dyed, matched and paired saddle hackles splayed outward/orange metallic Krystal Flash
Collar Hackle: Orange marabou

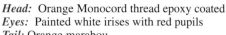
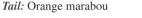

Head: Orange Monocord thread epoxy coated
Eyes: Painted white irises with red pupils
Tail: Orange marabou

Splayed Tarpon Fly, Key's Roach

Color: Brown/orange
Hook: L067M Billy Pate
Thread: Fluorescent orange flat waxed
Tail: Green pearl Krystal Flash/brown-dyed bucktail
Wing: Three fiery brown-dyed, matched and paired saddle hackles splayed outward/ pearl Krystal Flash
Collar Hackle: Brown-dyed bucktail
Head: Fluorescent orange flat waxed thread epoxy coated
Eyes: Painted yellow irises with black pupils

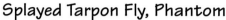

Splayed Tarpon Fly, Phantom

Color: Blue/black
Hook: L067M Billy Pate
Thread: Black Monocord
Tail: Black marabou
Wing: Three blue-dyed grizzly, matched and paired neck hackles splayed outward/navy Sparkle Flash
Collar Hackle: Black marabou/navy Sparkle Flash
Head: Black flat waxed thread epoxy coated
Eyes: Painted white irises with black pupils

Splayed Tarpon Fly, Pink Panther

Color: Purple/pink
Hook: L067M Billy Pate
Thread: Black Monocord
Tail: Purple marabou
Wing: Two purple, and one natural grizzly, matched and paired saddle hackle splayed outward/silver Sparkle Flash
Collar Hackle: Pink rabbit strip
Head: Black flat waxed thread, epoxy coated
Eyes: Painted white irises with black pupils

Splayed Tarpon Fly, Redhead Roach

Color: Black/red
Hook: L067M Billy Pate
Thread: Red flat waxed
Tail: Pearl Sparkle Flash/natural brown bucktail
Wing: Three natural grizzly, matched and paired saddle hackles splayed outward/pearl Flashabou
Collar Hackle: Natural brown bucktail
Head: Red flat waxed thread, epoxy coated
Eyes: Painted yellow irises with black pupils

Splayed Tarpon Fly, Revenge

Color: Pink
Hook: L067M Billy Pate
Thread: Shell pink flat waxed
Tail: Hot pink marabou/pink Krystal Flash
Wings: 1st: Two large hot pink and one natural grizzly neck hackles splayed outward on each side. 2nd: Pearl Krystal Flash
Collar Hackle: Flesh rabbit strip
Head: Shell pink flat waxed thread, epoxy coated
Eyes: Painted white irises with red pupils

Sten's Epoxydeceiver

Color: Blue/white
Hook: Mustad 34011
Thread: White flat waxed
Tail: Four to six white saddle hackles paired and matched on both sides/Large Day-Glo™ tubing
Body Hackle: Top 1/2: Blue bucktail/blue Sparkle Flash/peacock herl. Bottom 1/2: White bucktail
Head: Pearlescent tubing coated with epoxy
Eyes: Plastic Lure Eyes with yellow irises with black pupils
Note: The head makes this pattern more durable and look more realistic, however, there is a lot of time involved. If it is not done properly, you can lose the entire fly.

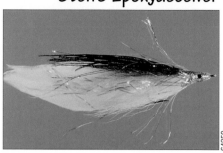

Sten's Epoxydeceiver

Color: Green/white
Hook: Mustad 34011
Thread: White flat waxed
Tail: Four to six white saddle hackles paired and matched on both sides/large Day-Glo™ tubing
Collar Hackle: Top 1/2: Green bucktail/green Sparkle Flash/peacock herl. Bottom 1/2: White bucktail
Head: Pearlescent tubing coated with epoxy
Eyes: Plastic Lure Eyes with yellow irises with black pupils

Sten's Epoxyhead

Color: Anchovy
Hook: Mustad 34007
Thread: White flat waxed
Body Hackle: Top 1/2: Green bucktail/green Sparkle Flash/blue bucktail/peacock herl
Collar Hackle: Bottom 1/2: White bucktail/ pearl Flashabou
Lateral Line: Silver Sparkle Flash
Throat: Red calf tail
Head: Pearlescent Mylar tubing coated with epoxy
Eyes: Plastic Lure Eyes with yellow irises with black pupils
Note: This is a great medium-sized baitfish pattern. Natural materials such as bucktail are more supple and allow a greater freedom of movement. The head is a good weight that permits the fly to be cast long distances.

Sten's Epoxyhead

Color: Gray minnow
Hook: Mustad 34007
Thread: White flat waxed
Tail: Rainbow Flashabou
Body: Rainbow Flashabou
Body Hackle: Top 1/2: White bucktail/pearl Krystal Flash/black bucktail/gray bucktail/peacock herl
Collar Hackle: Bottom 1/2: White bucktail/Pearl Flashabou
Lateral Line: Rainbow Flashabou
Throat: Red calf tail
Head: Pearlescent Mylar tubing coated with epoxy
Eyes: Plastic Lure Eyes with yellow irises with black pupils

64277

Sten's Epoxyhead

Color: Greenback baitfish
Hook: Mustad 34007
Thread: White flat waxed
Body Hackle: Top 1/2: White bucktail/green bucktail/green Sparkle Flash
Collar Hackle: Bottom 1/2: White bucktail/pearl Flashabou
Lateral Line: Pearl Krystal Flash
Throat: Red calf tail
Head: Pearlescent Mylar tubing coated with epoxy
Eyes: Plastic Lure Eyes with yellow irises with black pupils

64285

Sten's Epoxyhead, Vargas

Color: Blue/chartreuse/white
Hook: Mustad 34007
Thread: White flat waxed
Body Hackle: Top 1/2: White bucktail/rainbow Flashabou/chartreuse bucktail/blue/bucktail/peacock herl
Collar Hackle: Bottom 1/2: White bucktail/pearl Flashabou
Lateral Line: Pearlescent tubing
Throat: Red calf tail
Head: Pearlescent Mylar tubing coated with epoxy
Eyes: Plastic Lure Eyes with yellow irises and black pupils

64287

Sten's Epoxyhead

Color: Juvenile herring
Hook: Mustad 34007
Thread: White flat waxed
Body Hackle: Top 1/2: White bucktail/blue bucktail/blue Sparkle Flash
Collar Hackle: Bottom 1/2: White bucktail/pearl Flashabou
Lateral Line: Pearl Krystal Flash
Throat: Red calf tail
Head: Pearlescent Mylar tubing coated with epoxy
Eyes: Plastic Lure Eyes with yellow irises and black pupils

64289

Swimming Shrimp

Color: Tan
Hook: Mustad 34007
Thread: Tan Flymaster
Weight: Lead wire, large
Body: Tan chenille
Wing: Tan calf tail/one dark brown-dyed grizzly neck hackle on each side played outward
Head: Natural deer hair, spun

64299

Tentacle Shrimp

Color: Brown
Hook: Mustad 34007
Thread: Tan flat waxed
Tail: Root beer Krystal Flash/tan calf tail
Body: Tan flat waxed thread
Weed Guard: 30-pound monofilament
Antennae and Legs: White medium round rubber legs, striped with Pantone® marker
Eyes: Lead hourglass with painted yellow irises and black pupils
Head: Brown-dyed deer hair spun and trimmed

64300

Tic Crab

Color: Green
Hook: Mustad 34007
Thread: Tan monocord
Tail: 1st: Pearl Krystal Flash. 2nd: Gray marabou. 3rd: Two brown hackle tips splayed outward
Legs: White round rubber legs
Eyes: Chrome hourglass
Body: Green Furry Foam/gold glitter/hot glue
Note: The eyes are placed just behind the eye of the hook for proper sinking and swimming.

65502

Tic Crab

Color: Olive
Hook: Mustad 34007
Thread: Tan monocord
Tail: 1st: Pearl Krystal Flash. 2nd: Gray marabou. 3rd: Two brown hackle tips splayed outward
Legs: White round rubber legs
Eyes: Chrome hourglass
Body: Olive Furry Foam/gold glitter/hot glue

65504

Tic Crab

Color: Tan
Hook: Mustad 34007
Thread: Tan Monocord
Tail: 1st: Pearl Krystal Flash. 2nd: Gray marabou. 3rd: Two brown hackle tips splayed outward
Legs: White round rubber legs
Eyes: Chrome hourglass
Body: Tan Furry Foam/gold glitter/hot glue

Ultra Shrimp

Color: Tan
Hook: Mustad 34011
Thread: Clear nylon
Weed Guard: 25-pound monofilament
Tails: Tan Neer Hair
Body: Tan Antron dubbing
Rib: Clear nylon thread figure-eight
Body Hackle: Natural brown webby chicken hackle
Eyes: Monofilament burned, painted black and epoxy coated
Shellback: Clear drinking straw cut to form, epoxy coated
Note: Tails of Neer Hair are one piece tied-through the fly to help create bulk.

Turd Fly

Color: Bright pink
Hook: Mustad 34007
Thread: Shell pink flat waxed
Tail: Hot pink marabou/three strands pink Krystal Flash on each side
Body: Pink Ultra Chenille
Eyes: Stainless bead chain

Note: Brian O'Keefe designed this shrimp to be quiet and unobtrusive. A very successful pattern.

Yucatan Special

Color: Chartreuse
Hook: Mustad 34007
Thread: Chartreuse flat waxed
Tail: Pink Glo Bug yarn
Body: 1st: Silver flat #12 Mylar tinsel underwrap. 2nd: Chartreuse Amnesia monofilament over wrap
Eyes: Stainless bead chain
Wings: 1st: White calf tail. 2nd: Two strands pearl Krystal Flash on both sides
Head: Chartreuse flat waxed thread, epoxy coated

Turd Fly

Color: Pink
Hook: Mustad 34007
Thread: Shell pink flat waxed
Tail: Pink marabou/three strands pink Krystal Flash on each side
Body: Pale pink Ultra Chenille
Eyes: Stainless bead chain

Turd Fly

Color: Tan
Hook: Mustad 34007
Thread: Tan flat waxed
Tail: Tan marabou/three strands pearl Krystal Flash on each side
Body: Tan Ultra Chenille
Eyes: Stainless bead chain

Abel Automatics Inc, Camarillo CA 805/484-8789
Alaska Fly Shop, Fairbanks AK 907/456-3010
Angler's Emporium, Anchorage AK 907/279-3099
Angler's Inn, Salt Lake City UT 801/466-3921
Angler's Lane, Forest VA 804/385-0200
Angler's Workshop, Woodland WA 360/225-6359
Ashland Outdoor Store, Ashland OR 541/488-1202
Avid Angler, Seattle WA 206/362-4030
Back Country Fly & Tackle, Layton UT 501/775-0489
Baja Flycasters, Salem OR 503/393-5133
Bay Street Outfitters, Beaufort SC 803/524-5250
Bertrand's Sport Shop, Green Bay WI 920/432-1296
Big Foot Fly Shop, Vernal UT 435/789-4960
Bighorn Fly & Tackle, Harden MT 888/665-1321
Big Horn Mtn Sports, Sheridan WY 307/672-6866
Big Sky Flies & Guides, Emigrant MT 406/333-4401
Blackbird's Fly Shop, Victor MT 800/210-8648
Blue Heron Fly Shop, Idleyld Park OR 541/496-0448
Blue Mountain Anglers, Pendleton OR 541/966-8770
Blue Ribbon Flies, W Yellowstone MT 406/646-9365
Bob Marriott's Flyfishing, Fullerton CA 714/525-1827
Boca Grande Outfitters, Boca Grande FL 941/964-2445
Bonefish Bob's, Islamorada FL 305/664-9420
Boulder River Flyfishing, Kinston NC 800/723-8316
Brandywine Outfitters, Exton PA 610/594-8008
Brasington's Trail Shop, Gainesville FL 352/372-0521
Browner's Guide Service, Salida CO 800/826-6505
Bud Lilly's Trout Shop, W Yellowstone MT 800/854-9559
Caddis Fly Angling Shop, Eugene OR 541/342-7005
Captain Ed's Fly Fishing, Charleston SC 803/723-0860
Castaway Fly Fishing, Coeur d'Alene ID 800/410-3133
Cimarron Creek, Montrose CO 970/249-0408
Circle 7 Fly Shop, Fall River Mills CA 530/336-5827
Clearwater FlyFishing, Las Vegas NV 702/388-1022
Cope & McPhetres, Santa Clara CA 408/345-2640
Countrysport, Portland OR 503/221-4545
Creekside Angling Co, Issaquah WA 425/392-3800
Creekside Flyfishing Shop, Salem OR 503/588-1768
Cumberland Transit, Nashville TN 615/321-4069
Deep Water Cay, Ft Lauderdale FL 954/359-0488
Deschutes Canyon Fly Shop, Maupin OR 541/395-2565
Deschutes River Outfitters, Bend OR 541/388-8191
Dewing's Fly & Gun, W Palm Beach FL 561/655-4434
Dunsmuir Fly Fishing Co, Dunsmuir CA 530/235-0705
East'ard Variety, Harkers Island, NC 252-728-7149
Eric's Tackle Shop, Ventura CA 805/648-5665
Ernie's Casting Pond, Soquel CA 831/462-4665
Eureka Fly Shop, Eureka CA 707/444-2000
Evening Hatch, Coeur d'Alene ID 208/667-2726
Everglades Angler, Naples FL 941/262-8228
Firefly Outfitters, Boston MA 617/723-7211
Fish First!, Albany CA 510/526-1937
Fisherman's Headquarters, Ship Bottom, NJ 609/494-5739
Fisherman's Marine, Oregon City OR 503/557-3313
Fishermen's Spot!, Van Nuys CA 818/785-7306
Fishing Ambassadors, Countryside IL 708/482-4990
Fishing Headquarters, Dillon MT 406/683-6660

Fish On Fly Shop, Butte MT 406/494-4218
Flaming Gorge Lodge, Dutch John UT 801/889-3773
Fly Fishing Outfitters, Lafayette CA 925/284-3474
Fly Fishing Outfitters, San Francisco CA 415/781-3474
Fly Fishing Outfitters, Avon CO 800/595-8090
Fly Shop of Ft Lauderdale, Ft Lauderdale FL 954/722-5822
Fly Fishing Store, Bohemia NY 516/563-1323
Four Seasons Fly Shop, La Grande OR 541/963-8420
Fox Point Anglers, Fox Point WI 414/352-3664
Frisco Rod & Gun, Frisco NC 252/995-5366
Frying Pan Anglers, Basalt CO 970/927-3441
Gallatin River Guides, Big Sky MT 406/995-2290
Gary's Fly Shoppe, Yakima WA 509/457-3474
Gorge Fly Shop, Hood River OR 541/386-6977
Gorsuch Outfitters, Vail CO 970/476-4700
Grand Slam Outfitters, N Key Largo FL 305/367-3000
Great Outdoor Shop, Pinedale WY 307/367-2440
Grizzly Hackle, Missoula MT 800/297-8996
Hardy USA, Evergreen CO 303/679-1010
Harman's Fly Shop, Sheridan MT 406/842-5868
Hatch Finders Fly Shop, Livingston MT 406/222-0989
High Country Flies, Jackson WY 307/733-7210
Howsley's Fox Creek Store, Antonito CO 719/376-5881
Hyde Drift Boats, Idaho Falls ID 800/444-4933
Hunter Banks Co, Asheville NC 828/252-3005
Jack Dennis Sports, Jackson WY 307/733-3270
Jacklin's Inc, W Yellowstone MT 406/646-7336
International Angler, Pittsburg PA 800/782-4222
Juneau Flyfishing Goods, Juneau AK 907/586-3754
Key West Angler, Key West FL 305/296-0700
Kiene's Fly Shop, Sacramento CA 916/486-9958
Lost River Outfitters, Ketchum ID 208/726-1706
Mack's Fly Shop, Kodiak AK 907/486-4276
Mangrove Outfitters, Naples FL 941/793-3370
McAfee's Fly Shop, Anchorage AK 907/344-1617
McKenzie Outfitters, Medford OR 941/773-5145
Medicine Bow Drifters, Saratoga WY 307/326-8002
Montana Fly Company, Melrose MT 406/835-2621
Mountain Angler, Breckenridge CO 970/453-4665
Mtn Hardware & Sports, Truckee CA 530/587-4844
Mtn View Sports Center, Anchorage AK 907/563-8600
North Fork Anglers, Cody WY 307/527-7274
Northwest Outfitters, Coeur d'Alene ID 208/772-1497
Ole Florida Fly Shop, Boca Raton FL 561/995-1929
Park City Fly Shop, Park City UT 435-645-8382
Pine St Pawn & Flyfishing, Sandpoint ID 208/263-6022
Pomeroy Sports, Aspen CO 970/925-7875
Port Townsend Angler, Port Townsend WA 360/379-3763
Propp's Tackle, Spokane WA 509/838-3474
Quill Gordon Fly Fishers, Ft Smith MT 406/666-2233
Rainbow King Lodge, Iliamna AK 800/458-6539
Rainbow Lodge, South Fork CO 719/873-5545
Ramsey Outdoor, Paramus NJ 201/261-5000
Reno Fly Shop, Reno NV 702/827-0600
Rick's Lodge, Fall River Mills, CA 530/336-5300
Rocky Mountain Fly Shop, Ft Collins CO 970/223-7735

Rocky Point Marine, Redondo Beach CA 310/374-9858
Ruddick's Fly Shop, Vancouver BC 604/681-3747
Saltwater Fly Fisherman, Clearwater FL 813/443-5000
Scarlet Ibis, Corvallis OR 541/754-1544
Sea Boots, Big Pine Key FL 305/872-9005
Shasta Angler, Fall River Mills CA 530/336-6600
Silver Creek Outfitters, Ketchum ID 800/732-5687
Snake River Angler, Moose WY 307/733-2415
Spinner Fall Fly Shop, Salt Lake City UT 800/959-3474
Steamboat Inn, Steamboat OR 541/498-2533
St Peter's Fly Shop, Ft Collins CO 970/498-8968
Streamside Anglers, Tumwater WA 360/709-3337
Sunriver Fly Shop, Sunriver OR 541/593-8814
Sweeney's Sports, Napa CA 707/255-5544
Taylor Creek Fly Shop, Basalt CO 970/927-4374
Ted's Sport Shop, Lynnwood WA 206/743-9505
The Back Country, Vero Beach FL 561/567-6665
The Back Country Angler, Dillon MT 406/683-3462
The Blue Quill Angler, Evergreen CO 303/674-4700
The Fish Hawk, Atlanta GA 404/237-3473
The Fly Fisher, Lacey WA 360/491-0180
The Fly Fisher's Place, Sisters OR 541/549-3474
The Fly Fisherman Inc, Titusville FL 407/267-0348
The Fly Fishing Shop, Welches OR 503/622/4607
The Fly Hatch, Red Bank NJ 732/530-6784
The Fly Shop, Redding CA 800/669-3474
The Fly Smith, Marysville WA 360/658-9003
The Joseph Fly Shoppe, Joseph OR 541/432-4343
The Mad Flyfisher, Federal Way WA 253/945-7414
The Morning Hatch, Tacoma WA 253/472-1070
The Old Baldy Club Tackle, Saratoga WY 307/326-5222
The Patient Angler, Bend OR 541/389-6208
The Ram Sports Center, Jerome ID 208/324-3722
The Rod & Reel, Anchorage AK 907/561-0662
The Saltwater Angler, Key West FL 305/295-2585
The Sporting Tradition, Lexington KY 606/255-8652
The Sports Lure, Buffalo WY 307/684-7682
The Trout Fisher, Denver CO 303/369-7970
The Trout Fitter, Mammoth Lakes CA 760/924-3676
Three Rivers Fly & Tackle, Wasilla AK 907/373-5434
Trophy Waters, Klamath Falls OR 541/850-0717
Trout Country Fly Shop, Cassel CA 530/335-5304
Troutfitter, Syracuse NY 315/446-2047
Tsylos Park Lodge, Vancouver BC 604/682-1352
Turneffe Flats, Deadwood SD 800/815-1304
Twin River Anglers, Lewiston ID 208/746-8946
Two Guys Fly Shop, Lafayette CO 303/666-7866
Upstream Flyfishing, Los Gatos CA 408/354-4935
Valley Fly Fisher, Salem OR 503/375-3721
Virginia Creeper, Abington VA 540/328-3826
Waters West, Port Angeles WA 360/417-0937
West Branch Angler, E Syracuse NY 607/467-5525
Western Rivers Flyfisher, Salt Lake City UT 800/545-4312
Williamson River Anglers, Chiloquin OR 541/783-2677
World Wide Sportman, Islamorada FL 305/664-4615
Worley Bugger Fly Shop, Ellensburg WA 509/968-9216
Yellowstone Angler, Livingston MT 406/222-7130

Snapping Shrimp

Color: Tan/orange
Hook: Mustad 34007
Thread: Black Monocord
Body: Orange (butt) Antron dubbing
Thorax: Tan Antron dubbing
Wing: Brown FisHair

64221

Ordering program: On the bottom right-hand corner of each fly photograph is an item number that can be used through your local fly shop to order anything Frontier offers. Simply call and explain to your fly shop your desire to order flies tied by Frontier. They will be happy to forward the order and you should receive it within two weeks. Subject to stock on hand.

TROUT

PMD Extended Body Compara-dun, 23
PMD Flashback Nymph, 79
PMD Hairwing Dun, 23
PMD Loop Wing Emerger, 22
PMD Sparkle Dun, Pale Green, 22
PMD Sparkle Dun, Pale Olive, 23
PMD Sparkle Dun, Pale Orange,,23
PMD Twilight Parachute, Pale Olive, 24
PMD Twilight Parachute, Pale Pink, 24
PMD Poly Spinner, 24
Prince Nymph, 79
Prince Nymph, Flashy, 79
Renegade, 31
Robotic Stone, Golden, 55
Robotic Stone, Orange, 55
Royal Coachman Trude, 31
Royal Wulff, 31
RS2, Beige, 79
RS2, Gray, 79
RS2, Olive, 79
Rubber Leg Hare's Ear, Brown, 79
Rubber Leg Hare's Ear, Gold Ribbed, 80
Ruling Stone, Black, 55
Ruling Stone, Gold, 55
Ruling Stone, Olive, 55
San Juan Worm, Red, 80
San Juan Worm, Tan, 80
Scud, Gray/Olive, 80
Scud, Orange, 80
Sculpin, Articulated Woolhead, 80
Sculpin, Big Eye, 80
Serendipity, Green, 81
Serendipity, Red, 81
Serendipity, Tan, 81
Slick Water Caddis, Frontier Black, 43
Slick Water Caddis, Frontier Brown, 43
Slick Water Caddis, Frontier Cream, 44
Slick Water Caddis, Frontier Gray, 44
Slick Water Caddis, Frontier Olive, 44
Slick Water Caddis, Frontier Tan, 44
Slick Water Caddis, Frontier Twilight Blk, 43
Slick Water Caddis, Frontier Twilight Brn, 44
Slick Water Caddis, Frontier Twilight Crm, 44
Slick Water Caddis, Frontier Twilight Gray, 44
Slick Water Caddis, Frontier Twilight Olive, 44
Slick Water Caddis, Frontier Twilight Tan, 45
Soft Hackle, Partridge/Gray, 81
Soft Hackle, Partridge/Green, 81
Soft Hackle, Partridge/Hare's Ear, 81
Soft Hackle, Partridge/Yellow, 81
Soft Hackle, Pheasant Tail, 81
Soft Hackle, Starling, 81

Sparkle Dun, Twilight Pale Olive, 23
Sparkle Dun, Twilight Pale Orange, 23
Speckled Wing Dun, Quill Body, 17
Speckled Wing Spinner, 17
Spent Spinner, Gray Drake, 28
Spent Spinner, Natural Hare's Ear, 28
Tarantula, Frontier, 31
Tied-Down Caddis, 45
Trico Angel Wing Spinner, 29
Trico Angel Wing Spinner, Female, 29
Trico Black & White Parachute, 29
Trico Hairwing Dun, 29
Trico Hairwing Dun, Female, 29
Trico High & Dry Dun, 28
Trico High & Dry Dun, Female, 28
Trico Loop Wing Emerger, 28
Trico Parachute, Twilight, 29
Trico Parachute, Twilight Female, 29
Trico Parachute, Twilight Spinner, 29
Ugly Bug Nymph, 82
WD-40, Brown, 82
WD-40, Olive, 82
Whiz Banger Leech, Black/Chartreuse, 82
Whiz Banger Leech, Black/Pink, 83
Whiz Banger Leech, Chartreuse/Fluor Pink, 83
Whiz Banger Leech, Orange/Red, 83
Whiz Banger Leech, Red/Orange, 83
Woolly Worm, Black, 82
Woolly Worm, Brown, 82
Woolly Worm, Olive, 82
Yarn Body Stone, Gold, 55
Yarn Body Stone, Orange, 55
Zonker, 83
Zug Bug, 83

SALMON/STEELHEAD

Agitator, Black, 88
Agitator, Purple/Flame, 88
Agitator, Sandy Candy, 88
Alaskan Roe Bug, Chartreuse, 88
Alaskan Roe Bug, Orange, 88
Alaskan Roe Bug, Pink, 88
Articulated Leech, Black, 88
Articulated Leech, Purple, 88
Big Black Bunny Leech, 89
Big Flesh Bunny Leech, 89
Big Purple Bunny Leech, 89
Big Red Bunny Leech, 89
Blue Mack's Canyon, 89
Bomber, Martini Olive/Red, 89
Bomber, Martini Purple/Black, 89
Bomber, Martini Red/Black, 89

Bomber, Regular Natural/Chartreuse, 90
Bomber, Regular Natural/White, 90
Boss, 90
Comet, 90
Conrad, 90
Coppertop, 90
Cosseboom, 90
Cotton Candy, 90
Dan's Favorite, 91
Dark mack's Canyon, 91
Deep-Eyed Wog, 91
Doc Sprately, 91
Egg, Frontier Natural Chinook, 91
Egg, Frontier Natural Salmon, 91
Egg, Frontier natural Sockeye, 91
Egg, Frontier Natural Steelhead, 91
Egg, Frontier Natural Double Egg, 92
Eggo, Pink, 92
Eggo, Red, 92
Egg Sucking Leech, Black/Red, 92
Egg Sucking Leech, Purple/Pink, 92
Euphasid, 92
Eyed Shrimp, Chartreuse, 92
Eyed Shrimp, Orange/White, 92
Ferry Canyon, 93
Fly Dejour, 93
Freight Train, 93
General Practitioner, Black, 93
General Practitioner, Orange, 93
General Practitioner, Purple, 93
Glo Bug, Orange/Flame, 93
Glo Bug, Orange/Orange, 93
Glo Bug, Peach/Flame, 94
Glo Bug, Pink/Flame, 94
Golden Demon, 94
Grease Liner, Black, 94
Grease Liner, Orange, 94
Grease Liner, Peacock, 94
Green Butt Skunk, 94
Juicy Bug, 94
Kenai Special, 95
Krystal Bugger, Chartreuse, 95
Krystal Bugger, Orange, 95
Krystal Bugger, Pink, 95
Krystal Bugger, Red, 95
Limit Lander, 95
Mack's Canyon, 95
Muddler After Dinner Mint, Green, 95
Muddler After Dinner Mint, Purple, 96
Muddler After Dinner Mint, Red, 96
October Caddis, 96
Paint brush, 96

SALTWATER